UNIQUENESS
The Human Pursuit of Difference

PERSPECTIVES IN SOCIAL PSYCHOLOGY

A Series of Texts and Monographs • Edited by Elliot Aronson

INTRINSIC MOTIVATION
    By Edward L. Deci

SCHOOL DESEGREGATION
    By Harold B. Gerard and Norman Miller

HUMAN AGGRESSION
    By Robert A. Baron

UNIQUENESS: The Human Pursuit of Difference
    By C. R. Snyder and Howard L. Fromkin

SCHOOL DESEGREGATION: Past, Present, and Future
    Edited by Walter G. Stephan and Joe R. Feagin

A Continuation Order Plan is available for this series. A continuation order will bring delivery of each new volume immediately upon publication. Volumes are billed only upon actual shipment. For further information please contact the publisher.

UNIQUENESS
The Human Pursuit of Difference

C. R. Snyder

The University of Kansas
Lawrence, Kansas

and

Howard L. Fromkin

York University
Downsview, Ontario, Canada

PLENUM PRESS · NEW YORK AND LONDON

Library of Congress Cataloging in Publication Data

Snyder, C   R
  Uniqueness, the human pursuit of difference.

  (Plenum series in social psychology)
  Includes index.
  1. Individuality. I. Fromkin, Howard L., 1937-   joint author. II. Title.
III. Series.
BF697.S64   155.2   79-18764
ISBN 0-306-40376-5

© 1980 Plenum Press, New York
A Division of Plenum Publishing Corporation
227 West 17th Street, New York, N.Y. 10011

Printed in the United States of America

To Rebecca, naturally . . .
and
Zachary, Staci, Shannon, Joshua, and Adam
(new participants in ''the pursuit of difference'')

Foreword

My Red Shirt and Me

The red shirt incident begins with a rather ordinary red shirt. Not a brightly colored red shirt, not a dramatic cherry or firehouse red, more like a faded burgundy. But, for several days, my very identity was bound up in its redness. It was me, and I wore it with the pride a matador takes in his splendid cape, a hero in his medals of bravery, or a nun in her religious habit. I'll never forget the boundless joy I felt wearing that simple, pullover, short-sleeved red shirt in the hospital—or the rush of relief that I experienced when, at last, I decided to surrender it. However, we are getting ahead of our story, which starts a short time earlier with a most unfortunate accident.

A light flurry of wet snow had begun to fall as the university limousine turned the corner on its way from the Bronx campus of New York University to the downtown campus. Although eight of us were packed into the car and had resigned ourselves to the usual boring faculty meeting awaiting us, somehow a spontaneous air of joviality was created. Talk turned to the anti-Vietnam War activities some of us were engaged in at the college, when the driver's voice boomed: "Wanna hear my solution to the war?"

Our silence, bred of expecting the worst from such openers, was interrupted by the ever-courteous sociologist sitting next to the driver: "Why yes, of course, we would like you to share your opinion with us."

Instinctively, I knew this was no time for noblesse to oblige the driver class. We would be trapped in this container for nearly an hour while his solution was forged on an anvil of platitudes, stereotypes, and hate. Sure enough, prediction verified: ". . . Load all our bombers with nuclear warheads and blow all the gooks to hell."

Instead of biting the bullet in midair, our sociologist professor began to profess: ". . . Now that's not really an acceptable solution. It is comparable to losing at chess and deciding to win by kicking over the entire chess board." Obviously pleased by his metaphor, he continued, "Don't you see. . . ."

The driver didn't see—neither the point of the responsible rebuttal nor the irresponsible car skidding over the white lane-divider. A head-on smash! Screams, crying, moaning, blood, broken bones, silence.

I had been sitting in the jump seat behind the driver and my head bounced off the metal back of his seat into the nose of the psychologist behind me. One mild concussion for me, broken nose for my colleague, broken sternum and severed arteries for the driver. He died on the operating table at Fordham Hill Hospital, where we were all taken for emergency care.

While waiting to be X-rayed, I passed out, was revived in time to help the nurse remove my jacket, but then lapsed into unconsciousness.

When I opened my eyes some time later, I was strapped into a hospital bed on the "trauma ward." Intravenous fluid was being injected into an arm splotched blue-black from obvious misses with the IV needle. Through the haze the nurse's announcement rang loud and clear: "The man in the red shirt has come to." Temperature, blood pressure, and endless other medical reactions were taken. "Well, Red, you are sure the lucky one, the other Italian, the cab driver, what's his name, didn't pull through. Your X rays are negative, no fractures, just a concussion, some sprains, and a tear in your Achilles tendon. But you'll survive. Be outta here in less than a week. We'll take your red shirt off and give you clean pj's as soon as the IV can come out of your arm."

The trauma ward was more like a set of the prison camp in the old movie *Stalag 17* than a hospital. It was populated by society's trauma victims, mostly old winos who had fallen from grace down the stairs or into a hole, bums mugged for their last quarter, unemployed and homeless Puerto Ricans stabbed in a bar brawl, and other seamy citizens that you pass quickly by on skid row but would not choose to have as your next-door neighbor, admit to your country club, or share your local hospital. These were the comrades among whom I had been deposited.

Cursed the driver for inflicting this indignity (and pain) on me. Felt guilty since he died for his prowar opinions, substituted curses on the heads of the eloquent sociologist and the chairperson who called for the faculty meeting and the driver of the other car and. . . .

"Say, Red, you feel hungry yet? I'd like to get some of this nice hot soup into you. Also no dozing, keep alert, it's a bad sign to be nodding off, so don't do it. Talk to the other guys."

There was obviously no one to talk to on the trauma ward; the nurses were too busy since it was understaffed, and I had nothing in common with the rest of *them*. The ward was ugly, smelly, and for a hospital, remarkably dirty. The institutional vomit greengray paint was flaking off the walls; the outsides of the windows were covered with thick dust or maybe it was black moss. The high ceilings and barren walls created an echo-chamber effect with a constant din all day long and worse at night—with snoring and unreal, animal-like body sounds.

They were all uniformed in their grubby green pajamas, but not me. My red shirt set me apart—above—these slovenly masses. It stood out like a beacon of uniqueness. It proclaimed, "I don't belong here," "I am special," "I am an individual, not just a charity patient, and not one of them." My individuality had survived the accident. It was apparent to one and all that I was the "man in the red shirt" and not just an anonymous ward of society. They all realized it, too; no one bothered me, no one talked to me, no one irritated me by insisting on sharing their newspaper or extra food or whatever they were doing with each other. I was left alone. My red shirt did it. It created a color barrier; an instant caste system where red was special amid a sea of pukey green.

After some days of enjoying being so special, I was confounded at an impulse building somewhere in me to take off my red shirt. Earlier, when the IV had been removed, I told the nurse I did not want to try to take the red shirt off because my neck and back hurt and I didn't want to aggravate my condition. But now for some bizarre reason, I felt compelled to remove it, to rip it off, to give it up. "After all, how silly can I get?" "What's the big deal over a dirty, old red shirt?" "It wasn't even one of my favorite shirts, don't even know why I put it on in the first place." "Doesn't make sense to keep wearing it forever, does it?"

It was perhaps less than two minutes after I exchanged my red shirt for the hospital issue of green pj's that the guy in the next bed tossed me his copy of the *New York Daily News*.

"Waddya think about City Hall's upping the subway fare to fifty cents? What crooks!"

Then, in succession, came each of my other ambulatory ward mates, one to give me some extra sugar he had cached away since he noticed I always asked for, but never got, an extra lump; another to tell me some gossip about the head nurse and the resident; then there was the joke about the two Jews who . . . .

In turn, I shared the candies I had received, told them the gory details about the "big crash," kidded about whether anyone on the ward had died from lead poisoning of paint flakes in their food or from the nurses' forgetting to take the thermometers out that they were always shoving up us. We laughed, played rummy, made obscene comments about the staff, and united in our complaints about the tasteless mush they called food.

". . . Gee, I knew you was a regular guy, one of da bunch. Just because you be a little younger that don't mean we can't be friends, do it?"

"Thanks, not at all, we're gonna be buddies," I said, feeling the pride of having been accepted, of passing the friendship test, of being made part of their group, of our group.

And thus our young cucumber was slowly immersed in the vinegar barrel of life, not wanting to become just a pickle like all the others, but wanting even more to be of them and not apart, not isolated and alone. . . .

There are times and circumstances when we want to be noticed and to have our sense of individuality publicly acknowledged: when goodies and gold stars are being passed out, when we are "into" our hero thing, or when we want to connect with some special other person on a deeper level. But we don't step forward for life's shit details or want to go it alone through uncertain or dangerous terrain or call attention to our vulnerabilities when "evil eyes" are squinting. And then there are the nights when we want to suspend our conscience on the Golden Rule hanger and get down to the usually inhibited pleasures of acting out primitive impulses. Then we declare our sameness to the other animals of appetite rather than our uniqueness among the angels of reason.

Snyder and Fromkin's analysis of our quest for uniqueness helps us to understand the conditions that propel us to establish some sense of difference from others in our life space. Their original theory and assessment procedure allow us to appreciate individual differences in the need to be unique. Beyond the creative theorizing and scores of innovative experiments by the authors on different aspects of uniqueness, real and illusory, lies the contribution of this work in assembling here an impressive body of literature from diverse areas on individuality—and its loss.

While psychologists strive to make analytical sense of the processes, variables, and dynamics involved in this fascinating phenomenon, advertisers, we learn, are at work exploiting the uniqueness syndromes of potential buyers, and otherwise anonymous vandals are spray-painting their way to uniqueness with identification graffiti.

By helping us to know more about the human pursuit of being different, Snyder and Fromkin also give us insights into why it is imperative that each of us also surrenders to the equally powerful need to continually reassert the human connection.

My red shirt isn't so special in the dark, in a red-lit world, to the blind, or when I want my uniqueness to depend not on appearances but on more substantial stuff—the "real me." In consuming the ideas so lavishly served up by Snyder and Fromkin, you and I are treated to a more robust conception of self, identity, and uniqueness than anyone has ever prepared for us before. (And just in case you want to enjoy this reading in the proper frame of mind, I can get you a red shirt just like mine, wholesale.)

PHILIP G. ZIMBARDO

Stanford University
Palo Alto, California

Preface

Uniqueness is a concept that has fascinated individuals in a variety of fields for many years. We share this fascination and thus have worked to describe, organize, summarize, and add new perspectives on the research and the theoretical proposals advanced by individuals studying uniqueness. We offer the present book as a means of conveying the results of our efforts and as a means of pursuing our own needs for uniqueness.

For the reader with some background in psychology, it should be apparent that psychology is replete with theories and data suggesting that people are attracted to similar others (interpersonal attraction literature) and are prone to behave like others (conformity literature) in certain situations. While the literature in these areas indicates that people sometimes do not want to be different, it is our contention that there are many situations in which people *do* want to appear and feel different. By exploring this "pursuit of difference," the present book serves as a focal counterpoint to the previous interpersonal attraction and conformity literature. In addition, it seeks to examine difference from a positive angle, without the negative connotations of words like *deviance* and *abnormality*. We have adopted the term *uniqueness* in order to positively describe the "pursuit of difference."

In Part I of the book, we present our "case" for uniqueness. As a brief preview to our more formal theory and a review of research on uniqueness seeking, the first chapter traces evidence of the need for uniqueness through several forms of literary thought.

Having briefly established this anecdotal backdrop, we begin looking into the theory of uniqueness in Part II. The second chapter explores the research evidence related to the question, "Do birds of a feather always flock together?" While considerable data seem to indicate that the answer to this question is yes, we present our views on the limitations of the research paradigms and assumptions typically used in answering this question. In Chapter 3, we outline our theory of uniqueness and provide research data to support our view that individuals strive to maintain a moderate sense of difference relative to other people. In Chapter 4, we expand on our theory in a discussion of the characteristics of comparison others that are important to uniqueness-seeking behavior. We further elaborate on uniqueness theory in Chapter 5 by describing individual differences in the need for uniqueness and the role of these differences in uniqueness seeking.

All of us have a number of societally recognized attributes through which we establish our difference in relation to others. Part III describes four such characteristics, called *uniqueness attributes*. Chapter 6 discusses how commodities are sometimes considered symbols of a person's unique identity. Chapter 7 proposes that names serve as an important uniqueness attribute by providing us with a source of identity among the masses. Chapter 8 describes attitudes and beliefs as a way in which we derive a sense of difference relative to others. And Chapter 9 examines competitive performance as a means of establishing both positive and negative uniqueness relative to others.

Part IV was designed to look at uniqueness seeking "in perspective" by examining the role of uniqueness motivation in our present society. Chapter 10 begins this examination by discussing deindividuation (or the loss of uniqueness) and the potential repercussions of environments that deprive individuals of a sense of uniqueness. Chapter 11 continues by describing individuation (or the pursuit of difference) and the various environments in which we may establish a sense of uniqueness.

At this point, it is our pleasure to thank the many people who helped us with this project. Elliot Aronson, the series editor, provided a supportive atmosphere for the development of the manuscript. Phil Zimbardo graciously provided a commentary on the book. His "unique" zest for psychology is evident in the Foreword. Leonard R. Pace, our editor at Plenum, patiently supported us through our many rewrites (and missed deadlines). We also gratefully acknowledge the input of Jack Brehm, Sharon Brehm, Timothy C. Brock, Donn Byrne, Fritz Heider, Cheryl Newburg, John J. Sherwood, and Susan Streufert for their comments on earlier versions of portions of this manuscript. Additionally, we are indebted to Robert Augelli, C. Daniel Batson, Diane Boss, Jeffrey Brandt, Rick Dattore, Robert Dipboye, Janet R. Endelman, Irene Gurri, Charles A. Kiesler, Raanon Lipshitz, Alan Omens, Rebecca Snyder, Randee Jae Shenkel, Sundance Smith, and Lawrence S. Wrightsman, whose encouragement and intellectual challenges made this manuscript possible. A final thanks is due to our secretaries, Gerda Brouhard, Carol Hopkins, Winnie Kucera, Connie Morris, and Linda Speicher, whose patient work and understanding manner have expedited this project. The present research was supported by grants (Numbers 2160-7099 and 3075-60-0038) from the University of Kansas Graduate School Research Fund to the first author.

In writing the present book for a diverse audience, including undergraduates and professionals, we were reminded of an interchange between Franklin and Peppermint Patty in a "Peanuts" cartoon. In this cartoon, Patty sees that young Franklin is reading a psychology book and asks him about it. Franklin informs her that it is a pretty good psychology book because he can understand it. Patty quickly tells Franklin to forget it, for "no psychology book can be any good if you can understand it!" In the following pages, the reader can judge whether Franklin or Peppermint Patty was right.

C. R. SNYDER

Lawrence, Kansas

HOWARD L. FROMKIN

Toronto, Ontario, Canada

Acknowledgments

From *Pattern and Growth in Personality,* by Gordon W. Allport, p. 4. Copyright 1937, © 1961 by Holt, Rinehart, and Winston, Inc., New York. Reprinted by permission of the publisher.

From *Actress: Postcards from the Road,* by Elizabeth Ashley with Ross Firestone, p. 36. Copyright © 1978 by Elizabeth Ashley and Ross Firestone. New York: M. Evans and Company, Inc. Reprinted by permission of the publisher.

From "Letter" by E. E. Cummings. Copyright © 1955 by E. E. Cummings. In *A Miscellany,* edited by George J. Firmage. Reprinted by permission of Harcourt Brace Jovanovich, Inc., New York.

From *Selected Poems 1956-1968,* by Leonard Cohen, p. 212. Copyright © 1964, 1966, 1968 by Leonard Cohen. Reprinted by permission of Viking Penguin, Inc., New York.

From *Essays,* by Ralph W. Emerson, p. 53. Copyright, 1926 by Thomas Y. Crowell. New York. Reprinted by permission of Harper & Row, Publishers, Inc., New York.

From *Asylums: Essays on the Social Situation of Mental Patients and Other Inmates,* by Erving Goffman, p. 16. Copyright © 1961 by Erving Goffman. Reprinted by permission of Doubleday & Company, Inc., New York.

From *The Thoreau Centennial,* edited by Walter Roy Harding, p. 113. Copyright © 1964 by the State University of New York Press, Albany, New York. Reprinted by permission of the publisher.

From *A High Wind in Jamaica,* by Richard Hughes, pp. 134–135. Copyright 1929, 1957 by Richard Hughes. Reprinted by permission of Harper & Row, Publishers, Inc., New York.

From *Born to Win: Transactional Analysis with Gestalt Experiments,* by Muriel James and Dorothy Jongeward, p. 274. Copyright © 1971 by Addison-Wesley Publishing Company, Reading, Mass. Reprinted by permission of the publisher.

From "I'm Me" by Lynne Lehman. Unpublished manuscript, 1978. Reprinted by permission of the author.

From "A Faceless Defeat in War Against Anonymity," p. 79. In *LIFE.* Copyright © 1970 by Time, Inc., New York. Reprinted by permission of the publisher.

From "A Triumph with a Facade of Faces," p. 80. In *LIFE.* Copyright © 1970 by Time, Inc., New York. Reprinted by permission of the publisher.

From "Dare to Be Different" in *Hold to Your Dream,* by Helen Lowrie Marshall, p. 21. Copyright © 1965 by Doubleday & Company, Inc., New York. Reprinted by permission of the publisher and John S. Marshall.

From *The Psychological Impact of School Experience: A Comparative Study of Nine-Year-Old Children in Contrasting Schools,* by Patricia Minuchin *et al.,* p. 41. Copyright © 1969 by Basic Books, Inc., Publishers, New York. Reprinted by permission of the publisher.

From *Tolerance for Nonconformity,* by C.Z. Nunn, H.J. Crockett, and J.A. Williams, pp. 172–173. Copyright © 1978 by Jossey-Bass, Inc., San Francisco, Calif. Reprinted by permission of the publisher.

From *Appeals to the Special Person in Psychotherapy,* by Victor Raimy. Unpublished manuscript. University of Colorado, 1978. Reprinted by permission of the author.

From *Misunderstandings of the Self,* by Victor Raimy, p. 109. Copyright © 1975 by Jossey-Bass, Inc., San Francisco, Calif. Reprinted by permission of the publisher.

From *The Little Prince,* by Antoine de Saint-Exupéry, pp. 77-78. Copyright © 1943, 1971 by Harcourt Brace Jovanovich, Inc., New York. Reprinted by permission of the publisher.

From "The Illusion of Uniqueness," by C.R. Snyder, pp. 33–41. In *Journal of Humanistic Psychology,* 1978, *18*(3). Copyright © 1978 by the Association for Humanistic Psychology, Los Angeles, Calif. Reprinted by permission of the publisher.

From *Oddballs: The Social Maverick and the Dynamics of Individuality,* by Bernard G. Suran, p. 207. Copyright © 1978 by Bernard G. Suran. Reprinted by permission of Nelson Hall, Chicago, Ill.

From "Harrison Bergeron," in *Welcome to the Monkey House,* by Kurt Vonnegut, Jr. pp. 7–8. Copyright © 1961 by Kurt Vonnegut, Jr. New York: Delacorte Press/Semour Lawrence. Originally published in *Fantasy and Science Fiction.* Reprinted by permission of the publisher.

From *The Man on the Assembly Line,* by C. R. Walker and R. A. Guest, p. 169. Copyright © 1952 by Harvard University Press, Cambridge, Mass. Reprinted by permission of the publisher.

From "The Other Side of Unusual First Names," by R.L. Zweigenhaft, p. 294. In *Journal of Social Psychology,* 1977, *103,* 291–302. Copyright © 1977 by the *Journal of Social Psychology,* Provincetown, Mass. Reprinted by permission of the publisher.

A Case for Uniqueness

I'm Me

I'm me and nobody else
Not the girls down the street
With ribbons in their hair
Not Sue, or Jane
Or the girl with the bike
I don't even want to be Mike

I'm me and nobody else
I'm different in a strange sort of way
Sue and Jane like me for what I am
I still like Mike
With his Motor Bike

But I like me for what I am
Because I'm me and nobody else

—Lynne Lehman (Age 13)

Literary Precedents for Uniqueness

Uniqueness seeking is a phenomenon that has only recently become the subject of much systematic research and empirical investigation. However, as is often true of psychological principles, literary thought was exploring uniqueness seeking long before the phenomenon was investigated empirically. Therefore, as an introduction to more formal research on uniqueness, evidence for the need to see ourselves as unique is traced in the present chapter through several forms of literature.

While the literary references to be presented are not systematic research and do not yield unequivocal evidence regarding the uniqueness-seeking phenomena, they do reflect the observations of sensitive people and their opinions about significant behaviors within our culture. As such, the observations of these artists are offered as a complement to, not as a substitute for, our scientific inquiry.

The following quotations document our thesis that the need to see oneself as unique is a potent and continuous force in our society. That is, as compared to many psychological phenomena (see Gergen, 1973), the need to see oneself as unique is neither dated nor simply a symptom of a particular period in history.

American literature provides some excellent examples of the presence of the uniqueness theme in literary thought. The following excerpts from essays by Emerson and Thoreau emphasize the value these authors placed on individuality:

> I must be myself. I will not hide any taste or aversions. I will so trust that what is deep is holy, that I will do strongly before the sun and moon whatever inly rejoices me and the heart appoints. (Emerson, 1926, p. 53)

It is one of the great paradoxes—and equally redeeming fea-
tures—of human history and evolution that a scale of organized
society grows and as the gregarious and enveloping nature of
that society increasingly dominates the individual, the very
same process highlights the extreme individuality of the human
conscience. The more the conformist nature of society grows,
the more accented is the nonconformity of what the ancient
Hindus called the "atman"—the individual soul. It is the spirit
of nonconformity that has enriched the dialogue of human pro-
gress—no less, indeed, in the material fields than in the spirit-
ual. (Thoreau, in Nehru, 1964, p. 113)

In a more recent poem, Cohen (1968) echoes a somewhat similar theme:

> I wonder if my finger prints
> Get lonely in the crowd
> There are no others like them
> & that should make them proud. (p. 212)

While the above writers emphasize the positive nature of individuality, other writers from the early part of this century chose to
emphasize the negative nature of the *lack* of individuality. For-
mally designated as the literature of "der doppelgänger," many
novels were written with plots that focused on the main character's
anxiety over an anticipated confrontation with another identical
person (see Beebe, 1955; Bleiler, 1967; Chizhevsky, 1962; Guerard, 1967; Rosenfield, 1967).

The notion of a double first evoked negative or threatening
self-evaluation characteristics in the literature of German folklore.
In the late 18th and early 19th centuries, a group of German writers
known as the Dark Romanticists began to utilize the double as a
means of exploring the conflicting struggle of good and evil within
people (Bleiler, 1967; Gurri, 1975; Thompson, 1970). E.T.A. Hoffmann produced several stories in which the double was placed in
opposition to the self (Eigner, 1966; Spilka, 1959). For example, in
Hoffmann's "Signor Formica" (1967), Signor Capuzzi attends a
play where he sees an exact copy of himself. Capuzzi is shocked at
the sight of his double and, in an emotional fit, goes onstage to
quarrel with it. Capuzzi is apparently so threatened by this extreme
similarity that the challenge to his unique identity causes him to
leap to the stage and defend "himself."

The double theme is also evident in Russian literature through the work of such writers as Gogol (1969) and Dostoevsky (1958). For example, we see the negative reaction resulting from the appearance of the double in Dostoevsky's novel *The Double* (1958). This story begins to explore the psychogenic origin of the double. The principal character, Golyadkin, starts his double hallucination by attributing his peculiar behavior to "someone strikingly like me." Later, the double appears visually, eliciting a sense of curiosity, horror, and danger in Golyadkin. Trembling and questioning his sanity, Golyadkin flees in fright, only to meet his double repeatedly. As the story progresses, Golyadkin eventually sees "an infinite procession of precisely similar Golyadkins" and is taken away by his doctor. Golyadkin's illness appears to have resulted from his being forced to look closely at himself and at his own negative qualities and actions (Beebe, 1955; Chizhevsky, 1962; Rosenfield, 1967).

Guy de Maupassant (1903) wrote about his own autoscopic hallucinations in his story "He?" The central character in the story roams the city looking for friends. Returning to his apartment friendless, the character hallucinates "someone sitting in my armchair by the fire, warming his feet with his back turned toward me." As noted by Boyd (1926), this scene parallels Maupassant's own experience of returning to his apartment and seeing himself sitting in his chair. Maupassant comments on that scene by asking the reader, "If you had not a cool head, would't you be afraid?" One can infer from the character's responses in "He?" that Maupassant's feelings at the sight of the double were a combination of curiosity and danger.

Maupassant's mother believed that one of the causes of his autoscopic hallucinations was his friendship with the American novelist Henry James. This explanation may have been accurate, as James also had autoscopic hallucinations and used the double theme in his writing. For example, James's story "The Jolly Corner" (Edel, 1965) depicts the struggle of a person haunted by a double. This story reveals the curiosity and anxiety that Bryden, the central character, feels regarding his double (Dove, 1958). James describes Bryden as feeling, "Horror, with the sight . . . for the bared identity was too hideous as *his*. . . . The face, *that* face, Spencer Bryden's?— he searched it still, but looking away from it in dismay and denial" (James, 1909, p. 476). As the story unfolds,

Bryden spends more and more of his time trying to find differences between himself and his double. The story closes with Bryden's cry, "But this brute, with his awful face—this brute's a black stranger. He's none of *me*, even as I *might* have been" (p. 483).

The strongest feelings toward a double are probably portrayed in the short story "William Wilson" by the American writer Edgar Allan Poe (1927). In this story, the central character, Wilson, initially evidences ambivalence toward his double. He feels animosity and fear, yet curiosity and respect. The double had first appeared when Wilson was in grade school and has continued to follow him throughout his life. The threat of the double grows; as Wilson notes, "The feeling of vexation thus engendered grew stronger with every circumstance tending to show resemblance, moral or physical, between my rival and myself. . . . In a word nothing could more seriously disturb me . . . than any allusion to a similarity of mind, person, or condition existing between us" (pp. 14–15). As a final act of desperation, Wilson kills his double in a duel. Curiously, Wilson notices in terror that he has also injured himself and thus realizes the double is part of him. With the killing of his double, Wilson finally finds his identity.

As can be seen from the above glimpse at the double literature, those who wrote about doubles used differing story lines, but they described the characters' reactions to doubles in similar ways. Gurri (1975) highlighted these similarities in the following statement:

> After Dostoevsky established the double as a legitimate literary character, there appeared in all of the above mentioned stories a common response by the protagonist to his double. The character, usually in conflict, at first sensed a vague feeling of impending danger, coupled with an intense curiosity overriding it. The character pursued the double as though unable to stop himself, yet his anxiety was so great, he wondered if he could function at all. An obsession with the double was usually present along with a strange feeling of kinship. The actual confrontation with the double was extremely anxiety-producing and mobilized some form of defense. The defense employed included flight, unconsciousness, attack, denial, and death. All of the characters felt such a threat from the double to their individual and unique existence that they had to find a means, at times drastic, to cope. (p. 10)

Interestingly, the double literature is a rather accurate portrayal of an actual, albeit rare, clinical syndrome: autoscopic paranoia. Individuals with this particular type of paranoia develop belief systems characterized by delusions or visual hallucinations around the notion that they have an exact double who is trying to take over their existence. The terror engendered in clinical cases of autoscopic paranoia is the same kind of anxiety that is described in the double literature.

A similar kind of autoscopic fear is found in the classic (and recently reproduced) science fiction movie *Invasion of the Body Snatchers*. This movie portrays the terror of people who believe that they are being replaced by exact doubles from another planet. Likewise, another recent science fiction film, *The Clones*, also ex-

"Oh, come off it, Ashton! The only reason you decided to detest Chris Evert is because no one else does."

Drawings by Wm. Hamilton; © 1972 The New Yorker Magazine, Inc.

plores the fear that results from having an exact biological duplicate.

The astute reader will recognize that there are several alternative explanations for the fear that attends an anticipated confrontation with someone exactly like oneself. For the Dark Romanticists, the double signaled that the soul had left the body and death was thereby imminent (Bleiler, 1967; Guerard, 1967). More recent double themes seem to focus on the self-scrutiny provoked by a double and the resulting perceptions of one's own negative qualities or actions (Beebe, 1955; Chizhevsky, 1962; Gurri, 1975; Rosenfield, 1967). According to these themes, the perception of a double may evoke processes of conscience, much like a superego, that lead to anxiety and fear. While it is difficult to separate the death and the self-evaluation apprehensions, it is equally likely that the fear and the anxiety associated with a double are the results of threats to one's sense of uniqueness.

As will be observed throughout this book, another form of contemporary American literature, satire and humor, often reflects

Drawing by C. R. Snyder, 1979.

real societal concerns. As will be confirmed by any lecturer who has discovered the effectiveness of the word *sex* in evoking laughter from an audience, we often find humor in things that concern and confuse us. Accordingly, satire and humor sometimes address our need to see ourselves as unique and the sense of confusion that arise when our sense of uniqueness is lost.

References

Beebe, M. The three motives of Raskolnikov. *College English*, 1955, *17*, 151–158.

Bleiler, E. F. Introduction to E.T.A. Hoffmann. In E. F. Bleiler (Ed.), *The best tales of Hoffmann*. New York: Dover, 1967, pp. v-xxxiii.

Boyd, E. *Guy de Maupassant: A biographical study*. New York: President Publishing, 1926.

Chizhevsky, D. The theme of the double in Dostoevsky. In R. Wellek (Ed.), *Dostoevsky*. Englewood Cliffs, N.J.: Prentice-Hall, 1962, pp. 112–129.

Cohen, L. *Selected poems 1956–1968*. New York: Viking, 1968.

Dostoevsky, F. M. *The double*. G. Bird (Trans.). Bloomington: Indiana University Press, 1958.

Dove, G. N. The haunted personality in Henry James. *Tennessee Studies in Literature*, 1958, *3*, 99–106.

Edel, L. (Ed.). *Complete tales of Henry James*, vol . 12. New York: Lippincott, 1965.

Eigner, E. M. *Robert Louis Stevenson and romantic tradition*. Princeton, N.J.: Princeton University Press, 1966.

Emerson, R. W. *Essays*. New York: Thomas Y. Crowell, 1926.

Gergen, K. J. Social psychology as history. *Journal of Personality and Social Psychology*, 1973, *26*, 309–320.

Gogol, N. The nose. In L. J. Kent (Ed.), *The collected tales and plays of Nikolai Gogol*. New York: Modern Library, 1969, pp. 474–497.

Guerard, A. J. Concepts of the double. In A. J. Guerard (Ed.), *Stories of the double*. New York: Lippincott, 1967, pp. 1–14.

Gurri, I. The double. Unpublished manuscript, University of Kansas, 1975.

Hoffmann, E. T. A. Signor Formica. In E. F. Bleiler (Ed.), *The best tales of Hoffmann*. New York: Dover, 1967, pp. 308–376.

James, H. Jolly corner. In H. James, *The altar of the dead*. New York: Scribner's, 1909, pp. 435–485.

Maupassant, G. de. *Short stories: Margot's tapers and others*. New York: Review of Books, 1903.

Nehru, B. K. Henry David Thoreau: A tribute. In W. Harding (Ed.), *The Thoreau centennial*. Albany: State University of New York Press, 1964, pp. 112–119.

Poe, E. A. William Wilson. In E. A. Poe's, *The works of Edgar Allan Poe*. New York: Scribner's, 1927, pp. 5–32.

Rosenfield, C. The shadow within: The conscious and unconscious use of the double. In A. J. Guerard (Ed.), *Stories of the double*. New York: Lippincott, 1967, pp. 311–331.

Spilka, M. Kafka's sources for "The metamorphosis." *Comparative Literature*, *11*, 1959 (Fall), 289–307.

Thompson, G. R. (Ed.). *The great short works of Edgar Allan Poe*. New York: Harper & Row, 1970.

Need for Uniqueness: Theory and Research

Irrationally held truths may be more harmful than reasoned errors.

> —Thomas Henry Huxley, *Science and Culture*, xii, "The Coming Age of the Origin of Species"

The great tragedy of Science—the slaying of the beautiful hypothesis by an ugly fact.

> —Thomas Henry Huxley, *Collected Essays*, viii, "Biogenesis and Abiogenesis"

Research has shown you are attracted to people like you.

Do Birds of a Feather Always Flock Together?

PEANUTS

   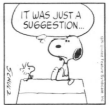

© 1979 United Feature Syndicate, Inc.

The introductory chapter provides a glimpse of the uniqueness-seeking phenomenon as revealed through literature. Based on such anecdotal evidence, it would seem that person-to-person encounters that result in self-perceptions of very high degrees of interpersonal similarity are likely to be a threat to a person's sense of uniqueness. Therefore, one would expect such threats of very high similarity to be noxious and aversive. Yet, at first glance, the vast majority of research does *not* support this contention. A careful analysis of this body of research, however, reveals a more complicated picture in which the negative and positive outcomes of interpersonal similarity vary systematically accordingly to the conditions that pose a threat to a sense of uniqueness. The following sections examine the prevailing theories and research on interpersonal similarity. Furthermore, limitations to such research are described, and the possibility of uniqueness seeking is introduced in the context of a new research paradigm.

Similarity and Approach Forces

The study of interpersonal similarity has reached almost epidemic proportions in psychology. A reader of either professional journals or various popular magazines and books frequently encounters the topic of interpersonal similarity. The theory and research in this area typically assert that greater interpersonal similarity is associated with more positive feelings. Likewise, greater interpersonal similarity is conceived of as being a powerful determinant of favorable reactions toward ourselves and other persons who are similar to us. For example, there is a cornucopia of studies that demonstrates that attitude similarity leads to greater interpersonal attraction than dissimilarity (Byrne, 1969, 1971; Byrne & Clore, 1967, 1970). Additionally, this positive influence of greater similarity has been reported on a variety of other dimensions, including abilities (Senn, 1971), economic conditions (Byrne, Clore, & Worchel, 1966), physical attributes (Pearson & Lee, 1903), race (Triandis & Davis, 1965), and personality (although inconsistently) (Byrne, Griffit, & Stefaniak, 1967).

The Stranger Paradigm: Greater Attraction to a More Similar Other Person

The theory and extensive research of Byrne (1971) and his colleagues have produced the most robust findings utilizing research procedures that are referred to as the *stranger paradigm*. In this paradigm, research participants[1] are recruited for an alleged study of first impressions. After arriving at the psychological research laboratory, individuals complete an attitude survey containing approximately 15 attitude items. Next, the experimenter col-

---

[1]The most common term for people who participate in psychology experiments is *subjects*. Generally, the authors will not employ this term because it implies a state of *total* subservience on the part of the person who participates in the experiment. In actuality, research participants are not totally subservient. Likewise, the term *subject* suggests that the experimenter adopts a superior role. Another point of information for the reader pertains to what kind of people serve in these experiments and why they do so. Participants in psychology experiments are often college freshmen and sophomores who take part in these experiments as one possible means of fulfilling the requirements of their introductory psychology courses.

lects the questionnaires of each person. While the research participants are supposedly waiting for other participants to complete their questionnaires, the experimenter prepares fictitious responses to the attitude surveys. The "other" questionnaires are prepared so as to vary in the degree of agreement with the participant's previously stated attitude positions. The experimenter returns and gives the person the fictitious attitude responses of an alleged "other participant." It is important to note that the research participants truly believe that they are going to meet this stranger. Each research participant then receives the questionnaire of an alleged stranger whom they are to meet. The proportion of similarity on this questionnaire is either 100% similarity (i.e., similarity on 15 out of the 15 attitudes), 80% similarity (i.e., 12 out of the 15 attitudes are similar), 66% similarity (i.e., 10 out of the 15 attitudes are similar), or 33% similarity (i.e., 5 out of the 15 attitudes are similar). People are then asked to read the questionnaire and form a "first impression" of this stranger prior to meeting him or her. Finally, the research participant completes two 7-point self-report items that measure his or her interpersonal attraction toward the stranger. The two items tap the extent to which the research participant (1) likes the other person and (2) would like to work with the other person. The total attraction score is the sum of these two scores (scores range from a low of 2 to a high of 14).

Byrne and other researchers have analyzed the research participants' responses to the stranger under each of the previously mentioned conditions of varying degrees of similarity. The results from several different experiments have demonstrated that the self-reported interpersonal attraction toward a stranger increases linearly as the degree of attitude similarity increases (e.g., Byrne, 1971).

Validation of Self-Studies: "Misery Loves Company"

Research in other response domains has shown that the selection of other persons to validate our opinions or abilities is determined, in part, by the degree of similarity between ourselves and the other persons with whom we choose to compare ourselves (Latane, 1966). In this regard, Festinger (1954) proposed that people have a need to evaluate their abilities and opinions by using some perceivable objective measure of reality. If such objective external sources are not available, individuals supposedly satisfy their need to evaluate themselves by comparing themselves with other people. Given a range of persons with whom to make comparisons, people tend to choose someone who is similar to them in abilities or opinions rather than someone who is dissimilar. According to Festinger (1954), comparisons with similar others are necessary for accurate self-appraisal.

Several experiments have supported Festinger's hypothesis about the choice of similar others for social comparison (Wheeler, 1966). Consider as an example the possibility of participating in an experience you know will be unpleasant. Would you want to be with a similar or a dissimilar person in such a circumstance? Research on this point would suggest that you would pick someone similar to yourself. But, similar in what sense? Darley and Aronson (1966) found that people who were led to believe that they were about to undergo a painful experimental procedure wanted to be with others who were also about to undergo such experimental procedures. Similarity of experience was evidently important to these people in making their choices. Along these same lines, Miller and Zimbardo (1966) performed an experiment in which people were given the information that they would be participating in a rather painful experiment. Results revealed that people chose to wait with others who had similar personalities (even though such individuals would not go though the painful experiment) in preference to waiting with others of dissimilar personalities who were to undergo the same painful experiment. Similarity of personality appears to have been a more important source of comparison than similarity of experience in this latter experiment.

The results of both of the aforementioned studies substantiate the notion that "Misery loves company." Other research also lends some support to this old saying. For example, the greater the uncertainty of an individual about his or her opinion (i.e., the greater the discrepancy between the individual and the group in the absence of physical reality), the greater will be the person's need to seek out comparisons with others whose opinions are perceived as being similar to his or her own opinion (see Gordan, 1966; Radloff, 1959).

Generalization of Similarity Studies

In still another area of research, Stotland and his colleagues (e.g., Stotland & Dunn, 1962; Stotland & Hillmer, 1962; Stotland, Zander, & Natsoulas, 1961) reported that the perception of similarity in a selected number of attributes evokes a tendency to assume similarity in other attributes. An example may be useful at this point. Stotland et al. recruited people for an alleged experiment about the nature and causes of personal tastes and preferences. Each person was escorted to a small room equipped with a microphone and earphones to permit communication with the experimenter and two other participants. In actuality, the "other two participants" were fictitious. The experimenter had prepared their responses earlier on tape recordings. First, each participant was asked to write (privately) his or her preference among eight pairs of brief musical compositions. After the choice had been made within each pair, the person heard the alleged preferences of each of the other two fictitious participants. Each person heard that his or her own preferences were highly similar to those of one of the bogus research participants and highly dissimilar to those of the other bogus research participant. Later in the experiment, people were asked to write their preferences for one of a pair of girls' names that were read aloud by the experimenter. After stating their choice, participants were asked to predict which names would be preferred by each of the two bogus participants. Results showed that the participants assigned their own preferences for girls' names to the participant with whom they had previously agreed on the musical preferences. Therefore, this study demonstrates that people who are convinced that they are similar to another person on a few characteristics may generalize this perceived similarity to other characteristics (e.g., names, in the aforementioned study).

Conformity and Persuasion Studies

Finally, the perception of similarity or agreement in judgments or opinions among other persons produces greater conformity with the judgments or opinions of the other persons (Allen, 1965; Asch, 1963, 1956; Crutchfield, 1955; Kiesler & Kiesler, 1969; Sherif,

*"A word to the wise, Benson. People are asking why
they don't see Old Glory on your bike."*

1935). Indeed, most people may have some difficulty in disputing the opinions of other people when the others are unanimous. A classic experiment in the area of social psychology serves as an illustration of this phenomenon. In this experiment by Asch (1963), a group of people (usually eight in number) were seated in a row in a psychological laboratory. They were first instructed to examine the length of a model line that appeared on a screen in front of them. Then, from a group of three lines of unequal length, they were asked to select the line that was the same length as the model line. The people were requested to give their answers aloud. It should be emphasized that there was only one "real" research participant in this experiment, and this person responded last. The remaining people were paid confederates who responded unanimously with incorrect judgments on certain trials. Thus, the actual research participant was confronted with a unanimous contradiction of his or her own perception of correctness. While there was variability among participants, Asch found distinct movement toward the majority's incorrect judgments, that is, the direction of the group's distortion of accuracy. Thus, when confronted with a group of individuals who are similar in their judgments but different from our own private judgments, we may tend to change our own judgments toward those of the similar majority.

In a somewhat similar experimental approach, it appears that similarity of opinions leads to greater persuasion (Berscheid, 1966; Bettinghous, 1968; Mills & Jellison, 1968). In a review of the relevant research, Simons, Berkowitz, and Moyer (1970) offered some conclusions regarding this relationship between similarity and persuasion. First, similarities between the communicator and the recipient of the communication must be relevant to the communication before similarity leads to greater persuasion than dissimilarity. Second, certain kinds of dissimilarities (e.g., particularly membership-group dissimilarities) contribute to attitude change and influence when the dissimilarities lead to perceptions of competence, fairness, prestige, etc. Third, the degree of influence by a similar or a dissimilar communicator depends on the extent to which the similarities or dissimilarities are perceived by the receiver as performing a function for the receiver in his or her capacity as a recipient of a particular message. For example, Brock (1965) varied whether a paint store salesperson's experiences in the use of a product were similar or dissimilar to the experience anticipated by the customer. Salespeople whose experiences were similar to the customer's experiences expected use of the product produced significantly greater shifts in customer purchasing decisions.

At this point, the reader may be convinced of the veracity of the saying that "Birds of a feather flock together." This belief may be even more obvious when we realize that we often prefer to be around, and may be influenced by, similar others. While it may be tempting to affirm this conclusion, the subsequent discussion may raise some qualifications for the reader.

Limitations on Similarity Notions

Preoccupation with the study of the "approach" forces that often accompany similarity can lead to the erroneous conclusion that similarity is *always* a positive state and rarely, if ever, aversive to the individual. In fact, it has been suggested that this need for uniformity does not take into account the variety of instances in which people emphasize their uniqueness rather than their similarity (Deutsch & Kraus, 1965). In this regard, there are at least two bodies of data indicating that it is inaccurate to assume that similarity *always* results in a positive state. First, evidence suggests that the approach or avoidance forces that attend interpersonal similarity are influenced by the other person's attributes and the motives that are aroused by these attributes in the particular situation. Second, it can be argued that the typically employed experimental manipulations of interpersonal similarity may not have aroused an extremely high degree of self-perceived similarity in the participants in such experiments. The following brief review of both communities of similarity research illustrates the need for some theoretical redress in order to account for these factors.

Attributes of the Similar Other

Data suggest that the favorable reactions resulting from interpersonal similarity may be limited to situations where the person does not receive information other than attitude similarity about the stimulus person. If the other person possesses characteristics that may have negative connotations, people may not be so consistent in their preference for similar others (Byrne & Lamberth, 1971; Cooper & Jones, 1969; Lerner & Agar, 1972; Novak & Lerner, 1968; Taylor & Mettee, 1971). For example, utilizing the stranger research paradigm described earlier in this chapter, Taylor and Mettee (1971) initially provided research participants with information showing that they were either similar or dissimilar to a person they were about to meet. Then, upon meeting the participant (actually a confederate), this other person acted in a very pleasant or obnoxious manner. Results revealed that people liked the similar other more than the dissimilar other when the other person was pleasant. However, when the other person was obnoxious, the research participants showed greater liking for the dissimilar stranger as compared with the similar stranger.

In a related study by Lerner and Agar (1972), similar other strangers were perceived as being more attractive and approachable when the similar and dissimilar persons were portrayed as "normal." However, people avoided a similar person more than a dissimilar person who was also "the cause of his own drug addiction." While this research certainly suggests a limitation to the notion that "birds of a feather flock together," the following analysis of the experimental procedures used to manipulate interpersonal similarity provides a more telling criticism.

The Experimental Manipulation of Interpersonal Similarity

Previous researchers have implicitly assumed that they have manipulated similarity so that the research participants have perceived that they are about to interact with another person who may have either a very low, moderate, or very high degree of similarity to them. But, have people truly believed that the other person is of high or very high similarity?

In most studies of similarity, greater persuasion, greater attraction, and greater assumed similarity *follow comparison of a small number of attributes* (e.g., 1 to 15 beliefs) *with only one other person*. Evidence on this topic demonstrates that the magnitude of self-perceived similarity in such experiments may *not* necessarily exceed the person's customary experiences or perceptions of moderate degrees of interpersonal similarity between himself or herself and members of the peer group. For example, Boss (1973) found that the experimental induction of similarity (analogous to those procedures described previously in the stranger paradigm) did *not* produce significant differences in the magnitude of self-perceived similarity between research participants in the "low-" and "high-" similarity conditions and participants in a control condition in which they did not receive information about the attitude profile of a stranger. That is, research participants who were given a high-similarity manipulation did not report a significantly higher sense of similarity relative to the hypothetical stranger than did a control group of people given no similarity information; moreover, the research participants given a low-similarity manipulation did not report a significantly lower sense of similarity relative to the hypothetical stranger than did a control group of people given no similarity information.[2]

Given the aforementioned results, one may begin to question the interpretation of similarity in the previous stranger-paradigm research, since such experiments may not have induced people to feel that they were *extremely similar* (or dissimilar) relative to the hypothetical other person. Without establishing a very high sense

[2]Although the high- and low-similarity conditions did not differ in terms of perceived similarity relative to a control group of people given no similarity feedback, it should be noted that the high-similarity condition did elicit a higher sense of similarity than the low-similarity condition.

of similarity, the best conclusion resulting from the previous stranger-paradigm studies is that a moderate degree of similarity relative
to another person results in a positive state. *Within the range of
similarity typically manipulated in these aforementioned studies*,
greater purported similarity has generated more positive responses
toward the other person. However, these studies do not allow one
to infer safely that the positive response toward another person
would result in circumstances where *very high* similarity results.
This is the case because very high levels of similarity typically
have not been manipulated in such studies.

If the reader imagines himself or herself as a participant in the
typical stranger-paradigm study, it becomes apparent why a very
high sense of similarity may not necessarily occur. Most of us are
aware of a multitude of dimensions on which we compare ourselves with others in order to form a self-concept. The relatively
small number of such dimensions or characteristics employed in
the stranger paradigm would still potentially allow us to speculate
that we are different on a variety of other characteristics. But
suppose we are given feedback that we are very similar to another
person on a much larger number of comparison attributes (say 50
or more). It then becomes much harder for us to reason that we
may be different on "other" characteristics. In such an instance, a
very high degree of interpersonal similarity is likely to be established. Also, consider the fact that each one of us may compare
himself or herself with more than one person. Suppose that we
were led to believe that we were similar to *several* people on a large
number of characteristics? Such feedback would potentially generate a sense of *very high interpersonal similarity*. These latter con-
ceptions of interpersonal similarity may suggest to the reader how
an extreme sense of interpersonal similarity may be established.

In order to provide a more definitive explanation of the various overall levels of similarity as utilized in uniqueness theory, the
reader should refer to Table I. Here, the reader may visualize the
factors that are associated with the particular levels of similarity
employed in uniqueness theory. For example, very high similarity
is hypothesized to occur when there is 95–100% similarity on 50 or
more comparison attributes relative to 2–10,000 other people. This
truly should reflect very extreme similarity. Likewise, high similarity is hypothesized to occur when there is 80–100% similarity on

Table I. Hypothesized Factors That Are Associated with Overall Levels of Similarity as Conceptualized in Uniqueness Theory

		Factors that contribute to overall level of similarity	
		Proportion of similarity on comparison attributes	Number of comparison attributes	Number of comparison others
Overall level of similarity as conceptualized in uniqueness theory	Very high	95–100%	50 or more (including attitudes, personality and physical characteristics, etc.)	2–10,000
	High	80–100%	30–50 (may include more than just attitudes)	1
	Moderate	60–100%	1–15	1
	Slight	10–50%	1–15	1
	Very slight	0–5%	1–15	1

approximately 30–50 comparison attributes relative to another person. It should be pointed out, however, that in the typical previous interpersonal-attraction research, neither this high nor very high level of similarity has been reached. Rather, the usual stranger-paradigm manipulations have been in the very slight to slight and moderate range, as depicted in Table I.

Having argued that previous research may not have manipulated interpersonal similarity into the high and very high ranges, it is now appropriate to explore how extreme similarity may threaten one's sense of uniqueness. The final section in this chapter begins this inquiry.

Extreme Similarity and Uniqueness Seeking

In contrast to the conclusions of the typical stranger-paradigm studies of interpersonal similarity, self-actualization theories provide justification for expecting unfavorable reactions and avoidance of similarity following social comparisons of many similar attributes with many similar persons. For example, the writings of Fromm (1941, 1955), Horney (1937), and Maslow (1962) suggest that people have a "need for separate identity" or a "need for uniqueness." Within this framework, situations that induce a loss of separate identity are said to evoke anxiety and leave the person in a state of insecurity.

Although rarely measured, it is likely that uniqueness-related behaviors have been evident in conformity experiments. For example, it is surprising that the negative feelings expressed by many conforming research participants and the behavior of research participants who did *not* conform on 68% of the trials in the classic Asch (1963) experiment have not attracted the attention of many psychologists. In this vein, it is interesting to note that Sherif and Hovland (1961) and Asch (1956) reported that some individuals maintained independence or changed in the direction that was opposite to the position advocated by the group. The people who refused to conform may have been exhibiting a stronger need to maintain their own individual integrity relative to the need to avoid appearing different and being ostracized by others (Asch, 1963; Homans, 1961; Pepinsky, 1961).

Psychologists who have performed reviews of the group pressure literature reveal a significant bias toward the study of conformity (see Allen, 1965; Bass, 1961; Blake & Mouton, 1961; Graham, 1962; Mann, 1959; Willis, 1965). Such reviews are striking because they continue to neglect other potential responses to group pressure, such as anticonformity or nonconformity and independence (Allen & Newtson, 1972; Krech, Crutchfield, & Ballachey, 1962). Given this context, however, it is important to acknowledge that a small number of researchers have explicitly recognized the need to study individual and situational determinants of anticonformity and independence (Allen, 1975; Jahoda, 1959; Stricker, Messick, & Jackson, 1970; Willis, 1970).

Since the experimental procedures of conformity research very likely induce feelings of sameness on some dimension or dimensions that are important to the person, the negative feelings expressed by many conforming research participants and the anticonforming or independent responses of other participants may reflect a frustration of the desire to see themselves as differentiated from the crowd (unique). If this conjecture is valid, it may also be hypothesized that any situation that induces strong feelings of interpersonal similarity may arouse negative affect. Following this logic, a series of experiments by Fromkin (1968, 1970) was conducted to evaluate the reactions to extremely high similarity. The hypotheses in these early uniqueness-theory studies were that very high degrees of similarity would be undesirable and would evoke behavior directed at eliminating the negative feelings (Fromkin, 1968). The experimental approach employed was known as the *test feedback method.* It provided research participants with fictitious test results from an extensive battery of tests that allegedly measured their personality, values, attitudes, interests, etc. Test results described research participants as either very highly or slightly similar to 10,000 of their peers on a large number of comparison attributes. How did the research participants respond to such an extreme sense of similarity?

The results of the test feedback method revealed that when the very high as compared to slight degrees of similarity were employed, research participants (1) generated a greater number of unique uses for a common object (Fromkin, 1968); (2) assumed greater dissimilarity from an unknown other person (Fromkin, 1968); and (3) exhibited greater preferences for experiences that were unavailable to other research participants (Fromkin, 1970). Although qualifications may be raised about each of these results, this early set of findings provides initial support for the assumption that very high degrees of self-perceived similarity are undesirable. These studies and others are presented in greater detail in Chapter 3 on the "Theory of Uniqueness."

While the findings mentioned in the previous paragraph seem to stand alone in opposition to the abundance of similarity research, it should be noted that the vast majority of other studies of interpersonal similarity involve comparisons of only a *relatively small number of attributes* between the research participant and only *one* other person. Thus, it may be hypothesized that the positive relationship between similarity and conformity, between similarity and liking, and between similarity and choice of comparison others is obtained only under conditions of *very slight to moderate degrees* of interpersonal similarity (see again Table I). Returning to the often-used analogy, then, it may be the case that "Birds of a feather do *not always* flock together." Rather, there appear to be situations in which birds want to be different from a flock[3]—and, as will be shown later in Chapter 5, some birds may want to be more different than others (i.e., there are individual differences in need for uniqueness).

References

Allen, V. L. Situational factors in conformity. In L. Berkowitz (Ed.), *Advances in experimental social psychology*, vol. 2. New York: Academic, 1965, pp. 133–170.

Allen, V. L. Social support for nonconformity. In L. Berkowitz (Ed.), *Advances in experimental social psychology*, vol. 8. New York: Academic, 1975, pp. 1–43.

Allen, V. L., & Newtson, D. Development of conformity and independence. *Journal of Personality an Social Psychology*, 1972, *22*, 18–30.

Asch, S. E. Studies of independence and conformity: A minority of one against a unanimous majority. *Psychological Monographs*, 1956, *70* (9, Whole No. 416).

Asch, S. E. Effects of group pressure upon the modification and distortion of

---

[3]See *Jonathan Livingston Seagull* (Bach, 1973) for an extrapolation of the need-for-uniqueness notion within the "flock" metaphor.

judgments. In M. H. Guetzkow (Ed.), *Groups, leadership and men.* Original copyright, Pittsburgh: Carnegie Press, 1951. Reissued, New York: Russell & Russell, 1963, pp. 117–190.

Bach, R. *Jonathan Livingston Seagull.* New York: Avon, 1973.

Bass, B. M. Conformity, deviation, and a general theory of interpersonal behavior. In I. A. Berg & B. M. Bass (Eds.), *Conformity and deviation.* New York: Harper, 1961, pp. 38–100.

Berscheid, E. Opinion change and communicator–communicatee similarity and dissimilarity. *Journal of Personality and Social Psychology*, 1966, *4*, 670–680.

Bettinghous, E. P. *Persuasive communication.* New York: Holt, Rinehart, & Winston, 1968.

Blake, R. R., & Mouton, J. S. Conformity, resistance, and conversion. In I. A. Berg & B. M. Bass (Eds.), *Conformity and deviation.* New York: Harper, 1961, pp. 199–229.

Boss, D. The relationship between low and high degrees of interpersonal similarity and increments and decrements in self esteem. Unpublished master's thesis, Purdue University, 1973.

Brock, T. C. Communicator–recipient similarity and decision change. *Journal of Personality and Social Psychology*, 1965, *1*, 650–654.

Byrne, D. Attitudes and attraction. In L. Berkowitz (Ed.), *Advances in experimental social psychology,* vol. 4. New York: Academic, 1969, pp. 36–86.

Byrne, D. *The attraction paradigm.* New York: Academic, 1971.

Byrne, D., & Clore, G. L. Effectance arousal and attraction. *Journal of Personality and Social Psychology*, 1967, *6* (4, pt. 2, 1–18).

Byrne, D., & Clore, G. L. A reinforcement model of evaluative responses. *Personality*, 1970, *1*, 103–128.

Byrne, D., & Lamberth, J. Cognitive and reinforcement theories as complementary approaches to the study of attraction. In B. I. Murstein (Ed.), *Theories of attraction and love.* New York: Springer, 1971, pp. 59–85.

Byrne, D., Clore, G. L., & Worchel, P. The effect of economic similarity–dissimilarity on interpersonal attraction. *Journal of Personality and Social Psychology*, 1966, *4*, 220–224.

Byrne, D., Griffitt, W., & Stefaniak, D. Attraction and similarity of personality characteristics. *Journal of Personality and Social Psychology*, 1967, *5*, 82–90.

Cooper, J., & Jones, E. E. Opinion divergence as a strategy to avoid being miscast. *Journal of Personality and Social Psychology*, 1969, *13*, 23–30.

Crutchfield, R. S. Conformity and character. *American Psychologist*, 1955, *10*, 191–198.

Darley, J., & Aronson, E. Self-evaluation vs. direct anxiety reduction as determinants of the fear-affiliation relationship. *Journal of Experimental Social Psychology Supplement*, 1966, *1*, 66–79.

Deutsch, M., & Krauss, R. M. *Theories in social psychology.* New York: Basic Books, 1965.

Festinger, L. A theory of social comparison process. *Human Relations*, 1954, *7*, 117–140.

Fromkin, H. L. Affective and valuational consequences of self-perceived uniqueness deprivation. Unpublished doctoral dissertation, Ohio State University, 1968.

Fromkin, H. L. Effects of experimentally aroused feelings of undistinctiveness upon valuation of scarce and novel experiences. *Journal of Personality and Social Psychology*, 1970, *16*, 521–529.

Fromm, E. *Escape from freedom.* New York: Farrar & Rinehart, 1941.

Fromm, E. *The sane society.* New York: Rinehart & Company, 1955.

Gordan, B. Influence and social comparison as motives for affiliation. *Journal of Experimental Social Psychology Supplement*, 1966, *1*, 55–65.

Graham, D. Experimental studies of social influence in simple judgment situations. *Journal of Social Psychology*, 1962, *56*, 245–269.

Homans, G. C. *Social behavior: Its elementary forms.* New York: Harcourt, Brace, & World, 1961.

Horney, K. *The neurotic personality of our time.* New York: Norton, 1937.

Jahoda, M. Conformity and independence—A psychological analysis. *Human Relations*, 1959, *12*, 99–120.

Kiesler, C. A., & Kiesler, S. B. *Conformity.* Reading, Mass.: Addison-Wesley, 1969.

Krech, D., Crutchfield, R. S., & Ballachey, E. L. *Individual in society.* New York: McGraw-Hill, 1962.

Latane. B. (Ed.). Studies in social comparison: Introduction and overview. *Journal of Experimental Social Psychology Supplement*, 1966, *2*, Supplement No. 1.

Lerner, M. J., & Agar, E. The consequences of perceived similarity: Attraction and rejection, approach and avoidance. *Journal of Experimental Research in Personality*, 1972, *6*, 69–75.

Mann, R. D. A review of the relationship between personality and performance in small groups. *Psychological Bulletin*, 1959, *56*, 241–270.

Maslow, A. H. *Toward a psychology of being.* New York: Van Nostrand, 1962.

Miller, N., & Zimbardo, P. Motives for fear induced affiliation: Emotional comparison or interpersonal similarity? *Journal of Personality*, 1966, *34*, 481–503.

Mills, J., & Jellison, J. M. Effect on opinion change of similarity between the communicator and the audience he addressed. *Journal of Personality and Social Psychology*, 1968, *9*, 153–159.

Novak, D. W., & Lerner, M. J. Rejection as a consequence of perceived similarity. *Journal of Personality and Social Psychology*, 1968, *9*, 147–152.

Pearson, K., & Lee, A. On the laws of inheritance in man: I. Inheritance of physical characteristics. *Biometrika*, 1903, *2*, 357–462.

Pepinsky, P. N. Social exceptions that prove the rule. In I. A. Berg & B. M. Bass (Eds.), *Conformity and deviation.* New York: Harper & Row, 1961, pp. 380–411.

Radloff, R. Opinion and affiliation. Unpublished doctoral dissertation. University of Minnesota, 1959.

Senn, D. Attraction as a function of similarity–dissimilarity in task performance. *Journal of Personality and Social Psychology*, 1971, *18*, 120–123.

Sherif, M. A study of some social factors in perception. *Archives of Psychology*, 1935, *27*, No. 187.

Sherif, M., & Hovland, C. I. *Social judgment: Assimilation and contrast effects in communication and attitude change.* New Haven, Conn.: Yale University Press, 1961.

Simons, H. W., Berkowitz, N. N., & Moyer, R. J. Similarity, credibility, and attitude change. *Psychological Bulletin*, 1970, *73*, 1–16.

Stotland, E., & Dunn, R. E. Identification, "oppositeness," authoritarianism, self esteem, and birth order. *Psychological Monographs*, 1962, *76*, (9, Whole No. 528).

Stotland, E., & Hillmer, M. L., Jr. Identification, authoritarian defensiveness, and self esteem. *Journal of Abnormal and Social Psychology*, 1962, *64*, 334–342.

Stotland, E., Zander, A., & Natsoulas, T. Generalization of interpersonal similarity. *Journal of Abnormal and Social Psychology*, 1961, *62*, 250–256.

Strickler, L. J., Messick, S., & Jackson, D. N. Conformity, anticonformity, and independence: Their dimensionality and generality. *Journal of Personality and Social Psychology*, 1970, *16*, 494–507.

Taylor, S. E., & Mettee, D. R. When similarity breeds contempt. *Journal of Personality and Social Psychology*, 1971, *20*, 75–81.

Triandis, H., & Davis, E. Race and belief as determinants of behavioral intentions. *Journal of Personality and Social Psychology*, 1965, *2*, 715–725.

Wheeler, L. Motivation as a determination of upward comparison. *Journal of Experimental Social Psychology Supplement*, 1966, *1*, 27–31.

Willis, R. H. Conformity, independence, and anti-conformity. *Human Relations*, 1965, *18*, 373–388.

Willis, R. H. The conscientious cartographers: A fable inspired by Strickler, Messick, and Jackson. *Journal of Personality and Social Psychology*, 1970, *16*, 508.

Theory of Uniqueness

Theoretical formulations in psychology are frequently evaluated in terms of how plausible they appear to the reader, their contribution to the derivation of testable hypotheses, and the number of established data that they can encompass satisfactorily. Related to the first issue, the reader will be the judge of how plausible the theory appears after reading the subsequent chapters. With regard to the second issue, it is probably accurate to say that the present theory does generate hypotheses that are testable through empirical procedures. Furthermore, the theory also attempts to explain and integrate a wide variety of research findings from different response domains. Equally importantly, however, the theory seeks to provide some insights into important social phenomena. At this point it is appropriate to introduce the theory of uniqueness.

Similarity as a Self-Attribute

The predictions of uniqueness theory utilize the concept of self as a basic explanatory dynamic. In order to develop the concept of self in the present context, it is first necessary to define various relevant terms. In the following discussion, *person* refers to the perceiver. *Comparison other(s)* refers to an individual(s) with whom the person is comparing himself or herself. A *comparison attribute* is a "percept or cognition by which the individual designates himself and discriminates persons, either himself or other persons" (Sherwood, 1970, p. 42). Some examples of attributes are tall, pretty, funny, or cruel. Attributes can be ordered into *attribute categories,* such as personality traits, attitudes or opinions, and physical characteristics. A person can perceive that his or her opinions, physical characteristics, etc., are (slightly, moderately, or highly) similar to those of another person. A *self* (person) *attribute* is the perceptual outcome of such interpersonal comparisons or the specific location that the person assigns himself or herself; for example, I am (slightly, moderately, or extremely) similar to another person or persons. An *identity dimension* is defined from the point of view of the perceiver as a "set of person attributes which have a common core of meaning" (Miller, 1963, p. 676).

The encoding of a set of self-attributes onto a particular identity dimension requires conceptual leaps that represent abstractions from self-perceptions to interpretive or evaluative dimensions. In this regard, the common core of meaning attached to any one set of self-attributes can vary among different persons. However, there are probably common identity dimensions along which most people perceive themselves. In the present context, it is theorized that uniqueness is one such identity dimension. The hypothetical process by which people encode their similarity self-attribute on an identity dimension of uniqueness is described in the subsequent paragraphs.

Simply put, the foregoing discussion suggests that a person compares himself or herself with other people and that as a result of this process, the person perceives some degree of similarity relative to other people. Thus, it is assumed that similarity becomes salient as a result of the social comparison processes (see Snyder, 1975a,b,c; Snyder & Batson, 1974). This degree of similarity is a self-attribute that is then interpreted by the person. This interpretation process occurs on an identity dimension that represents an evaluative continuum. In the case of similarity, we hypothesize that people principally encode the degree of similarity self-attribute information on a uniqueness identity dimension. That is, people evaluate the acceptability of their similarity perception based on a uniqueness identity dimension. The hypothesized encoding of degree of similarity information on the uniqueness identity dimension is shown in Figure 1.

As can be seen in the hypothesized encodings shown in Figure 1, a person who perceives a very slight similarity relative to another person encodes this information as having low acceptability (Point A); slight similarity is encoded as having moderate accepta-

UNIQUENESS IDENTITY DIMENSION

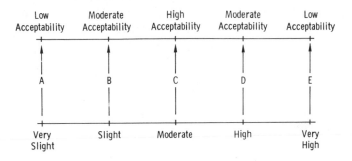

SIMILARITY SELF-ATTRIBUTE

Figure 1. Hypothesized encoding of degree of similarity self-attribute information on the uniqueness identity dimension.

bility (Point B); moderate similarity is encoded as having high acceptability (Point C); high similarity is encoded as having moderate acceptability (Point D); and very high similarity is encoded as having low acceptability (Point E).[1] Thus, it is hypothesized that moderate similarity generates the highest sense of acceptability on the uniqueness identity dimension and that increases *or* decreases relative to moderate similarity both lessen the degree of encoded acceptability.

The rationale for this hypothesized encoding process is that most people may believe that exceedingly high or low similarity deviates from reality, both as they have experienced it and as they would like to perceive it. In regard to reality *as we actually perceive it*, we learn that people vary somewhat on physical characteristics because of differing genetic backgrounds; moreover, we learn that people differ somewhat from each other because of differing environmental backgrounds (see Chapter 11 for a more detailed discussion of these topics). Therefore, in an actuarial sense, we may come to perceive that we are moderately similar relative to other people. This moderate similarity thus translates to a maximal sense of acceptability on the person's uniqueness identity dimension. In

[1]The approximate operational definitions of the very slight, slight, moderate, high, and very high overall levels of similarity are the same as those hypothesized previously in Table I, Chapter 2.

regard to reality *as we would like to perceive it*, we are motivated to seek some sense of difference relative to others. Because of this motivation, a moderate level of similarity may be perceived as having the highest acceptability on the uniqueness identity dimension. Overall, therefore, the moderate level of similarity should be encoded as having maximal acceptability on the uniqueness identity dimension because of both reality-based *and* motivation-based factors.

If the self-attribute of similarity exhibits the aforementioned uniqueness encoding process, then it is logical to speculate that predictable emotional and behavioral reactions to varying degrees of similarity should result. In this context, the level of acceptability on the uniqueness identity dimension represents an evaluative reaction that influences subsequent predicted emotional and behavioral responses. Such emotional and behavioral reactions are consistent with self-theories that maintain that evaluative and motivational states are part of the coding process of identity dimensions (MacLeod, 1951; Miller, 1963; Sherwood, 1970; Wylie, 1961). These predictions are addressed in the following section.

Emotional and Behavioral Predictions of Uniqueness Theory

The degree of interpersonal similarity that one person perceives relative to another person or persons plays a central role in uniqueness theory. *That is, the emotional and behavioral outcomes of interpersonal similarity depend on the magnitude of self-perceived similarity relative to the person(s) with whom we are comparing ourselves.*

First, consider a person's emotional reaction to another person. According to the theory, the most positive emotional reaction should result when a person feels a *moderate* amount of similarity relative to another person. The moderate degree of similarity is hypothetically most pleasant because the person may encode such information on the uniqueness identity dimension as having the highest degree of acceptability for both reality-based and motivation-based reasons. In those instances where the magnitude of similarity exceeds the moderate range, the person should begin to react more negatively emotionally. Thus, when a person feels a *very high* degree of similarity relative to another, a negative emotional reaction should occur. The negative emotional reaction to very high similarity results because the individual encodes such information as having low acceptability on the uniqueness identity dimension. In those instances where the magnitude of similarity falls below the moderate range, the person also begins to evidence a more negative emotional reaction. For example, if a person feels a *very slight* similarity relative to another, this may generate a strong negative reaction. This negative emotional reaction to very slight similarity results because this information is encoded as having low acceptability on the uniqueness identity dimension. Overall, therefore, the theory would predict a *curvilinear* relationship between emotional reactions as a function of degree of similarity relative to another person. This hypothetical curve is shown in Figure 2.

At this point, the reader may be surprised to learn that feedback that he or she is *very* different (i.e., very slightly similar to another) can generate a negative emotional response. This discovery may seem especially surprising considering the title of the present book, *Uniqueness: The Human Pursuit of Difference.* The best

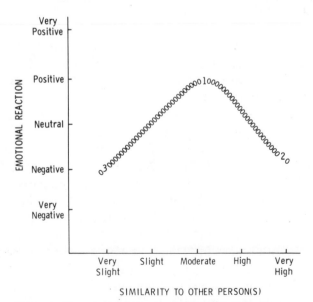

Figure 2. Hypothesized emotional reactions to another person as a function of similarity relative to that person.

way of comprehending this apparent paradox is to realize that the theory predicts that the most positive emotional reactions result from *some* intermediate sense of difference relative to other people. When we are made to feel as if we are *very little different* (i.e., have extremely high similarity), we do not not like such a state, *just as we do not like it when we are made to feel extremely different* (i.e., having very slight similarity). Emotionally, therefore, our pursuit of difference may be best conceptualized as a pursuit of *some* degree of dissimilarity relative to other people.

To this point, we have described the *emotional reactions* that are hypothesized according to the theory. Next, we shall attempt to explain how uniqueness theory addresses the *behaviors* that result when a person is confronted with various degrees of similarity relative to another person (or other persons).

When a person feels a moderate amount of similarity relative to another, according to uniqueness theory that person experiences a positive emotional reaction *and simultaneously expresses no change in behavior.* Since this moderate amount of similarity is associated with a positive emotional state, the person does not have to engage in behaviors that would either enhance or detract from the moderate degree of similarity relative to another person. This point of no change is depicted as Point 1 on Figure 3. It should be noted that Point 1 on Figure 3 reflects the degree of change that should correspond to the positive emotional state reflected in Point 1 on Figure 2. As can be seen in Figure 3, in those instances where the magnitude of similarity exceeds the moderate level, the person begins to manifest stronger changes toward dissimilarity. In other words, when confronted with feedback that a person is very highly similar to another, that person will try to behave so as to lessen the similarity. In this regard, Point 2 of Figure 3 reflects the change toward dissimilarity that corresponds to the negative emotional state that is reflected in Point 2 on Figure 2. In those instances where the magnitude of similarity falls below the moderate range, the person may change his or her behavior so as to become more similar to the other person. That is, when we receive feedback that we are very slightly similar relative to another, we may attempt to change our behavior so as to enhance the similarity. Point 3 of Figure 3 portrays the amount of change toward similarity that corresponds to the negative emotional state that is reflected in Point 3 of Figure 2.

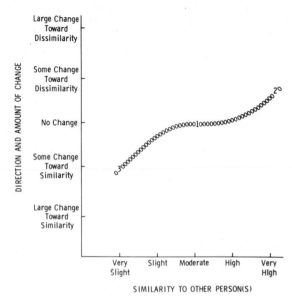

Figure 3. Hypothesized direction and amount of change as a function of similarity relative to another person.

The shape of Figure 3 suggests that the uncomfortable emotional reactions to very high similarity and very slight similarity are associated with behavioral maneuvers to reestablish a moderate sense of difference. Again, it should be emphasized that "the pursuit of difference" is *not* a phenomenon whereby people seek to behaviorally establish their *total* difference relative to others. On the contrary, the theory suggests that people behaviorally strive to maintain *some* sense of difference relative to others.

While the present theory obviously addresses the emotional and behavioral reactions that result from the entire range of similarity, the subsequent discussions of data and examples, in this and other chapters, often emphasize the reactions resulting in the range from moderate to very high similarity. The reason for this focus is that psychologists have already expended considerable verbiage on people's negative reactions to extreme dissimilarity (very slight similarity) as well as on people's attempts to "fit in" and increase their similarity when they feel very different. (The reader is directed to the sources cited in Chapter 2 that illustrate how people avoid the low range of similarity.) As can be seen in the present model, it is acknowledged that extreme difference does generate unpleasant emotions and attempts at "fitting in." What is new and potentially revealing about the present model is that it also predicts that it is unpleasant for people to perceive that they are not at all different (i.e., they are extremely similar to another). Likewise, the model suggests that people attempt to avoid this feeling of lacking uniqueness and therefore pursue behavioral maneuvers in order to achieve a moderate sense of difference.

Having briefly stated the uniqueness theory in terms of emotional and behavioral reactions, we will now discuss the various studies that are relevant to uniqueness theorization.

Research on Emotional Reactions

Emotion: Mood Scale Study

According to uniqueness theorization, a person's emotional reaction should be curvilinearly related to degree of similarity relative to another person (see again Figure 2). Fromkin (1972) performed the following experiment to test this hypothesis.

Research participants initially completed an official-looking test, which consisted of 90 items that were constructed to appear as if they measured personality traits, interests, values, etc. The format of the items was similar to those items typically employed in "freshman orientation" at this particular state university. The research participants responded on computer "mask-sense" cards. The research participants were later returned a five-page computer printout of their test results. The feedback each person received was actually bogus, and depending on the similarity condition to which the person was randomly assigned, the research participant was led to believe that he or she was very highly, highly, moderately, or slightly similar to "10,000 other college students who have taken the same test." This similarity manipulation was accomplished by showing the research participant his or her score on a large number of dimensions relative to the average of 10,000 other students. That is, an O appeared on a 50-dot line for the average of the 10,000 other students, and an X appeared on that same line for the research participant's score on this item. Thus, by varying the distance between the X's and O's, the experimenter could lead the research participant to believe that he or she was either very highly, highly, moderately, or slightly similar to other students.

After receiving this similarity feedback, research participants were asked to complete a mood rating scale. This mood scale consisted of several affect words that could be summed in order to rate each person's overall emotional response (Mood Adjective Checklist; Nowlis & Green, 1965). What were people's emotional responses to the various degrees of similarity? Generally, the emotional responses were consistent with the curvilinear relationship predicted by the uniqueness theory. Descriptively, the emotional response became more positive from the slight to moderate similarity conditions, and then the emotional response became less positive from the moderate to high to very high similarity conditions. Statistically, this curvilinear pattern was significant for the male research participants, although it did not reach significance for the females.

In summary, therefore, the results of the Fromkin study are generally consistent with the model. What is especially noteworthy is that the emotional response eventually becomes less positive when a person believes that he or she is highly or very highly similar to other people. Likewise, there appears to be some intermediate level of similarity (e.g., "moderate") that elicits the most positive emotional response.

Emotion: Self-Esteem Study

In the previous study, we were given information about how people feel in a situation in which they are led to believe that they are similar to others (in varying degrees). Another way of conceptualizing our emotional reaction to such similarity feedback is to examine what happens to a person's feelings about *himself or herself* in such a situation. A measure of self-esteem taps such a personal emotional response.

Ganster, McCuddy, and Fromkin (1977) performed the following study in order to explore the effects of interpersonal similarity on a person's self-esteem. In this study, research participants responded to attitude questionnaires that contained either 15 or 30 items. This questionnaire constituted the first independent variable. After responding to each item by pressing a button on a computer console, the research participant was given feedback about how a great number of other students had responded to the same question. The similarity independent variable in this study was either 33% or 80% similarity on the attitude items. By way of the video console, in the 33% similarity condition research participants received feedback that showed their responses were exactly the same as the modal response of the 10,000 other students on 33% of the attitude items. On the remaining items, the bogus modal position was two categories away from the research participant's response. In the 80% similarity condition, the bogus feedback indicated that the research participant's responses were exactly the same on 80% of the items. On the remaining items, the bogus modal position was two categories removed from the response made by the research participant.

Before and and after receiving the similarity feedback (33% versus 80%) on either 15 or 30 items, the research participants completed the Coopersmith (1967) Self-Esteem Scale. This scale consists of 58 self-descriptive statements, such as "I'm easy to like" and "I'm pretty sure of myself." A self-esteem score is derived by adding the number of agreements with positive statements and the number of disagreements with negative statements. Finally, it should be noted that the scale was divided into odd- and even-numbered items in order to create a 29-item pre-(before)-measure of self-esteem and a 29-item post-(after)-measure of self-esteem. Thus, a self-esteem change score was calculated by subtracting the prescore from the postscore. Using this approach, a positive change score reflected an increase in self-esteem, and a negative change score reflected a decrease in self-esteem.

Results showed that self-esteem *increased for the 15-item feedback* when the research participants were given 80% as compared to 33% similarity feedback. Conversely, self-esteem *decreased for the 30-item feedback* when the research participants received 80% as compared to 33% similarity feedback. The reader should consider these results in the light of the uniqueness theory predictions. As similarity *on 15 items* increased from 33% to 80%, it may be reasoned that the person experiences a change from slight to moderate similarity. As can be seen in the hypothetical curve shown in Figure 2, an increase in positive emotion (self-esteem, in this case) should occur under the circumstances where similarity increases from the slight to moderate range. This is what occurs. As similarity *on 30 items* increases from 33% to 80%, it may be reasoned that the person probably experiences a change from moderate similarity to high similarity. Again, as can be seen in the hypothetical curve of Figure 2, a decrease in positive emotion (self-esteem) should occur when similarity increases from the moderate to high range. This is also what occurs. Evidently, therefore, the number of items by which similarity is established may contribute to the magnitude of similarity in the eyes of the person (see again Table I, Chapter 2).

Emotion: Physical Distance Study

The previous two studies examining the emotional reactions to varying degrees of interpersonal similarity employed self-report measures. Using a different approach, Snyder and Endelman (1979) utilized a measure of interpersonal distance as a means of examining the emotional reactions to varying degrees of similarity. These researchers reasoned that interpersonal distance may serve as a sensitive indicator of emotional response, since previous research shows that greater physical distances are associated with less interpersonal attraction and/or are a reaction to threat (Argyle, 1975; Byrne, Baskett, & Hodges, 1971; Evans & Howard, 1973; Mehrabian, 1972). Additionally, these researchers argued that the interpersonal distance measure may be preferable to the self-report measures because it is more unobtrusive (Isaac & Michael, 1971; Webb, Campbell, Schwartz, & Sechrest, 1966).It should be noted that this latter assertion has received some support in social interaction settings. That is, nonverbal behaviors may serve as a "leakage" channel that is less susceptible to conscious censoring than self-report behavior (Argyle, 1975; Ekman & Friesen, 1968).

Initially, Snyder and Endelman (1979) had research participants complete a self-report inventory consisting of 70 items. Among these items were (1) 20 adjectives (e.g., *ambitious* and *energetic*), on which people rated the degree to which each adjective applied to them (1 = "always," to 9 = "never"); (2) 20 attributes (e.g., "I consider my self-control to be . . ."), on which people rated the degree to which they possessed those attributes (1 = "extremely low," to 9 = "extremely high"); (3) 20 attitudes (e.g.,

"Democracy is the best form of government in the world today"), on which people rated their agreement (1 = "very strongly agree," to 9 = "very strongly disagree"); and (4) 10 demographic variables (height, weight, hometown, etc.). During a subsequent "waiting" period, the experimenter left the room and constructed a bogus inventory of a hypothetical person with whom the research participant was to interact. The bogus profile was constructed so as to be 5% similar, 50% similar, or 95% similar to the profile completed by the research participant. These profiles represented one of the three similarity conditions (slight, moderate, or high) to which the research participant was randomly assigned.

Next, the research participant was asked to read the profile of the other person with whom he or she was to interact. The rationale was to help the person "know a little something" about the other person before meeting him or her. After the research participant had read the other's profile, he or she was ushered into another room, where two chairs were pushed up against each other. On one chair (the one supposedly belonging to the other student) were some books and a coat. Feigning a look of mild disorganization, the experimenter told the research participant that the other person had probably just stepped out and would be back in a couple of minutes. The experimenter then pointed to the empty chair and instructed the person to take a seat so that he or she would be able to begin interacting with the other person when he or she returned. The experimenter then left the room to "find the other person" (who was obviously not to be found!).

After approximately five minutes, the experimenter returned and measured the distance that the research participant had created between the front edges of the two chairs. Descriptively, the results showed that research participants in the 50% (moderate) similarity condition sat closest to the "other person's" chair, while research participants in the 5% (low) and 95% (high) similarity conditions sat at greater distances. Statistically, this pattern of results was significant and was consistent with the emotional "distancing" that would be predicted by the uniqueness model.

In summary, therefore, in all three previously mentioned studies on emotional reactions to varying degrees of similarity, a similar pattern of results emerges. People tend to experience a moderate degree of interpersonal similarity as positive, and when the degree of similarity becomes very high or very slight, then a more aversive emotional reaction occurs.

Self-Presentation Reactions

In addition to the aforementioned predicted emotional reactions, uniqueness theory predicts that people will engage in a variety of self-presentation behaviors aimed at maintaining a moderate sense of difference relative to other people. The following subsections explore such behaviors.

Perceived Similarity Study

Imagine a study in which one group of research participants is given feedback that they are 20% similar relative to another person, a second group of research participants is given feedback that they are 50% similar relative to another person, and a third group of research participants is given feedback that they are 80% similar relative to another person. Instead of merely examining the usual self-reported attraction to this hypothetical other, suppose that the research participants in the various similarity conditions are asked to report how similar they are to the other person. Uniqueness theory would predict that a motivated distortion process should occur under these circumstances. That is, a person informed that he or she is highly similar to another person should misremember or distort this information so that *less* similarity is perceived. Conversely, a person informed that he or she is only slightly similar to another person should misremember or distort this information so that *more* similarity is perceived. Finally, a person given moderate similarity information should be the most emotionally comfortable and therefore should report relatively little change in the perceived similarity.

Byrne and Griffitt (1969) reported a study in which the results are consistent with this theorization. Initially, research participants completed a lengthy true–false personality scale (the Repression–Sensitization Scale by Byrne, Barry, & Nelson, 1963). Next, depending on the similarity condition to which research participants were randomly assigned, the person was led to believe that he or she was either 20%, 50%, or 80% similar to a stranger that he or she was going to meet. This similarity was manipulated by showing the research participant how another person had filled out half of the Repression–Sensitization Scale. The bogus other person appeared to have responded the same as the research participant on either 20%, 50%, or 80% of the true–false items.

Two measures of perceived similarity were employed. The first measure was a direct, verbalized percentage-similarity estimate in which the research participant marked the similarity on a scale ranging from 0% to 100% similarity. The second measure was a more indirect one that tapped projected similarity. On this measure, the research participants estimated how the stranger had filled out the other one-half of the Repression–Sensitization Scale items. The results of this study are shown in Table II.

Table II. Perceived Similarity (Direct and Indirect Measures) as a Function of Manipulated Similarity[a]

Perceived similarity	Manipulated proportion of similarity		
	20%	50%	80%
Direct verbalized measure	37%	50%	66%
Indirect projected measure	46%	58%	73%

[a]From Byrne and Griffitt (1969), p. 182.

As can be seen in Table II, the 80% similarity people *lessened* their perceived similarity, and the 20% similarity people *increased* their perceived similarity. Likewise, the 50% similarity people appeared to evidence relatively little distortion in their perceived similarity. This same pattern of results has been obtained in subsequent studies that were conceptually or operationally similar to the Byrne and Griffitt study (Smith, 1975; Snyder & Batson, 1974).

Uniqueness theory predicts that these changes in perceived similarity will result because a person strives to maintain the perception that he or she is moderately similar to other people. However, another plausible explanation needs to be considered for these results. This other explanation is based purely on a statistical notion.[2] That is, the people informed that they were either 80%, 50%, or 20% similar to the other person could have merely "for-

[2]This explanation is known as "regression toward the mean."

gotten" their similarity relative to the other person. In such a case, people may report some intermediate level of similarity because they were just "guessing." This guessing would not necessarily be a *motivated* misperception toward moderate similarity, as would be predicted by uniqueness theory. Rather, the guessing would result merely because the research participants had forgotten the initial similarity information.

Is this apparent distortion toward intermediate similarity merely a product of a rather dispassionate forgetting process, or is there a motivating force behind the forgetting? In other words, do we present ourselves as having an intermediate level of similarity to another person or persons merely because we cannot remember how similar we may be and we therefore just make a "good guess" that we are somewhat similar? Or do we purposefully seek to maintain an intermediate level of difference relative to others?

A further examination of the previously mentioned Ganster, McCuddy, and Fromkin study (1977) suggests that people purposefully strive to avoid a high sense of similarity relative to others. The reader may recall that research participants in this study were given feedback on either 15 or 30 items that they were either 33% or 80% similar to 10,000 other college students. In addition to the self-esteem measure that has already been discussed, research participants were asked (1) "How similar were the other college students' attitudes to your own?" and (2) "What percentage of your attitudes were the same as those of other college students?" Responses to both items were essentially the same. If the magnitude of similarity is perceived in a manner that is veridical to the manipulations, then increments in the number of similar attitude items (e.g., from 15 to 30 items) should have produced increments in the magnitude of self-perceived similarity under both the 33% similarity and the 80% similarity conditions. As expected, under the 33% similarity conditions, the magnitude of self-perceived similarity increased from 15 to 30 items. However, under the 80% similarity conditions, *the reverse was true*; that is, 15 attitude items produced significantly greater self-perceived similarity than 30 attitude items.

Ganster *et al.* (1977) suggested that research participants in the highest similarity conditions (i.e., 80% similarity on 30 attitude items) may have chosen to respond defensively by focusing selectively on items that showed their *dissimilarity*. Unexpectedly, the combined manipulation of proportion of similarity and number of attitudes facilitates such selective attention processes. That is, under the 15-item condition, there were 3 attitude items that showed the subjects to be dissimilar to the other students. In contrast, under the 30-item condition, there were 6 items that showed the subjects to be dissimilar. Thus, there were twice as many dissimilar items under the 30-item condition as under the 15-item condition. Whatever the particular underlying process, however, it should be emphasized that "forgetting" cannot be invoked to explain these results. Rather, a plausible hypothesis is that those people who were confronted with 80% similarity on 30 items sought to lessen this degree of similarity because it threatened their sense of uniqueness.

One other experiment is worthy of mention with regard to how people perceptually handle high similarity. In this study by Fromkin, Brandt, Dipboye, and Pyle (1974), it is informative to note how people given high similarity feedback reacted. Research participants initially completed a 60-item attitude scale. Prior to a hypothetical meeting with several "strangers," the person was sequentially shown a profile of how each or the other three strangers had completed the attitude scale. In each case, the "stranger's" attitude responses were just the same (100% similarity) as those of the research participant. After reading each "stranger's" attitude scale, the research participants completed a self-report scale asking them to rate how similar they were to the stranger. Thus, these self-reported similarity ratings were taken after the research participant saw each of the three "identical strangers." Results showed that *perceived similarity decreased* from the first to the second to the third stranger.

If the research participants in the aforementioned study were responding with veridical perceptions of the first, second, and third strangers, there should be no differences in the perceived similarity for each stranger. Reflecting on these results, Fromkin *et al.* (1974) suggested that when confronted with a high degree of similarity relative to others, people "tend to defensively distort the information toward less perceived similarity between themselves and similar person(s)" (p. 17).

Based on the total set of results related to perceptual reactions to high degrees of similarity, it appears that people may indeed distort or avoid high-similarity feedback. This conclusion is supported further when one considers the previously mentioned studies in which moderate similarity is emotionally experienced as being more positive than either slight or high similarity. Likewise, further studies mentioned subsequently in this chapter suggest that something other than a simple forgetting process is occurring when people react to either slight or extreme similarity.

Conformity Behavior Study

As was noted in Chapter 2, psychologists have conducted considerable research on conformity behavior. Within this research context, uniqueness theory predicts that conformity behavior should decrease as the degree of similarity to another person or persons increases into the high-similarity range. This prediction is shown in the hypothetical curve of Figure 3. Duval (1972) performed an experiment that produced data relevant to this prediction.

In a procedure similar to that employed by Fromkin (1968), female research participants were randomly assigned to similarity conditions that delivered *false* feedback demonstrating that either 5% or 50% or 95% of 10,000 other college students agreed with their "ten most important attitudes." Following this similarity manipulation, the research participants were asked to estimate the number of dots on each slide in 10 sets of slides. On the *first* slide in a pair, each person estimated the number of dots without feedback. On the second slide in each pair, which was identical to the first slide, research participants made their estimates after hearing two confederates make estimates that were 150–200 dots greater than the research participant's response to the first slide. Analyses of two measures of conformity (e.g., amount of change and frequency of change scores) yielded only one finding that is noteworthy in the present context. The degree of similarity effect showed that conformity significantly *decreased* as the proportion of similar others increased (Duval, 1972). This effect of degree of similarity supports the notion that high similarity relative to other people may elicit forces of avoidance, that is, tendencies toward dissimilarity (less conformity).

Attitude Change Studies

Uniqueness theory predicts that people should actually change their attitudes when they feel that other people have adopted the same attitudes. This should be especially prevalent when a person is given feedback that he or she is extremely similar to other people on an attitude that he or she previously believed to be different. That is, people should strive to maintain the uniqueness of their "different" attitudes. Weir (1971) performed two studies related to this topic.

In a first study, research participants completed a 20-item attitude questionnaire by rating their attitude position on each item and their perception of the "average college student's" position on each item. In a second meeting, half of the research participants were given false feedback that a large number of their peers had selected the same position on attitudes that the person *believed to be different* from those held by the average college student. This group will be called the *uniqueness-deprived* group. The other half of the research participants were given false feedback that their peers had selected the same position on attitudes that the research participant *believed to be similar* to those of the average college student. This group will be called the *uniqueness-not-deprived* group. The research participants were then asked to listen to five aesthetic preferences of the "other" (actually confederates) research participants and give their own aesthetic preference ratings to these same five items. The measure of interest in this study was the extent to which the aesthetic preferences of the research participants deviated from the supposed preferences of other research participants. Results revealed that the research participants in the uniqueness-deprived group evidenced more deviation in aesthetic attitudes on all five items than the uniqueness-not-deprived group.

In a second study, Weir (1971) provided a modified replication and expansion of the first study. Initially, research participants filled out a 30-item attitude questionnaire in which they rated (1) their own attitudes; (2) their estimated position of the average college student; and (3) how important it was for them to maintain the difference between their position and the position of the average college student. Next, research participants were randomly assigned to one of three attitude feedback conditions. In the *differ-ences-of-high-importance* condition, people were given feedback about how others responded to their five attitude items that were of high importance in terms of maintaining a difference. In the *differ-ences-of-low-importance* condition, people were given feedback about how others responded to their five attitude items that were of low importance in terms of maintaining a difference. In the *no-difference* condition, people were given feedback on the five items on which they believed that their attitudes were the same as the average college student's.

In a second meeting, the research participants again rated themselves on the five attitude items. This second self-report of attitudes occurred after the person heard the responses of two other supposed research participants to the same attitude items. In actuality, the "other" participants were confederates, and it was made to appear that these other two people either responded with (1) the same response as the research participant's original position (the uniqueness-deprived condition) or (2) the research partici-pant's original estimate of the average college student's response on each of the five items (the uniqueness-not-deprived condition). This second variable was uniqueness deprivation.

The research participant's change away from their original attitude position on each of the five attitude items served as the dependent variable in this experiment. Results revealed that the people who were in the uniqueness-deprived condition changed their attitudes more over the course of the five items than did those people who were in the uniqueness-not-deprived condition. Like-wise, the attitude change for the uniqueness-deprived people was more marked on the high important-attitude-difference items than on the low important-attitude-difference items. This latter finding suggests that there may be a certain number of attitudes held by people that especially serve to maintain their sense of uniqueness relative to other people. (See the discussion in Chapter 8 of how attitudes may serve as a vehicle for uniqueness presentation or maintenance.)

Overall, therefore, the Weir studies suggest that people at-tempt to change their attitudes when they believe that others have coopted many of their own opinions. It is as if people have to reestablish their sense of difference by changing their opinions, and it should not be surprising that this uniqueness-seeking behavior is magnified when attitudes that people had theretofore believed were different are involved.

Unique Uses Test

According to uniqueness theorization, if the individual is made to feel highly similar to another person or persons, that individual should engage in behaviors that demonstrate his or her differences. Under such high-similarity conditions, the person should become highly sensitive to opportunities to redefine himself or herself as having some sense of difference. Fromkin (1968) provided a test of uniqueness theory by exploring this question.

In order to examine the possibility that people seek to reestablish their differences after receiving high similarity feedback, Fromkin first sought to find a measure of uniqueness seeking other than the previously mentioned measures of emotional response and self-presentation. In this regard, the Unusual Uses Test (Guilford, 1950) was employed to test uniqueness theory. The Unusual Uses Test requires people to think of unusual uses for common everyday objects. Since performance on the Unusual Uses Test has been shown to increase following training procedures, task instructions, and verbal reinforcement (see Freedman, 1965; Maltzman, 1960), it was reasoned that this measure could provide a sensitive measure of uniqueness-seeking behavior. More specifically, Fromkin (1968) hypothesized that people would generate more "unique" uses for an object following experimentally produced feelings of high similarity than would be the case following slight-similarity feedback.

Initially, research participants completed a 90-item questionnaire on personality traits, values, opinions, beliefs, abilities, interests, etc. When they returned for the second session, they were randomly assigned to one of two similarity conditions and were then given feedback that they were either highly similar or slightly similar to "10,000 other students who had previously completed the questionnaire." That is, the research participant received bogus computer-printout feedback showing that he or she responded at a very similar or dissimilar point on each questionnaire relative to the other students. This feedback was made salient to the participants by a 50-dot line for various items. For example, in the high-similarity condition, the research participant's position (an X) was virtually at the same position (an O) of the average of 10,000 other students.

Finally, after receiving the similarity feedback, the research participant was given the instructions for the Unusual Uses Test. The instructions emphasized that the person was to write as many unique uses for an object as he or she could generate. Further, research participants were informed that these unique uses would be scored relative to the answers of "hundreds of other college students." Then, the participants were given two minutes to generate as many unusual uses as they could for a shoe. Using a variety of ways to measure unique uses, all results showed that the high-similarity-condition people generated a significantly greater number of unique uses for the shoe than people in the slight-similarity condition. (This finding was especially strong for the female as compared with the male research participants.) In brief, therefore, this study is consistent with the uniqueness theory prediction that very-high-similarity feedback should prompt the person to engage in any behavior that he or she perceives as a means of reestablishing some sense of difference.

Valuation of Scarce Experiences Study

Fromkin (1970) reasoned that people would become especially desirous of participating in rare or scarce activities if they had been made to feel very highly similar to other people. The logic may be that the experiencing of unusual activities serves as a means of refuting the feedback that one is very similar to other people. In other words, scarce activities serve to maintain a moderate sense of difference. (See Chapter 6 for a further discussion of how a variety of commodities may serve to maintain a sense of uniqueness.)

As a first step in the "scarce experience" study, Fromkin had research participants complete a 90-item questionnaire on a variety of traits, values, hobbies, etc. Research participants used "electrographic pencils" and "mark-sense" scoring sheets. After the person had completed the questionnaire, he or she was told to wait while the questionnaire was "run through the computer." In a few minutes, the experimenter returned and gave each person feedback. This feedback was in actuality bogus but was developed so as to make it appear that the research participant was either very highly similar or only slightly similar to 10,000 other students who had previously taken the test.[3] (This similarity manipulation was conducted in the same fashion as that described for the 1968 Fromkin study in the previous section.)

After the similarity feedback, the research participants were informed that they could now begin the psychology experiment (earlier the people had been told that the purpose of the questionnaire was to collect some normative data for the Educational Research Agency, which was not part of the psychology department). Each research participant was given a booklet titled "Experiment SB2, The Simulation of Psychedelic Experiences." This booklet informed the participants that they would have the possibility of participating in four "psychedelic-like environments" (simulated with multicolored stroboscopic lights). Further, because of time constraints, each research participant was told that he or she could participate in only one of the four environments. At this point, one environment was described as being available only one hour per week. It represented the *unavailable* experience. In actuality, of course, the unavailable room "just happened" to be open during the one hour the research participant had available. A second environment was described as being available at all times and represented the *plentiful* experience. Finally, research participants rated (1) how much they wanted to participate in each environment; (2) how long they wanted to spend in the environment; and (3) their willingness to relinquish each of the environments.

Under the slight-similarity condition, there were no differences in the research participants' ratings of the scarce and plentiful environments. However, under the high-similarity condition, the unavailable experience was rated significantly higher on all three measures than the plentiful experience. That is, under the high- as compared with the slight-similarity condition, the research

---

[3]Parts of the design for the Fromkin (1970) study are deleted in the present explanation in order to simplify the discussion. It should be emphasized, however, that the results of the conditions not discussed are totally consistent with the present condensed summary.

participants (1) rated the unavailable experience as more desirous than the plentiful experience; (2) wanted to spend more time in the unavailable experience; and (3) were less willing to give up the unavailable experience.

Why would people express such preferences? By seeking the unavailable as compared with the plentiful experience, the high-similarity people were evidently presenting themselves as being the sort of persons who do not like to experience "the same old things." This self-presentation of uniqueness-seeking behavior may serve both to convince the person that he or she has some sense of difference and to convince the experimenter of the same thing. In the case of this experiment, the psychedelic experience served as a potential valuable commodity by which the person made to feel very similar could reassert his or her other differences. As Brock (1968) put it, "the greater the need to be unique, the greater will be valuation and effectiveness of commodified stimuli" (p. 272).

Concluding Comment on Uniqueness Theory

The foregoing experiments have addressed the basic predictions of the uniqueness model. An important component of this model predicts that when the magnitude of similarity becomes very high, then (1) negative emotional responses should occur and (2) people should behave so as to reestablish their differences.[4] Three experiments have been presented in support of the contention that the increase from the moderate to the very high range of similarity results in an aversive emotional response. Likewise, several studies suggest that people may engage in a motivated perceptual–cognitive distortion process whereby the perception of very high similarity is lessened. This distortion process may be a means of redefining oneself as having *some* sense of difference. Finally, four experiments showed that people may engage in a variety of behaviors so as to maintain some sense of difference relative to others.

[4]It should again be emphasized that the total uniqueness model makes predictions regarding reactions (emotional and behavioral) relative to the entire range of similarity (very slight to very high). The emphasis in the present conclusion, however, is on the reactions resulting from a moderate to very high level of similarity.

These latter experiments are noteworthy because they contain at least four distinct response domains (from perceptual anticonformity, attitude change, and object usage to desire for an activity).

References

Argyle, M. *Bodily communication.* New York: International Universities Press, 1975.

Brock, T. C. Implications of commodity theory for value change. In A. G. Greenwald, T. C. Brock, & T. M. Ostrom (Eds.), *Psychological foundations of attitudes.* New York: Academic, 1968, pp. 243–275.

Byrne, D., Barry, J., & Nelson, D. Relation of the revised Repression–Sensitization Scale to measures of self-description. *Psychological Reports,* 1963, *13,* 323–334.

Byrne, D., Baskett, G. D., & Hodges, L. Behavioral indicators of interpersonal attraction. *Journal of Applied Social Psychology,* 1971, *1,* 137–149.

Byrne, D., & Griffitt, W. Similarity and awareness of similarity of personality characteristics as determinants of attraction. *Journal of Experimental Research in Personality,* 1969, *3,* 179–186.

Coopersmith, S. *The antecedents of self-esteem.* San Francisco: Freeman, 1967.

Duval, S. Conformity on a visual task as a function of personal novelty on attitudinal dimensions and being reminded of the object status of the self. Unpublished doctoral dissertation, University of Texas, 1972.

Ekman, P., & Friesen, W. V. Nonverbal behavior in psychotherapy research. In J. M. Shlien (Ed.), *Research in psychotherapy,* vol. 3. Washington, D.C.: American Psychological Association, 1968, pp. 179–216.

Evans, G. W., & Howard, R. B. Personal space. *Psychological Bulletin,* 1973, *80,* 334–344.

Freedman, J. L. Increasing creativity by free-association training. *Journal of Experimental Psychology,* 1965, *69,* 89–91.

Fromkin, H. L. Affective and valuational consequences of self-perceived uniqueness deprivation. Unpublished doctoral dissertation, Ohio State University, 1968.

Fromkin, H. L. Effects of experimentally aroused feelings of indistinctiveness upon valuation of scarce and novel experiences. *Journal of Personality and Social Psychology,* 1970, *16,* 521–529.

Fromkin, H. L. Feelings of interpersonal undistinctiveness: An unpleasant affective state. *Journal of Experimental Research in Personality,* 1972, *6,* 178–182.

Fromkin, H. L., Brandt, J. M., Dipboye, R. L., & Pyle, M. Number of similar strangers and feelings of undistinctiveness as boundary conditions for the similarity attraction relationship: A bridge between different sand-boxes. *Institute for Research in the Behavioral, Economic, and Management Sciences,* Paper No. 478, Purdue University, 1974.

Ganster, D., McCuddy, M., & Fromkin, H. L. Similarity and undistinctiveness as determinants of favorable and unfavorable changes in self esteem. Paper presented at the Midwestern Psychological Association, Chicago, 1977.

Guilford, J. P. Creativity. *American Psychologist*, 1950, *5*, 444–454.

Isaac, S., & Michael, M. B. *Handbook in research and evaluation*. San Diego, Calif.: Edits Publishers, 1971.

MacLeod, R. B. The place of phenomenological analysis in social psychology. In J. H. Rohrer & M. Sherif (Eds.), *Social psychology at the crossroads*. New York: Harper, 1951, pp. 215–241.

Maltzman, I. On the training of originality. *Psychological Review*, 1960, *67*, 229–242.

Mehrabian, A. *Nonverbal communication*. Chicago: Aldine-Atherton, 1972.

Miller, D. R. The study of social relationships: Situation, identity, and social interaction. In S. Koch (Ed.), *Psychology: A study of science*, vol. 5. New York: McGraw-Hill, 1963, pp. 639–737.

Nowlis, V., & Green, R. F. Factor analytic studies of the mood adjective checklist. *Technical Report No. 1*, Office of Naval Research: Contract—668 (12), 1965.

Sherwood, J. J. Self actualization and self identity theory. *Personality: An International Journal*, 1970, *1*, 41–63.

Smith, C. S. Self-definition change as a function of interpersonal similarity: A test of a psychological spacing model. Unpublished master's thesis, University of Kansas, 1975.

Snyder, C. R. The comparison process and "classroom" performance. In I. K. Goldberg (Ed.), *Audio seminars in education*. Fort Lee, N.J.: Sigma Information, 1975. (a)

Snyder, C. R. The comparison process and student "personality." In I. K. Goldberg (Ed.), *Audio seminars in education*. Fort Lee, N.J.: Sigma Information, 1975. (b)

Snyder, C. R. The development of the comparison process. In I. K. Goldberg (Ed.), *Audio seminars in education*. Fort Lee, N.J.: Sigma Information, 1975. (c)

Snyder, C. R., & Batson, C. D. The balanced interpersonal perception of differences and similarities: A model of psychological distance. Paper presented at the Western Psychological Association, San Francisco, 1974.

Snyder, C. R., & Endelman, J. R. Effects of degree of interpersonal similarity on physical distance and self-reported attraction: A comparison of uniqueness and reinforcement theory predictions. *Journal of Personality*, 1979, *47*(3), 492–505.

Webb, E. J., Campbell, D. T., Schwartz, R. D., & Sechrest, L. *Unobtrusive measures: Nonreactive research in the social sciences*. Chicago: Rand McNally, 1966.

Weir, H. B. Deprivation of the need for uniqueness and some variables moderating its effects. Unpublished doctoral dissertation, University of Georgia, 1971.

Wylie, R. C. *The self concept: A critical survey of pertinent research literature*. Lincoln: University of Nebraska Press, 1961.

4

Corollaries of Uniqueness Theory: The Nature of the Comparison Other Persons

Given the initial body of information described in the previous chapter, the reader may be more convinced that there is some support for the "pursuit of uniqueness." However, there are further refinements of the theory that need to be considered at this juncture. In the experiments mentioned in the previous chapter, the reader should note that the research participants were given similarity feedback relative to some other stranger or strangers. In each case, however, the research participants were given a minimal amount of information other than similarity about the "other person(s)." Suppose that you are given additional value-laden information about another person? Maybe you are told that a person is an "ex-con," insane, or brilliant. Perhaps the "other" person is a member of a group that you hold in esteem, such as your sorority, fraternity, lodge, club, or organization. Maybe the "other" person is a member of some other organization or group that you do not like. What predictions does the uniqueness model make about your emotional behavioral reactions under these circumstances? The present chapter addresses these questions.

Reactions to Another Person Who Is Either "Negative" or "Positive"

The state of self-perceived similarity implies a prior comparison of attributes with another person(s). With information only about neutral similar comparison attributes, the emotional and behavioral reactions to varying degrees of similarity should conform to the predictions depicted in Figures 2 and 3 of Chapter 3. However, it is not uncommon to perceive that the characteristics of the comparison other are either attractive and desirable or unattractive and undesirable. Therefore, corollaries to the aforementioned uniqueness theory predictions need to be established in order to accommodate reactions to such other people.

The emotional and behavioral reactions to another person who exhibits negative, neutral, or positive characteristics are shown in Figures 4 and 5. The curves for the neutral information are the same as those discussed in the previous chapter (i.e., Figures 2 and 3 of Chapter 3).

The knowledge that another person possesses some particularly negative characteristic should predispose people toward a more negative emotional response than the situation where such negative information is not available. The hypothetical curve depicting the emotional response to another person with a negative characteristic is shown in Figure 4. This curve indicates that the most positive emotional response to another person with a negative characteristic may result under a slight degree of similarity. As similarity increases to the moderate, high, and very high ranges, the hypothesized emotional response becomes quite negative.

The knowledge that another person possesses some particularly positive characteristic should generate a more positive emotional response than the instance where either neutral or negative information is available about the "other" person. The hypothetical curve depicting the emotional response to a person with positive characteristics indicates that the most positive emotional response may come under conditions of high similarity. As similarity decreases to the moderate, slight, and very slight ranges, the hypothesized emotional responses become more negative.

In examining the behavioral responses predicted in Figure 5, it should be noted that comparisons with another person who has negative characteristics mostly result in changes toward dissimilarity; conversely, comparisons with another person who has positive characteristics mostly result in changes toward similarity. The predicted curve for the neutral-information other reveals a relatively equal amount of change toward similarity and toward dissimilarity. In regard to the curves hypothesized for the emotional and behav-

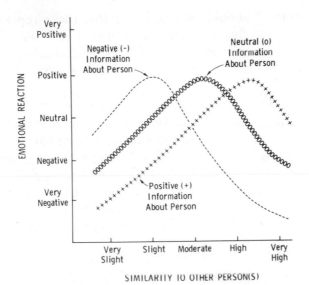

Figure 4. Hypothesized emotional reaction to another person as a function of similarity relative to that person and type of information about the person.

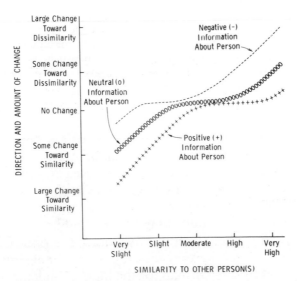

Figure 5. Hypothesized direction and amount of change as a function of similarity relative to another person and type of information about that person.

ioral responses, it should be cautioned that these represent only rough estimates of the responses to a "negative" and "positive" other person. This is by necessity the case because there has been little research that has generated data relevant to these hypothetical curves.

One study that may give the reader an idea of the emotional response to a positive or negative other person was performed by Taylor and Mettee (1971). As a cover story to enhance the plausibility of receiving similarity feedback relative to another person, female research participants initially completed a lengthy series of sentence completion, true–false, and adjective checklist items. At this point, the research participant received bogus feedback showing that she was either highly similar or slightly similar to another person with whom she was to interact. Next, the research participant briefly interacted with this "other" person. In actuality, the other person was a confederate who was trained to behave in either an *obnoxious* or a *pleasant* fashion. (This represents an example of the negative and positive characteristics we are describing in this section.) In the obnoxious-other condition, the confederate criticized the research participant's college and her reasons for attending it. In fact, the obnoxious person said:

> "My grades are really good and I have the money, so I'm transferring. I went to BU (Boston University) for an interview last weekend. What a laugh that was! I really psyched that guy out. You know how most people get nervous at interviews? You probably do. Well, I never do. I figured out what he wanted me to say ahead of time and said it. After that interview, they'll have to let me in." (Taylor & Mettee, 1971, p. 77)

In the pleasant condition, the confederate merely engaged the research participant in a friendly discussion. After the brief interchange with either the obnoxious or the pleasant other, the research participant completed a self-report liking measure.

Under the pleasant-other condition, the research participants reported significantly greater liking for the highly similar than for the slightly similar other. Conversely, under the obnoxious-other condition, the research participants reported significantly greater liking for the slightly similar than for the highly similar other.

In a study that was conceptually similar to the Taylor and Mettee study, Lerner and Agar (1972) led research participants to believe that they were either highly or slightly similar to either a "normal" person or a drug addict. The measure of interest in this study was an emotion-related approach–avoidance index that tapped the extent to which the research participant wanted to meet the other person. For the normal condition, people reported a significantly higher desire to meet the highly similar as compared with the slightly similar other person; conversely, for the drug addict condition, research participants reported a significantly greater desire to meet the slightly similar as compared with the highly similar other person. If the reader utilizes the hypothesized curves show in Figure 4, some correspondence between the emotional responses occurring in the Taylor and Mettee and the Lerner and Agar studies and those predicted may be discerned. That is, high as compared to slight similarity generates a more positive emotional response when the other person has some positive characteristic (e.g., pleasantness or "normality"); conversely, the slight as compared with the high similarity generates a more positive emotional response when the other person has some negative characteristic (e.g., obnoxiousness or drug addiction).

The aforementioned studies give some indication of possible emotional reactions to a negative or a positive other person who is either slightly or highly similar. Another study is worthy of mention because it utilized a measure that is more related to behavior that may either increase or decrease similarity relative to another person. In this study by Cooper and Jones (1969), the design was somewhat similar to the Taylor and Mettee study. That is, male research participants were initially led to believe that they were either highly or slightly similar to another person (a confederate) who acted in either a nonobnoxious or an obnoxious manner. The extent to which the research participants changed their opinions either toward or away from the other person (on attitude items) represented the measure of opinion convergence or divergence. The results revealed that for the nonobnoxious-other condition, there were no significant changes in attitudes for the high- as compared with the low-similarity conditions. However, under the obnoxious-other condition, the research participants reported significantly greater opinion divergence under the high-similarity condition as compared with the slight-similarity condition. As can be seen in comparing these results with those hypothesized in Figure 5, the predicted greater attitude change toward dissimilarity was obtained under conditions of high as compared with slight similarity relative to a negative (obnoxious) other. On the other hand, the predicted greater attitude change toward similarity under conditions of slight as compared with high similarity for the positive (nonobnoxious) other was not obtained. Further research is obviously needed to test the possible behavioral repercussions of varying degrees of similarity relative to a positive or a negative other person.

Uniqueness Relative to a "Negative" Other Person: Underlying Mechanism

The aforementioned corollaries to uniqueness theory and the results of the experiments discussed suggest that it may be especially important to maintain a sense of difference relative to a person with some negative characteristic. Why is this so? Several previous explanations address this issue. A first interpretation of these findings follows Lerner's (1969) "just world" hypothesis. Under this conception, similarity relative to a stigmatized person is especially threatening because it implies that a negative outcome (e.g., drug addiction) can happen to anyone, including oneself. Furthermore, such negative outcomes need not happen merely to those who "deserve" it. A second explanation of the special aversiveness of the similarity relative to a negative other is that people may fear that they are being "associatively miscast" with a negative other person. Cooper and Jones (1969) found support for this hypothesis in their study. A third explanation is offered by Taylor and Mettee (1971). They suggest that when persons are motivated to evaluate the "goodness" of their own attributes via social comparison, similarity increases the *saliency* of the other person's attributes. Given attributes that are negatively valent, the attributes are perceived as especially unfavorable. Similarity relative to another person with unfavorable attributes implies that one may possess the undesirable trait. This leads to the fear that one may actually possess the negative characteristic. (This explanation is similar in some ways to both the "just world" and "associatively miscast" explanations.)

In the previous chapter on the theory of uniqueness, a hypothetical process by which similarity information is encoded on a uniqueness identity dimension was presented. This process (see again Figure 1 of Chapter 3) reflects the predicted encoding that occurs when neutral information is available about another person. In Figure 6, the reader can see the hypothetical encoding process by which degree of similarity information is encoded on a uniqueness identity dimension *for a negative other person.* In the case of a negative other person, it is hypothesized that a slight degree of similarity should elicit the highest encoded acceptability on the uniqueness identity dimension (Point B on Figure 6). The reason for this hypothesized highest point of encoded acceptability is that the typical person probably perceives himself or herself as having slight similarity relative to a negative person for both reality- and motivation-based reasons. Thus, this slight level of similarity relative to a negative other person may represent the most acceptable encoding on the uniqueness dimension. What is especially noteworthy about Figure 6 is that increases in similarity beyond the slight range (i.e., points B to C to D to E) are progressively encoded as having lower acceptability. Thus, greater similarity relative to a negative other should result in stronger aversive emotional reactions and behavioral maneuvers aimed at establishing dissimilarity.

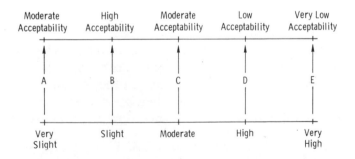

UNIQUENESS IDENTITY DIMENSION
FOR NEGATIVE OTHER PERSONS

Moderate Acceptability	High Acceptability	Moderate Acceptability	Low Acceptability	Very Low Acceptability
A	B	C	D	E
Very Slight	Slight	Moderate	High	Very High

SIMILARITY SELF-ATTRIBUTE

Figure 6. Hypothesized encoding of degree of similarity information on the uniqueness identity dimension for negative other persons.

The currently hypothesized uniqueness-identity-dimension encoding interpretation for a negative other is consistent with the previously mentioned "just world" interpretation, the "associatively miscast" interpretation, and the saliency interpretation. In fact, the uniqueness-identity-dimension encoding interpretation may reflect a more parsimonious means of combining the other interpretations. That is, a slight level of similarity relative to a negative other may be encoded as having highest acceptability on the uniqueness-identity-dimension because of "just world," "associatively miscast," and saliency considerations.

Whatever the particular dynamics, it appears that the negative attributes of a comparison other may be influential determinants of emotional and behavioral responses. When the person is aware of negative attributes of the comparison other, high degrees of similarity result in negative emotional reactions and attempts at establishing dissimilarity. Thus, we may be motivated to maintain a sense of difference relative to a stigmatized person.[1] Finally, it is important to highlight the fact that the pivotal point of comparison (in terms of change in emotional response and behavior) with a negative other occurs somewhere in the *slight*-similarity range. As one proceeds beyond this point toward greater similarity, people especially seek to establish their differences if there is a genuine threat that they may be similar to a "stigmatized" other.

Uniqueness Relative to a "Positive" Other Person: Underlying Mechanism

As can be seen in Figure 4, the increasing similarity from very slight to high similarity relative to a positive other person results in increases in positive emotion. People theoretically tolerate a higher degree of similarity relative to a positive other person than they do for either a neutral or a negative other. As shown in Figure 7, the high degree of similarity (Point D) should be encoded as having the

---

[1]However, it should also be noted that as one proceeds to *very* slight similarity *relative to a negative other*, then there is some change in the curves depicted in Figures 4 and 5. This is theoretically the case because such *extreme* (slight similarity) feedback may generate only a moderate level of acceptability. This state is less comfortable than the high acceptability of slight similarity and hypothetically should result in attempts at reestablishing some higher sense of similarity.

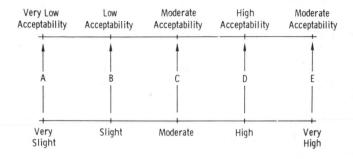

UNIQUENESS IDENTITY DIMENSION
FOR POSITIVE OTHER PERSONS

SIMILARITY SELF-ATTRIBUTE

*Figure 7. Hypothesized encoding of degree of similarity information
on the uniqueness identity dimension for positive other persons.*

highest acceptability on the uniqueness-identity-dimension. The rationale for this hypothesized highest point of encoded acceptability is that the typical person may perceive himself or herself as having a high degree of similarity relative to a positive other person for both reality- and motivation-based reasons. This point of high degree of similarity should therefore reflect the highest level of acceptability for the person comparing himself or herself to a positive other person. Thus, as can be seen in Figure 7, increases from very slight to high similarity relative to a positive other person (Points A to B to C to D) should be progressively encoded as having higher acceptability on the uniqueness identity dimension.[2]

Groups and Uniqueness: Membership Attributes

Often a person has information about another individual other than positive or negative characteristics. Such information may

[2]Despite the potential benefits that may flow from a sense of similarity relative to a "positive" person, it should be emphasized that at some *very* high level of similarity, the individual's uniqueness may be threatened. That is, even for a positive other person, there should be some lessening of the acceptability on the uniqueness-identity-dimension associated with *very* high similarity. Thus, it is only when the level of similarity relative to a positive other person becomes *very* high that the circumstances are experienced less positively and uniqueness-seeking behaviors may be expected.

involve the other person's sex, race, age, etc. This information indicates whether or not a person is a member of one's own reference group. The following discussion addresses the role of groups in defining one's sense of uniqueness.

Groups that are selected as criteria for attitude formation and self-evaluation have been referred to as *reference groups* (Hyman, 1942, 1960; Merton, 1957). A reference group is any group against which the person evaluates himself or herself (whether or not the person actually belongs to the group). A positive reference group is made up of people who are viewed favorably by a person; conversely, a negative reference group is made up of people who are viewed unfavorably by a person. As we noted in Chapter 2, various theorists hold that the relatively high degree of uniformity in attitudes or behavior among members of any single reference group occurs because these groups serve a normative function by setting and enforcing standards of belief and behavior (e.g., Kelley, 1952). By participating in groups comprised of similar others, theorists such as Festinger (1954) maintain that a person may get very accurate self-appraisal information. Restated, this means that the drive for accurate self-appraisal results in the individual's seeking others who are somewhat similar.

The power of groups to achieve uniformity on certain beliefs resides in their potential to satisfy a diversity of socioemotional needs of their membership. Deviations from these standards are punished with rejection (see Schachter, 1951), unless the deviant member has achieved high status by accumulating idiosyncratic credits by means of prior conformity (Hollander, 1958). Indeed, some moderate degree of commonality in beliefs that are related to the purposes or goals of the group are most probably the *raison d'être* for the initial selection of a particular group as a reference group. Therefore, it is likely that reference groups are characterized by at least a small number of beliefs that are uniformly adopted by the membership because these beliefs are related to the accomplishment of specific goals or purposes of the group (Cartwright & Zander, 1960). We shall refer to these beliefs as *membership attributes*.

For example, members of the KKK share a belief system that favors segregation and supremacy for whites over blacks. The cartoon on page 67 illustrates this shared belief system as a premise.

Members of the NAACP share a belief system that favors desegregation and equal rights for whites and blacks. Members of the Black Panthers may share a belief system that espouses the supremacy of blacks over whites. Similarly, specific beliefs about God and specific traditions such as dietary practices are common to most members of any particular religious reference group. Thus, orthodox Mormons abstain from drinking alcoholic beverages and orthodox Jews abstain from eating certain kinds of meat and shellfish.

"My wife just joined the Ku Klux Klan."

When systems of beliefs that are shared by the majority of group members serve the function of defining the group goal, the adoption of these group-defining beliefs, or at least public compliance, is often required to retain membership. Thus, some degree of attribute similarity is expected among members of a particular reference group as the basis for aspiration toward and/or the maintenance of membership in a particular reference group. Indeed, since beliefs are often linked to important personal values, positive self-regard may result when a person perceives similarity to reference group members on group-defining attributes.

Similarity to positive reference group members on these group-defining attributes can also produce some sense of difference relative to others. At first glance, it may seem paradoxical that interpersonal *similarity* to the attributes of comparison others can serve as a means to confirm one's uniqueness. A more detailed examination reveals how this can happen. By definition, group-defining attributes serve to *distinguish* the goals of the reference group from the larger population of *other* groups. That is, when one is similar on group-defining attributes to members of one's reference groups, that person is at the same time different from the *larger nonmember* population of other reference groups. For example, consider the musician who comes to define his or her unique identity from other individuals (the ''squares'') in terms of occupation (see Becker, 1964). While sharing certain talents, beliefs, and behaviors with other musicians, the musician may gain a sense of differentiation by comparing ''his'' or ''her'' group with the groups comprised of individuals with other occupations, interests, talents, etc. Or consider a female strongly involved in the women's movement who achieves a strong sense of difference by focusing on the differences in her group and other groups (antiliberation, males, etc.).

Another example shows how a group identification may simultaneously generate a sense of difference *and* societal rewards (e.g., jobs and money). A minority group member applying for admission to school or for a job may not only achieve a sense of difference from nonminority applicants but may also get the job because of the desire on the part of schools and the employers to recruit minority candidates. This is a situation where one can assert differences by being a member of a particular group *and* also receive potential additional benefits from society. This phenomenon is depicted in the cartoon on this page.

Language serves as an excellent example of one group's attempt to maintain a behavior different from that of another group. Using the example of blacks within American society, it has been argued that "jive" as a special language enables blacks to maintain or declare a sense of difference from the white society. Similarly, it has been suggested that the perpetuation of distinct languages in various countries results from a need for a separate identity for each country (Fishman, 1972). Thus, in a more general sense, nationalism and the accompanying special language may reflect one

Robert Day/*SPORTS ILLUSTRATED.* Copyright © 1955 Time, Inc.

people's desire to be different from another group or country of people.

One's unique social identity may also be defined by his or her membership in several groups simultaneously (Fromkin, 1973; Lemaine, 1974; Tajfel, 1972). The sum total of an individual's group identities becomes another means by which one can confirm his or her uniqueness. According to George Simmel (1955), the French sociologist, the greater the number of group affiliations and group roles, the more improbable it is that another individual will exhibit the same configuration. Each new group with which the person becomes affiliated "circumscribes him more exactly, more unambiguously, and more uniquely" (p. 140). Thus, one cannot become a member of a particular group without differentiating oneself from other people. For, as Simmons (1969) has stated, "in the very act of accepting and complying with the ideology of one social world you will often find yourself automatically violating the ideologies of other groups and persons" (p. 4).

Even when the group definition or categorization is performed on a random or arbitrary basis, several experiments have shown that group members have different attitudes and behave differently toward members of "their" group and members of the "other" groups (Billig, 1971; Rabbie & Horwitz, 1969; Sherif, Harvey, White, Hood, & Sherif, 1961; Tajfel, Billig, Bundy, & Flament, 1971). Therefore, one not only attains a sense of difference by centering on the differences between one's group and another group, but one may also generate even greater accentuation of the differences. This is especially true when there are rewards involved, and it is critical for one's group to have "more" of a particular characteristic than another group in order to attain rewards. This latter pattern of accentuating differences between groups is often called *discrimination* (see Fromkin & Sherwood, 1974). The cartoon on page 71 conveys the "us" and "them" phenomenon, with the accompanying discrimination. It is important to note, however, that the process of deriving a sense of difference in comparing one's group with another group does *not* necessarily lead to discriminatory behavior. The process of perceiving the world in terms of "them" and "us" does, though, seem to be a fairly prevalent intergroup phenomenon that is consistent with uniqueness theorization.

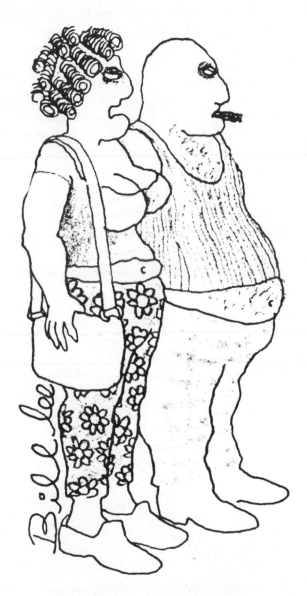

"Just lookit those damn filthy long-haired
degenerate hippie bums over there."

Before proceeding to an examination of how a person may react to another person who is a member of either a positive or a negative reference group, it may be appropriate to review the role of membership attributes. In this regard, it is hypothesized that *membership attributes* result when the majority of members of any particular reference group adhere normatively to a system of beliefs that (1) serve the function of group goal definition and (2) define the reference group as distinct from other groups. How people react to a dissimilar or similar other person who is a member of either a positive or a negative reference group is addressed in the following section.

Reactions to Positive and Negative Reference Group Members Who Vary in Similarity

In light of the theory and research on the comparison function of reference groups, it is likely that people prefer to compare their attributes with members of the *same* reference group. In general, college students would be more attentive to information about the attitudes of other college students than to information about high school students' attitudes; plumbers would be more attentive to information that compares their attitudes with the attitudes of other plumbers than to information about artists' attitudes; adults would be more attentive to information about the similarity of their attitudes to those of other adults than to information about teenagers' attitudes; and females would be more likely to respond to information about the degree of their similarity to other females than to information about males. If the reference group is very important to a person, then this group takes on the status of a positive reference group. For example, for a college football player, a reference group is college students, while a positive reference group would potentially be made up of college students who are football players. Any reference group whose membership (or potential membership) is highly valued by a person may be considered a positive reference group.

The emotional and behavioral predictions for a person who is a member of a positive reference group should be the same as those shown in the curves for the "positive information about other person" depicted previously in Figures 4 and 5. That is, the emotional reactions should generally increase up to a high degree of similarity. Likewise, people should tend to strive behaviorally for similarity relative to a positive reference group member up to a high level of similarity.[3] The reason for these predicted positive emotional and behavioral responses is that a high degree of similarity relative to a positive reference group should be encoded as having the highest degree of acceptability on the uniqueness-identity-dimension. Thus, the encoding process should be the same as that described previously for a positive other person (see Figure 7). Generally, therefore, the enhanced similarity relative to a positive reference group should serve to validate the perceived acceptability on the uniqueness-identity-dimension of one's attitudes, beliefs, behaviors, etc. (See, for related discussions, Hakmiller, 1966; Thornton & Arrowood, 1966; Wheeler, 1966). Additionally, by becoming a more identifiable member of the positive reference group, the person is also achieving the satisfaction of becoming different from members of other groups.

In contrast to comparisons made with members of a positive reference group, the comparison other may be identified as a member of a group that has *undesirable* characteristics. In this regard, it should be emphasized that we are also influenced by persons or groups whom we dislike. In these situations, the person or group is referred to as the *negative reference group* because we are generally motivated to avoid similarity to members of such groups. Thus, the emotional and behavioral predictions for a person who is a member of a negative reference group should be the same as those shown in the curves of Figures 4 and 5 that pertain to the "negative information about the other person." As can be seen in these curves, greater similarity to another person who is a member of a negative reference group generates a more negative emotional response and

[3]At some very high level of similarity relative to the positive reference group, however, the emotional and behavioral responses should change because the individual's uniqueness is being threatened. That is, in spite of the rewards that accrue to the person as he or she becomes more similar to a positive reference group, there is a point of very high similarity at which the rewards begin to lessen. In such instances the feedback that one is very similar to another person, even though that other person is a member of a positive reference group, serves to highlight the fact that the person *may not be different at all* (e.g., "He's just another typical college football player"). At this point, uniqueness-seeking behaviors would be expected to appear.

more uniqueness-seeking behaviors. The reason for these predicted negative emotional and behavioral responses is that a slight degree of similarity relative to a negative reference group is encoded as having the highest degree of acceptability on the uniqueness-identity-dimension. Therefore, the encoding process relative to a negative reference group should be the same as that described previously for a negative other person (see Figure 6).

Very often, obviously, a negative other person is responded to not only because he or she may have some stigmatized negative characteristic but also because he or she is a member of a negative reference group. Whether or not the other person has a negative characteristic and is also perceived as being a member of a negative reference group, the predictions (Figures 4, 5, and 6) from the corollaries to uniqueness theory are the same.

Concluding Comment on Uniqueness Theory

In summary, the present and previous chapters have outlined the basic theory and corollaries regarding the emotional reactions and behavioral responses to varying degrees of interpersonal similarity feedback. In brief, it has been theorized in the previous chapter that we typically perceive some intermediate level of similarity relative to other people as being the most perceptually acceptable state on a uniqueness-identity-dimension. In turn, it is hypothesized that we are most emotionally satisfied with a moderate level of similarity relative to other people. Likewise, it is postulated that we strive to maintain this moderate sense of similarity when we are made to feel either *very* slightly similar or *very* highly similar to other people. Research evidence that has been generated to this date is discussed, and in the present chapter, suggestions have been made to establish corollaries to the central notions of the theory. These corollaries are posited so that we may understand how people react to varying degrees of interpersonal similarity when information is available about whether the other person (1) has a positive or negative characteristic and/or (2) is a member of a positive or negative reference group.

This overall theory, including the corollaries, may serve as a vehicle for understanding how people seek to maintain a moderate sense of difference relative to other people. In subsequent chapters, we examine the various topics that further contribute to an understanding of this uniqueness-seeking phenomenon. In these subsequent discussions, the reader should keep in mind the central tenet of the uniqueness theory. In this regard, we are *not* proposing that people have an unquenchable thirst and total desire to be different from their fellow humans. Rather, we would suggest that the "pursuit of difference" represents a striving to maintain a moderate sense of dissimilarity relative to other people. Subsequent chapters and future research will provide a further scrutiny of this modest proposal.

References

Becker, H.S. *Outsiders.* New York: Free Press, 1963.

Billig, M. G. Categorization and similarity in intergroup behavior. Unpublished paper, Bristol University, 1971.

Cartwright, D., & Zander, A. (Eds.). *Group dynamics: Research and theory* (2nd ed.). Evanston, Ill.: Row & Peterson, 1960.

Cooper, J., & Jones, E. E. Opinion divergence as a strategy to avoid being miscast. *Journal of Personality and Social Psychology,* 1969, *13,* 23–30.

Festinger, L. A theory of social comparison processes. *Human Relations,* 1954, 7, 117–140.

Fishman, J. A. *Language and rationalism: Two integrative essays.* Rowley, Mass.: Newbury House, 1972.

Fromkin, H. L. The psychology of uniqueness: Avoidance of similarity and seeking of differentness. *Institute for Research in the Behavioral, Economic, and Management Sciences.* Paper No. 438, Purdue University, 1973.

Fromkin, H. L., & Sherwood, J. J. (Eds.). *Integrating the organization: A social psychological analysis.* New York: Free Press, 1974.

Hakmiller, K. L. Need for self-evaluation, perceived similarity, and comparison choice. *Journal of Personality and Social Psychology,* 1966, Supplement # 1, 49–54.

Hollander, E. P. Conformity, status, and idiosyncrasy credit. *Psychological Review,* 1958, *65,* 117–127.

Hyman, H. H. The psychology of status. *Archives of Psychology,* 1942, No. 269.

Hyman, H. H. Reflections on reference groups. *Public Opinion Quarterly,* 1960, *24,* 383-396.

Kelley, H. H. Two functions of reference groups. In G. E. Swanson, T. M. Newcomb, & E. L. Hartley (Eds.), *Readings in social psychology* (rev. ed.). New York: Holt, Rinehart, & Winston, 1952, pp. 410–415.

Lemaine, G. Social differentiation and social conformity. *European Journal of Social Psychology,* 1974, *4,* 17–52.

Lerner, M. J. On the just world. In A. Pepitone (Chm.), *Social psychology of freedom, justice and responsibility.* Symposium presented at the American Psychological Association, Washington, D.C., 1969.

Lerner, M. J., & Agar, E. The consequences of perceived similarity: Attraction and rejection, approach and avoidance. *Journal of Experimental Research in Personality*, 1972, *6*, 69–75.

Merton, R. K. *Social theory and social structure* (rev. ed.). Glencoe, Ill.: Free Press, 1957.

Rabbie, J. M., & Horwitz, M. Arousal of ingroup–outgroup bias by a chance win or loss. *Journal of Personality and Social Psychology*, 1969, *13*, 269–277.

Schachter, S. Deviation, rejection, communication. *Journal of Abnormal and Social Psychology*, 1951, *46*, 190–207.

Sherif, M., Harvey, O. J., White, B. J., Hood, W. R., & Sherif, C. W. *Intergroup conflict and cooperation: The robbers cave experiment.* Norman: University of Oklahoma Press, 1961.

Sherwood, J. J. Self actualization and self identity theory. *Personality: An International Journal*, 1970, *1*, 41–63.

Simmel, G. *Conflict and the web of group affiliations* (trans. by R. Bendix). Glencoe, Ill.: Free Press, 1955.

Simmons, J. L. *Deviants.* Berkeley, Calif.: Glendessary Press, 1969.

Tajfel, H. La categorisation sociale. In S. Moscovici (Ed.), *Introduction à la psychologie sociale.* Paris: Larousse, 1972, pp. 272–302.

Tajfel, H., Billig, M. G., Bundy, R. P., & Flament, C. Social categorization and intergroup behavior. *European Journal of Social Psychology*, 1971, *1*, 149–178.

Taylor, S. E., & Mettee, D. R. When similarity breeds contempt. *Journal of Personality and Social Psychology*, 1971, *20*, 75–81.

Thornton, D. A., & Arrowood, A. J. Self evaluation, self enhancement, and the locus of social comparison. *Journal of Experimental Social Psychology Supplement*, 1966, *1*, 40–48.

Wheeler, L. Motivation as a determination of upward comparison. *Journal of Experimental Social Psychology Supplement*, 1966, *1*, 27–31.

Individual Differences in Need for Uniqueness

In the previous chapters, data have been presented to support the contention that people exhibit a need to manifest their uniqueness in various situations. Although the striving for uniqueness appears to be influenced by situational factors, it is also logical to speculate that different people evidence different degrees of uniqueness motivation in similar circumstances. That is, there are probably *dispositional individual differences* among people with regard to their uniqueness motivation. For example, one person may grow up strongly desiring to be unique, while another person may develop a low need for uniqueness. In this regard, the reader may imagine certain acquaintances who may exhibit a rather strong desire for uniqueness; conversely, other acquaintances may be rather low in their desire for uniqueness. And how do you, the reader, estimate your desire for uniqueness? Perhaps after reading the present chapter, which reports the development and validation of an individual differences measure of a need for uniqueness, the reader may begin to more specifically answer this latter question.

Examples: People with High and Low Needs for Uniqueness

One way of understanding the difference between a person who has high as compared to a low need for uniqueness is to examine how such people describe themselves. What does the person who has a high need for uniqueness say about himself or herself? The following statement by an individual named Zeke reveals the perspective of a person with a high need for uniqueness:

> I don't like being called an average guy. Sometimes it seems like most of the people I know want to be like each other. They usually dress, act, and think the same. What others think about you seems to be very important to people. Most people would rather just go along with the crowd than really speak or act the way they want. Not me though . . . I used to get in situations where I wanted to do or say something, but I was kind of afraid of what others would think. But finally, when I was in college I got fed up with this sort of thing, because I would get mad at myself for not speaking out more. So now I usually say what I think, even when other people may think that I'm kind of weird. Maybe I am, but that's OK. Actually, I do think I am different from other people, and I'm proud of it. If people get bent out of shape because of something I strongly believe, that's their problem. And just because a bunch of people will tell you how to think or act, that doesn't necessarily mean they are right. That Vietnam thing is a good example. Back in 1966 and 1967, people were giving me a hard time because I thought we should get out of Vietnam. It's cases like that one that make me want to continue being a unique person.

What about the other end of the spectrum—the person with a low need for uniqueness? A person named Dennis portrays himself in the following way:

> Ever since I was a teenager, and probably before that, I have pretty much gone along with what other people say or do. This works fine for me. I guess you could say I am a pretty typical type of person. I'd much rather just be quiet and agree with people than cause some sort of disagreement. That makes me very uncomfortable. Generally, I think we're all better off if we try to cooperate and get along with each other. So, I try to find out why others say and do the things they do. Usually, most people have pretty good reasons for what they do, and in the long run, it is silly to question what others say. This is especially true of your supervisors. On the whole, I've found that the executives in my company know what they are doing. In fact, I think that I like it best when I'm given some direction. For example, I didn't mind my army days that much. Everything was clear as to what we were to do, and we performed similar jobs. The structure wasn't too bad either. Well, I'm probably just most comfortable when I'm "one of the guys."

What Is Your Need for Uniqueness?

The aforementioned examples may have stimulated the reader to speculate about his or her need for uniqueness. How would you assess yourself? Most people probably can make a reasonable guess. However, these estimates are approximations at best. Therefore, in order to provide a rapidly obtained, reliable, and valid measure of need for uniqueness, the authors developed the Need for Uniqueness Scale (Fromkin & Lipshitz, 1976; Snyder & Fromkin, 1977). Before proceeding further, the reader may wish to complete the Need for Uniqueness Scale and calculate his or her score.

Directions: The following statements concern your perceptions about yourself in a variety of situations. Your task is to indicate the strength of your agreement with each statement, utilizing a scale in which *1* denotes strong disagreement, *5* denotes strong agreement, and *2, 3,* and *4* represent intermediate judgments. In the blank preceding each statement, place a number from 1 to 5 from the following scale

1	2	3	4	5

Strongest   Strongest
disagreement   agreement

There are no "right" or "wrong" answers, so select the number that most closely reflects you on each statement. Take your time and consider each statement carefully.

_2_   1. When I am in a group of strangers, I am not reluctant to express my opinion publicly.

_5_   2. I find that criticism affects my self-esteem.

_5_   3. I sometimes hesitate to use my own ideas for fear they might be impractical.

_5_   4. I think society should let reason lead it to new customs and throw aside old habits or mere traditions.

_2_   5. People frequently succeed in changing my mind.

_3_   6. I find it sometimes amusing to upset the dignity of teachers, judges, and "cultured" people.

_4_   7. I like wearing a uniform because it makes me proud to be a member of the organization it represents.

_1_   8. People have sometimes called me "stuck-up."

_2_   9. Others' disagreements make me uncomfortable.

_5_ 10. I do not always need to live by the rules and standards of society.

_2_ 11. I am unable to express my feelings if they result in undesirable consequences.

_3_ 12. Being a success in one's career means making a contribution that no one else has made.

_1_ 13. It bothers me if people think I am being too unconventional.

_2_ 14. I always try to follow rules.

_2_ 15. If I disagree with a superior on his or her views, I usually do not keep it to myself.

___ 16. I speak up in meetings in order to oppose those whom I feel are wrong.

   —   17.   Feeling "different" in a crowd of people makes me feel uncomfortable.

   —   18.   If I must die, let it be an unusual death rather than an ordinary death in bed.

   —   19.   I would rather be just like everyone else than be called a "freak."

   —   20.   I must admit I find it hard to work under strict rules and regulations.

   —   21.   I would rather be known for always trying new ideas than for employing well-trusted methods.

   —   22.   It is better always to agree with the opinions of others than to be considered a disagreeable person.

   —   23.   I do not like to say unusual things to people.

   —   24.   I tend to express my opinions publicly, regardless of what others say.

   —   25.   As a rule, I strongly defend my own opinions.

   —   26.   I do not like to go my own way.

   —   27.   When I am with a group of people, I agree with their ideas so that no arguments will arise.

   —   28.   I tend to keep quiet in the presence of persons of higher rank, experience, etc.

   —   29.   I have been quite independent and free from family rule.

   —   30.   Whenever I take part in group activities, I am somewhat of a nonconformist.

   —   31.   In most things in life, I believe in playing it safe rather than taking a gamble.

   —   32.   It is better to break rules than always to conform with an impersonal society.

In order to calculate your total Need for Uniqueness Scale score, first reverse each of the individual scores on items 2, 3, 5, 7, 9, 11, 13, 14, 17, 19, 22, 23, 26, 27, 28, and 31. That is, on these items only, perform the following reversals: 1 to 5, 2 to 4, 3 to 3, 4 to 2, and 5 to 1. Then, on these 16 reversed items, mark through your original score and put the reversed score in the blank. Finally, add up your scores on all 32 items. The higher your score, the higher your need for uniqueness as measured by the uniqueness scale. Remember, this scale was developed to measure *not* how different you actually may be but rather the magnitude of your desire or need to be unique.

To see how your need for uniqueness compares with that exhibited by other people, refer to Table III. Here, the uniqueness scale scores of 1,404 students (658 females and 746 males) from the University of Kansas and Purdue University are presented. As you can see, if you are "average" in your need for uniqueness, then you would have obtained a score of approximately 100. If you scored above 128, you were manifesting a relatively high need for uniqueness (i.e., a score that is 2 standard deviations above the mean, or higher than 98% of the other people who have taken the test). Conversely, if you scored below 72, you were exhibiting a relatively low need for uniqueness (i.e., a score that is 2 standard

Table III. Percentile Scores Corresponding to Raw
Uniqueness Scale Score for College Students[a]

Raw score		Percentile (%)	Raw score		Percentile (%)
67 (or less)	=	1	101	=	52
68	=	2	102	=	55
69	=	2	103	=	57
70	=	2	104	=	60
71	=	2	105	=	62
72	=	2	106	=	65
73	=	3	107	=	67
74	=	4	108	=	69
75	=	5	109	=	72
76	=	6	110	=	74
77	=	7	111	=	77
78	=	8	112	=	79
79	=	9	113	=	82
80	=	10	114	=	84
81	=	11	115	=	85
82	=	12	116	=	86
83	=	13	117	=	87
84	=	14	118	=	88
85	=	15	119	=	89
86	=	16	120	=	90
87	=	18	121	=	91
88	=	21	122	=	92
89	=	23	123	=	93
90	=	26	124	=	94
91	=	28	125	=	95
92	=	31	126	=	96
93	=	33	127	=	97
94	=	35	128	=	98
95	=	38	129	=	98
96	=	40	130	=	98
97	=	43	131	=	98
98	=	45	132	=	98
99	=	48	133	=	98
100	=	50	134 (or more)	=	99

[a]The percentile scores are based on a sample of 1,404 (658 female
and 746 male) undergraduate students at the University of Kansas and Purdue University.

deviations below the mean, or higher than only 2% of the other
people who have taken the test). Overall, males and females tend
to score similarly on the uniqueness scale.

Initial Steps in Scale Development

Now that you know your need for uniqueness as measured by the uniqueness scale, it is appropriate to ask in more detail what the scale scores mean. Likewise, is the scale valid as a measure of need for uniqueness? A good way to answer these questions is to "step into the shoes" of the authors and to retrace some of the procedures that were involved in the development of the scale. Hopefully, the subsequent discussion will help the reader understand the process of developing an individual-differences scale, whether the scale measures need for uniqueness, anxiety, depression, assertiveness, or any of the many other constructs that psychologists use. Furthermore, the description of the uniqueness scale development and validation may aid the reader in better understanding the concept of need for uniqueness.[1]

Although the final uniqueness scale was made up of 32 items, it was initially necessary to start out with a much larger pool of potential items. Thus, 300 items were either selected from existing scales or written to correspond with the definitions, theory, hypotheses, and research presented in the previous chapter. A description of a person with a high need for uniqueness was developed from the theory. This description emphasized anticonformity, independence, self-esteem, and inventiveness. Four judges independently rated each of the items according to the criterion: "How much do you think responses to this item would discriminate between people who have a high as compared with a low need to see themselves as unique?" Items were rated on a 5-point scale (1 = not at all discriminating, to 5 = very discriminating). Of the total pool of 300 items, 117 were retained for further analysis because the judges were able to agree that each each of these items had at least "good" validity (a score of 4 on a 5-point scale).

Next, this pool of 117 items was reduced to the 32 items now comprising the scale. This reduction was done by selecting only those items that correlated positively with a scale of *autonomy* and negatively with a scale of *succorance*. The logic for this selection procedure was that people with a high need for uniqueness should be relatively free from the social constraints of other people.

[1]The initial and subsequent scale construction is reported in detail in other manuscripts (Fromkin & Lipshitz, 1976; Snyder & Fromkin, 1977).

Therefore, higher-need-for-uniqueness people should score higher on an autonomy scale. Additionally, high-need-for-uniqueness people should seek relatively less support from other persons. Thus, higher-need-for-uniqueness people should score lower on a succorance scale. (The autonomy and succorance scales of the Personality Research Form [Jackson, 1967] were correlated with the 117 uniqueness items.) Other reasons for reducing the pool of 117 items to 32 items are related to convenience and brevity; that is, it is easier and faster to administer and respond to a scale with less items!

The Problem of Response Sets

Very often measures of individual differences are criticized because individuals' responses can be explained in terms of response sets. Response sets can be thought of as cognitive stances (ways of thinking) that people adopt while completing an individual-differences measure. The most common response set, for example, is one in which the individual attempts to respond to a scale so as to make the most favorable impression. This is known as responding to test items in the socially desirable direction. If scores on any individual-differences measure bear a strong relationship to social desirability, then it is most parsimonious to explain the scale as tapping social desirability.

In order to test whether responses on the uniqueness scale were explicable in terms of a response set in which people sought to appear in the best possible light, several studies were performed to correlate uniqueness scale scores with scores on measures of social desirability (e.g., the social desirability scale of the Personality Research Form [Jackson, 1967] and the Marlowe–Crowne Social Desirability Scale [Crowne & Marlowe, 1964]). In four separate studies, the uniqueness scale did *not* correlate significantly with social desirability, and thus, the scale was judged to have met the criterion of *not* being explicable in terms of social desirability.

Reliability

Another important characteristic of an individual-differences scale is reliability, or the test's consistency over time. The issue here is that a person's response to the scale at one time should be reasonably consistent with that person's response to the scale at a later time. This consistency over time is known as *test–retest reliability.*

Two studies were performed to establish the test–retest reliability of the uniqueness scale. In a first study, 80 Kansas undergraduate students (40 males and 40 females) took the uniqueness scale on two separate occasions, separated by a two-month interval. This same procedure was replicated with a second group of 99 introductory psychology students at the University of Kansas with an interval of four months between administrations of the test. For both studies, the test–retest correlations between scores on the two occasions were highly positive. From the results of these two studies, the uniqueness scale appears to have an acceptable test–retest reliability.

Subcomponents to the Need for Uniqueness

One question of interest regarding the uniqueness scale is the possibility that the overall scale is comprised of particular subcomponents. In order to further explore the internal structure of the uniqueness scale, we performed a factor analysis on the uniqueness scale responses of 475 undergraduates at the University of Kansas. (Factor analysis is a statistical procedure for determining if there are subcomponents to the total scale.) Three major factors emerged from the above analysis. Factor 1 is made up of items 2, 3, 5, 9, 11, 12, 13, 17, 19, 22, 23, 26, 27, 28, and 31. These items evidently reflect a *lack of concern regarding others' reactions to one's different ideas, actions,* etc. Factor 2 is made up of items 4, 6, 7, 10, 14, 18, 20, 21, 29, 30, and 32. These items appear to represent a *person's desire to not always follow rules.* Factor 3 is comprised of items 1, 8, 15, 16, 24, and 25. These items appear to tap a *person's willingness to defend his or her beliefs publicly.* Therefore, while the overall uniqueness scale reflects a desire or need to manifest one's uniqueness, the scale does appear to have particular subcategories that contribute to the total score.

Each of the aforementioned subcategories of items is very consistent with the tenets of uniqueness theorization. For example, the high-need-for-uniqueness person publicly displays and defends his or her ideas (Factor 3) and is not very concerned about others' reactions to the uniqueness of his or her ideas (Factor 1). Not surprisingly, the high-need-for-uniqueness person does not appear overly desirous of following traditional (and external) rules (Factor 2). One picture that emerges of the person who is highly desirous of uniqueness, therefore, is that he or she is not concerned with external sources of control (e.g., other people) but is guided by internal needs and desires. If the reader recalls the personal statement of Zeke (the high-need-for-uniqueness man appearing earlier in this chapter), this sense of internal control emerges. In this regard, further research is warranted to address the relationship between the uniqueness scale and a measure of locus of control (see Phares, 1976; Rotter, 1966). (Locus of control is an individual-differences scale that measures whether a person feels controlled by external events or internal causes.)

Does Need for Uniqueness Relate to Other Individual-Differences Measures?

An individual-differences measure should not have a very strong relationship with any other measure that is already in existence. Why? The best answer is that the psychological literature is already populated by an enormous number of scales. Therefore, it is incumbent upon the developer of a scale (need for uniqueness, in this case) to demonstrate that the new scale does not have an extremely high correlation with other existing scales. In this regard, several correlational studies have indicated that the uniqueness scale does not evidence strong relations with selected other scales (Snyder & Fromkin, 1977; Borden & Kreiger, 1977). For example, measures of "Enjoys Being Center of Attention," "Is a Leader," "Desires Recognition," and "Feels Superior" all evidence relatively small positive correlations with uniqueness scale scores. Predictably, the person scoring higher in need for uniqueness also reports himself or herself as being independent in opinions and relatively low in anxiety (especially as it relates to social situations or audiences). Overall, these results indicate that the uniqueness scale does not have exceedingly strong correlations with selected other scales. It should be cautioned, however, that there may be other existent scales (not measured in previous research) that may bear stronger correlations with the uniqueness scale. Nevertheless, the present studies do lend support to the notion that the uniqueness scale has reasonable discriminant validity.

So far, we have presented information regarding the development of the uniqueness scale. By way of review, the scale evidently surpasses the normal psychometric characteristics required of an individual-differences measure. More specifically, the uniqueness scale appears to be reliable across time (test–retest reliability), different from other scales (discriminant validity), and not explicable in terms of social-desirability responses.

Having made a case for the psychometric characteristics of the scale, we may now demonstrate that the scale measures what it purports to measure: desire for uniqueness. The subsequent studies test the construct validity of the scale. The first step in this research process was to derive a number of predictions about the behavior of people who would obtain different need-for-uniqueness scores. Then, people were recruited for experiments after they had completed the uniqueness scale. If people "behaved" in a fashion that was consistent with predictions stemming from their desire for uniqueness as measured by the scale, then the scale was said to have received *construct validational* support.

Peer-Rating Validation Study

If the motivation for uniqueness behaviors is tapped by the uniqueness scale, then it may be predicted that certain observable behaviors should reflect this need. That is, a person's desire to be unique should show up in his or her behavior. If over time a person observes another in a sufficient number of situations, then the observer should be able to accurately estimate the need for uniqueness in the other person. Therefore, a friend should be able to accurately judge a friend's uniqueness-seeking behavior.

In order to test the above reasoning, an experiment was performed in which undergraduate students were asked to bring a friend "who knows them well" to the study. The friend and the research participant were then placed in separate rooms. The research participant completed the uniqueness scale under the usual instructions. The friend, however, was asked to rate the research participant using a modified version of the uniqueness scale. The modified version changed each item from the first to the second person. For example, Item 1 was changed from "When I am in a group of strangers, I am not reluctant to express my opinion publicly" to "When (s)he is in a group of strangers, (s)he is not reluctant to express his/her opinions publicly." The friend rated the research participant on each item according to his or her knowledge of the person's behavior.

The friends' ratings of the research participants using the modified uniqueness scale were correlated with the research participants' scores on the uniqueness scale. A statistically significant positive correlation resulted. This correlation indicated that the uniqueness scale reflects behaviors that are interpersonally observable and thus "verifiable." One inference from this study is that need for uniqueness, as measured by the uniqueness scale, evidently manifests itself publicly. This finding should not be surprising when one remembers the factors that comprise the uniqueness scale. These factors reflect a willingness to publicly display one's ideas, beliefs, etc., even when this public display may result in rule breaking and/or reactions from others.

Word-Association Validation Study

One way of showing one's need for uniqueness may be to engage in activities that are unusual relative to the activities of other people. It is predicted, therefore, that people who are high in need for uniqueness should conform less to norms than people who are low in need for uniqueness, thereby exhibiting unique behaviors. For instance, high-need-for-uniqueness individuals would be expected to be less conforming in their language and word associations. In this regard, early research has shown that when people are asked to read a word and then respond with the first word that comes to mind, they give certain associations (i.e., SHORT–long, TABLE–chair) more frequently than others (i.e., SHORT–fat, TABLE–candle) (Horton, Marlowe, & Crowne, 1963). Thus, it was reasoned that adherence to a statistical norm is revealed through frequency of common word associations. Therefore, word associations should be influenced by one's need for uniqueness. Specifically, it is predicted that high-need-for-uniqueness people should generate more unusual word-association responses than research participants who were low in need for uniqueness. The following study was conducted by Brandt to test the relationship between scores on the uniqueness scale and commonality of word associations.

In Brandt's dissertation (1976), people were asked to fill out the uniqueness scale along with a 33-item word-association test (Horton *et al.*, 1963). Each research participant's word responses were assigned a commonality score based on the frequency of their occurrence among all research participants. A higher commonality score reflected a greater number of common word associations. The negative correlation between the uniqueness scale scores and the commonality scores showed that, as predicted, individuals who obtained higher-need-for-uniqueness scores tended to give less common word associations. Based on these results, it may be hypothesized that language is a vehicle for the manifestation of uniqueness.

Group Validation Studies

There are several groups that may serve as criteria against which to measure a need for uniqueness. This may be true because these groups have membership "qualifications" that differ from the characteristics of other people in general. As described in Chapter 4, these "qualifications" are defined as membership attributes. By becoming a member of a particular group, the person may define himself or herself as being different from the larger non-member population and thereby achieve a sense of uniqueness. A good example is liberation groups, where the members define their sense of difference as being "positive" and even gain a sense of enhanced self-esteem from such differences. Members of women's movement groups, for example, may see their behaviors and attitudes about sex-role–related matters as being different from those held by other women. Additionally, gay liberation group members may see their behaviors and attitudes about sexual activities as being different from most others in their society. Another group of people that may see themselves as being different from other people is MENSA. MENSA is an organization for very intelligent people. The entrance requirement for MENSA is a score in the top 2% on any one of several achievement or intelligence tests. These people gather for discussions and programs. Of special interest, the MENSA brochure describes the organization as being for unique individuals. Based on their group membership characteristics, it was predicted that all three groups of people (women's movement, gay liberation, and MENSA) should score higher on the uniqueness scale than a control group of college students who were of the same age.

In order to test this hypothesis, members of each of these groups completed the uniqueness scale. Mean uniqueness scale scores for each of these three groups were then compared with the mean score of a control comparison group of college students. The uniqueness scale scores for the women's movement ($M = 123.75$), the gay liberation ($M = 118.43$), and the MENSA ($M = 123.08$) groups were all significantly higher than the mean for the control comparison group ($M = 104.57$).

Social-Comparison Validation Study

If a person's need to be unique relative to other people is measured by the uniqueness scale, then a person with a high as compared with low need for uniqueness should rate himself or herself as more different in a variety of situations. The same result should occur when a person with a high as compared with low need for uniqueness is asked to compare himself or herself with another person in a particular situation. In order to test this latter hypothesis, an experiment was performed in which high (top 20%) and low (bottom 20%) scorers on the uniqueness scale were recruited for a subsequent experiment on "friendship formation." Research participants listened to a 10-minute audiotaped talk in which a college sophomore described himself, and they were instructed to compare themselves carefully with this other person. Finally, research participants were asked to make an overall judgment as to how similar to or different they were from the other person on a 9-point scale (1 = very similar, 3 = moderately similar, 7 = moderately different, 9 = very different). As hypothesized, the results showed that the high-need-for-uniqueness research participants saw themselves as more different from the individual on the tape than did low-need-for-uniqueness research participants (Ms = 8.18 and 3.65, respectively).

Dispositional and Situational Uniqueness and Self-Esteem Validation Study

Situational similarity feedback that either confirms or contra-
dicts dispositional[2] uniqueness (as measured by the uniqueness
scale) should have predictable influences on people. For example,
an increase in self-esteem should occur in situations when the
high-need-for-uniqueness person is given low-similarity feedback
(i.e., is told that he or she is different from others) as compared
with being given high-similarity feedback (i.e., is told that he or she
is similar to others); on the other hand, a decrease in self-esteem
should occur in situations when the low-need-for-uniqueness person is given low-similarity feedback (i.e., is told that he or she is
different from others) as compared with high-similarity feedback
(i.e., is told that he or she is similar to others). As previously described in Chapter 3 (pages 39–40), Ganster, McCuddy, and Fromkin (1977) performed the following experiment as a test of this
prediction.[3]

In this study, people scoring either high or low on the uniqueness scale were recruited for the experiment. After arriving at the
research laboratory, the research participants completed a measure of self-esteem. Next, they filled out an attitude questionnaire
and were informed that their responses to the questionnaire were
either very similar to those of previous college students or were
quite different. After this situational feedback, research participants completed the self-esteem measure for the second time. The
research participant's change in self-esteem from the first to the
second testing served as the measure of interest in this study. As
predicted, results revealed that increased similarity generated a
significant decline in self-esteem in high-need-for-uniqueness re-

[2]Dispositional or trait characteristics represent behaviors that are relatively consistent across a variety of situations for a given person. Thus, a high scorer on
the uniqueness scale should fairly consistently manifest this high need for
uniqueness; likewise, a low scorer on the uniqueness scale should fairly consistently manifest this low need for uniqueness.
[3]The previous description of this experiment did not include a discussion of the
need-for-uniqueness variable. An analysis of the influence of high and low need
for uniqueness was deferred because the individual-differences variable was
deemed most appropriate in the context of the present chapter.

search participants and a significant increase in self-esteem for low-need-for-uniqueness research participants.

Implications for Uniqueness Theory: Individual-Differences Corollaries

At this point, the reader should have a good idea of the general strategy that has been employed to validate the uniqueness scale. Perhaps the reader may envision other studies that could generate validational tests of the scale. For example, in conjunction with theoretical statements and empirical data mentioned in Chapters 3 and 4, it seems reasonable to suggest that persons who are high as compared with low in need for uniqueness will, under high situational similarity, (1) experience greater negative affect and (2) exhibit greater changes in the direction of dissimilarity.

Some amplification of these predictions is warranted at this point. In this regard, the influence of varying needs for uniqueness (i.e., high, average, or low) on emotional reactions to degree of interpersonal similarity are illustrated in Figure 8. Here, it can be

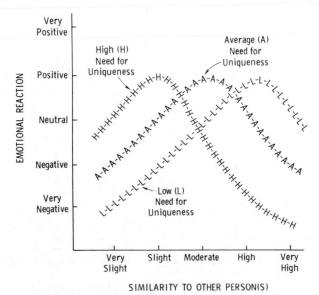

Figure 8. Hypothesized emotional reaction to another person as a function of similarity relative to that person and need for uniqueness.

seen that a high-need-for-uniqueness person should hypothetically exhibit the strongest positive emotional response in the slight range of similarity. As the degree of interpersonal similarity becomes higher, the high-need-for-uniqueness person should exhibit increasingly negative emotional reactions. Conversely, the low-need-for-uniqueness person should hypothetically exhibit the strongest positive emotional response in the high range of similarity. As the degree of interpersonal similarity becomes lower, the low-need-for-uniqueness person should exhibit increasingly negative emotional reactions.

The influence of varying needs for uniqueness (i.e., high, average, or low) on behavioral responses to degree of interpersonal similarity are illustrated in Figure 9. These hypothetical curves portray how a high-need-for-uniqueness person engages mostly in changes toward dissimilarity relative to others, while the low-need-for-uniqueness person engages mostly in changes toward similarity relative to others. Behaviorally, the high-need-for-uniqueness person should typically accentuate differences; the low-need-for-uniqueness person should accentuate similarities.

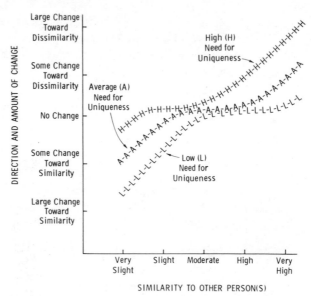

Figure 9. Hypothesized direction and amount of change as a function of similarity relative to another person and need for uniqueness.

It should be apparent to the reader that the hypothetical emotional response curves (Figure 8) and the behavioral change curves (Figure 9) for the high-need-for-uniqueness person are the same as those previously hypothesized for a negative-reference-group person in Chapter 4. Likewise, the hypothetical emotional curve and the behavioral change curve for the low-need-for-uniqueness person are the same as those hypothesized in Chapter 4 for a positive-reference-group person. The underlying reason for the similarity of the high-need-for-uniqueness and negative-reference-group curves is that similarity information should be encoded on the uniqueness identity dimension in a like manner. In both cases, the highest encoded acceptability on the uniqueness identity dimension should occur in the slight similarity condition. Likewise, the reason for the similarity of the low-need-for-uniqueness and positive-reference-group curves is that similarity information should be encoded on the uniqueness identity dimension in a like manner. In both cases, the highest encoded acceptability on the uniqueness identity dimension should occur in the high-similarity condition. At another level of analysis, this similarity of hypothesized curves indicates that *most* other people may represent a negative reference group for high-need-for-uniqueness people, while *most* other people may represent a positive reference group for a low-need-for-uniqueness person. That is, a high-need-for-uniqueness person does not want to be like the masses (negative connotation), and a low-need-for-uniqueness person wants to be like the masses (positive connotation).

Overall, therefore, the existing findings for the uniqueness scale suggest the necessity of developing corollaries in uniqueness theory in order to incorporate need for uniqueness as an individual-differences variable.

Application Exercises: Uniqueness Wheels

At this point, the reader should have an idea of his or her need for uniqueness. The following exercises are based on the premise that there are individual differences in need for uniqueness. Unlike the uniqueness scale, however, the uniqueness wheel exercise examines a person's perceived differences (1) relative to specific people and (2) on a variety of dimensions of comparison. The uniqueness wheel exercise enables a person to derive a vivid pictoral representation of perceived differences relative to another person. Therefore, this exercise may be used in a classroom setting as well as in management-training and therapeutic arenas (Snyder, 1979). Before discussing the uniqueness wheel in further detail, it first may be most useful for the reader to complete the following exercise.

Directions: The purpose of this exercise is for you to look at the ways in which you are similar to or different from your acquaintances on a variety of dimensions. Below you see several items on which you can compare yourself with an acquaintance according to the following comparison scale:

1	2	3	4	5	6	7	8	9

| Exactly
alike | Very
similar | | | | | Very
different | | Totally
different |

In the blank preceding each item place the number (1 through 9) that signifies how different or similar you are in comparison with your acquaintance.

I. Most Acceptable Acquaintance—Same Sex

Take about a minute and imagine your most acceptable acquaintance or a best friend who is of the same sex as you. Imagine a scene in which you have been with this person; think about how this person looks and acts. When you have an image of this person, go ahead and rate how similar or different you are (1 through 9) on the following items:

__ self-confidence	__ racial attitudes
__ conformity	__ overall physical appearance
__ anxiety	__ attractiveness
__ cooperativeness	__ intelligence
__ competitiveness	__ creativity
__ shyness	__ grades in school
__ dominance	__ athletic ability
__ happiness	__ career interests
__ religious beliefs	__ recreational interests
__ political views	__ socioeconomic background
__ attitudes about sex	__ lifestyle

In order to plot your uniqueness wheel, you merely mark a point (1 through 9) that corresponds to your response on each of the 22 dimensions and then join each of the points with a connecting line. An example of this process is given by Zeke, our high-need-for-uniqueness person who responded to the *Most Acceptable Acquaintance—Same Sex* in the following manner:

7	self-confidence	3	racial attitudes
5	conformity	7	overall physical appearance
4	anxiety	7	attractiveness
3	cooperativeness	4	intelligence
6	competitiveness	7	creativity
7	shyness	5	grades in school
6	dominance	5	athletic ability
3	happiness	5	career interests

$\frac{2}{2}$ religious beliefs $\frac{5}{4}$ recreational interests
$\frac{3}{}$ political views $\frac{}{3}$ socioeconomic background
        attitudes about sex   lifestyle

These responses are plotted on the uniqueness wheel in Figure 10.

   Plot your uniqueness wheel for your most acceptable acquaintance of the same sex on the wheel in Figure 11.

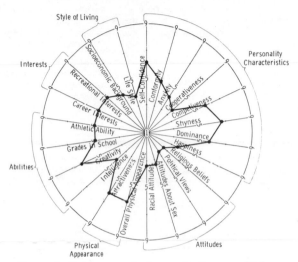

Figure 10. Uniqueness wheel example: the case of Zeke.

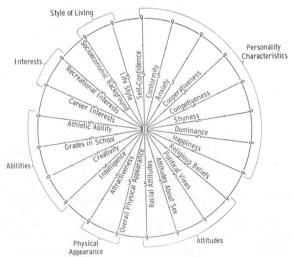

Figure 11. Uniqueness wheel: Most Acceptable Acquaintance—Same Sex.

Before describing the characteristic responses to this exercise, it may prove informative if the reader completes three other uniqueness wheels. After completing each exercise, plot your uniqueness wheel.

II. Most Acceptable Acquaintance—Opposite Sex
Take a minute to imagine your most acceptable acquaintance or best friend (can be girlfriend, boyfriend, or spouse) who is the opposite sex from you. Again, imagine a scene in which you have been with this person; think about how this person looks and acts. When you have an image of the person go ahead and rate how similar or different you are on the following items:

__ self-confidence	__ racial attitudes
__ conformity	__ overall physical appearance
__ anxiety	__ attractiveness
__ cooperativeness	__ intelligence
__ competitiveness	__ creativity
__ shyness	__ grades in school
__ dominance	__ athletic ability
__ happiness	__ career interests
__ religious beliefs	__ recreational interests
__ political views	__ socioeconomic background
__ attitudes about sex	__ lifestyle

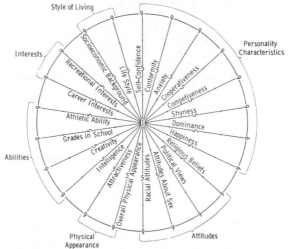

Figure 12. Uniqueness wheel: Most Acceptable Acquaintance—Opposite Sex.

III. Most Unacceptable Acquaintance—Same Sex
Take a minute to imagine your most unacceptable acquaintance, a "personal enemy" of sorts, who is the same sex as you. Imagine a scene in which you have been with this person; think about how this person looks and acts. When you have an image of the person, go ahead and rate how similar or different you are on the following items:

__ self-confidence	__ racial attidues
__ conformity	__ overall physical appearance
__ anxiety	__ attractiveness
__ cooperativeness	__ intelligence

- competitiveness
- shyness
- dominance
- happiness
- religious beliefs
- political views
- attitudes about sex

- creativity
- grades in school
- athletic ability
- career interests
- recreational interests
- socioeconomic background
- lifestyle

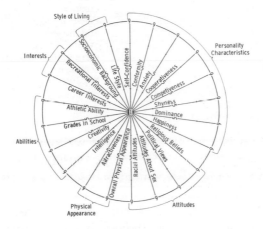

Figure 13. Uniqueness wheel: Most Unacceptable Acquaintance—Same Sex.

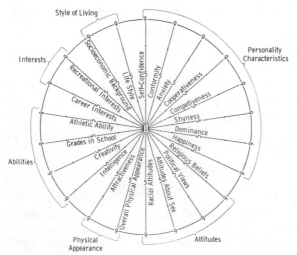

Figure 14. Uniqueness wheel: Most Unacceptable Acquaintance—Opposite Sex.

IV. Most Unacceptable Acquaintance—Opposite Sex

Take a minute to imagine your most unacceptable acquaintance, a "personal enemy" of sorts, who is the opposite sex from you. Imagine a scene in which you have been with this person; think about how this person looks and acts. When you have an image of the person, go ahead and rate how similar or different you are on the following items:

__ self-confidence	__ racial attitudes
__ conformity	__ overall physical appearance
__ anxiety	__ attractiveness
__ cooperativeness	__ intelligence
__ competitiveness	__ creativity
__ shyness	__ grades in school
__ dominance	__ athletic ability
__ happiness	__ career interests
__ religious beliefs	__ recreational interests
__ political views	__ socioeconomic background
__ attitudes about sex	__ lifestyle

Interpreting the Uniqueness Wheels

Several consistent patterns emerge when people complete this exercise (Snyder, 1979). A first finding is that close acquaintances are portrayed as being more similar on a variety of dimensions than the unacceptable acquaintances. Thus, our "personal enemies" are nearer to the far edges of the uniqueness wheel, as evidenced by the connected-line pattern. Indeed, it may be postulated that we take special efforts to maintain that we are quite different from a person we do not like. (See previous chapter for a discussion of either a negative-comparison other or a negative reference group.)

A second finding of this exercise is that even for a close acquaintance, most people find that they define themselves as being somewhat different from the other person on certain dimensions. In looking at the dimensions that are particularly important to a person, this perceived difference is especially evident (even for a close acquaintance). This may be the case because there are certain dimensions or attributes through which it is important for each person to maintain a sense of uniqueness. For some people, this may be through personality characteristics, while for others it may be through attitudes.[4]

[4]One revealing spinoff of the uniqueness wheel exercise is to have your close acquaintance of the same or the opposite sex complete the uniqueness wheel using you as the object person. Then, you can compare your perceptions of each other. Often, there are delightful inconsistencies between the two uniqueness wheel profiles. Surely, in such cases, one or probably both people are misperceiving the reality of such differences.

Another characteristic of uniqueness wheels is their intermediate patterning. That is, whether the wheel is for an acceptable or an unacceptable same- or opposite-sex person, people typically evidence a pattern that is neither entirely the same nor entirely different from the comparison-other person. While it is the case that the pattern for an acceptable acquaintance is closer to the center of the wheel, and the pattern for an unacceptable acquaintance is closer to the outer edges of the wheel, it should be emphasized that the patterns generally are in the intermediate range of similarity. This is consistent with uniqueness theory in that people are perceiving a moderate amount of similarity relative to others. While the aforementioned reasoning may appear to offer support for the uniqueness theory, it should be cautioned that there is another, equally plausible interpretation. Since people rarely use the extremes in responding to rating scales, people would naturally be expected to display some intermediate levels of difference on the uniqueness wheel exercise.

One final characteristic of these wheels is worthy of mention. Typical results of the uniqueness wheel demonstration reveal that people with a high as compared with a low need for uniqueness (as measured by the uniqueness scale) evidence different sizes of wheels. That is, the connected-line pattern for high-need-for-uniqueness people is farther out from the center point than is the case for the low-need-for-uniqueness people. This usually results whether or not the person is of the same sex or is a most acceptable or most unacceptable acquaintance. Evidently, therefore, the need for uniqueness is related to our perception of how different we actually are on a variety of dimensions. Whether or not need for uniqueness influences these perceptions of how different we actually are, or vice versa, cannot be definitively determined from such demonstrations. It should be recalled, however, that we have reasoned previously in this chapter that high-need-for-uniqueness people should accentuate their differences relative to other people. Furthermore, it is entirely consistent with the validation studies done on the uniqueness scale to conclude that high-need-for-uniqueness people *perceive* themselves as being different from other people. Whether this difference is just something that high-need-for-uniqueness people merely think exists or it really does exist is not certain. It may be that the high-need-for-uniqueness person is especially susceptible to the "pluralistic ignorance" or "illusion of uniqueness" phenomena that we shall discuss in Chapters 6 and 8. That is, the high-need-for-uniqueness person may just be ignorant of the fact that he or she is actually very similar to another person or persons on a variety of dimensions. Perhaps the most accurate statement in this regard is that high-need-for-uniqueness individuals partly accentuate their differences relative to other people and that part of this perceived difference is related to the realistic fact that they are somewhat different from other people.

Concluding Comment on Need for Uniqueness

Throughout this chapter, the reader has been exposed to empirical data and exercises revealing that there may be individual differences in the need to be unique. Undoubtedly, there are some of us who do appear to have a special need to manifest our uniqueness. Marshall (1967), in her poem entitled "Dare to Be Different," provides encouragement to such people:

> Dare to be different; life is so full
> Of people who follow the same push-and-pull.
> Poor, plodding people who other than name,
> Try to pretend they're exactly the same.
> God made men different; there never will be
> A replica soul of you and me.
> The Charm—the glory of all creation
> Rests on this very deviation.
> Your charm—your glory, too,
> Lies in being uniquely you—
> Lies in being true to your best,
> That part of you different from all the rest. (p. 21)

References

Borden, R. J. & Kreiger, W. Sex differences in social anxiety: A multivariate examination. Unpublished manuscript, Purdue University, 1977.

Brandt, J. M. *Behavioral validation of a scale measuring need for uniqueness.* Unpublished doctoral dissertation, Purdue University, 1976.

Crowne, D. P., & Marlowe, D. *The approval motive: Studies in evaluative dependence.* New York: Wiley, 1964.

Fromkin, H. L., & Lipshitz, R. A construct validity method of scale development: The Uniqueness Scale. *Institute for Research in the Behavioral, Eco-*

    nomic, and Management Sciences (Paper No. 591). West Lafayette, Ind.: Purdue University, 1976.

Ganster, D., McCuddy, M., & Fromkin, H. L. Similarity and undistinctiveness as determinants of favorable and unfavorable changes in self-esteem. Paper presented at the Midwestern Psychological Association, Chicago, 1977.

Horton, D. L., Marlowe, D., & Crowne, D. P. The effect of instructional set and need for social approval on commonality of word association responses. *Journal of Abnormal and Social Psychology*, 1963, *66*, 67–72.

Jackson, D. N. *Personality Research Form Manual*. Goshen, N.Y.: Research Psychologists Press, 1967.

Marshall, H. L. *Hold to your dream*. Denver: Helvern Press, 1967.

Phares, E. J. *Locus of control in personality*. Morristown, N.J.: General Learning Press, 1976.

Rotter, J. Generalized expectancies for internal versus external control of reinforcement. *Psychological Monographs*, 1966, *80* (1, Whole No. 609).

Snyder, C. R. Need for uniqueness and the uniqueness wheel exercise. Unpublished manuscript, University of Kansas, 1979.

Snyder, C. R., & Fromkin, H. L. Abnormality as a positive characteristic: The development and validation of a scale measuring need for uniqueness. *Journal of Abnormal Psychology*, 1977, *86*, 518–527.

III

Uniqueness Attributes

The Way to Be Unique

Being unique is sometimes my aim
Just to avoid being the same
Here are two basic rules
(Ignored only by fools)

First, know those differences
The ones that are not condoned
Second, pursue those differences
Where society lets you alone

—Anonymous undergraduate student
University of Kansas, 1979

Commodities As Uniqueness Attributes

What Is a Uniqueness Attribute?

As noted in the second chapter, there are many mechanisms that may account for the high degree of attitudinal and behavioral consistency we see frequently in groups (see Kiesler & Kiesler, 1969). "Normal" behavior becomes formalized in society, and people are rewarded for compliance and punished for deviations (Goffman, 1963). The reader may easily imagine unusual behaviors that may quickly bring strong social disapproval and mistreatment (see Becker, 1963; Clinard, 1968; Freedman & Doob, 1968; Goffman, 1963; Lofland, 1969; Matza, 1969; Palmer, 1970; Schur, 1965, 1969). In this regard, it is at times striking to see society's quick and strong response to a person who has deviated from the norm (Schachter, 1951). Equally striking, however, is the *lack* of response that a society will typically give to someone who is behaving "normally." Given this situation, we may be expected to develop a cautiousness in showing ourselves to be unique. Fortunately, however, society provides some socially acceptable attributes whereby people may manifest their differentness; these characteristics are called *uniqueness attributes.*

Before examing uniqueness attributes, it may be useful to examine the dynamics of uniqueness seeking within the context of an exchange theory of social behavior (see Fromkin & Snyder, 1980). When couched in an exchange theory perspective, conformity or similarity to other persons may be seen as a means of attaining valued outcomes or rewards (or to avoid negative consequences or costs) (Nord, 1969). In the most general sense, we conform in order to engage in an exchange in which we either get social approval or avoid disapproval. This process of gaining approval or avoiding disapproval is often purchased at some *cost* to the individual. That is, a person frequently has to deny himself or herself one activity in order to engage in another activity. Thus, it seems reasonable to assume that when a person complies with the norms of opinion and/or behavior of a group, he or she may, at the same time, experience feelings of interpersonal similarity that threaten his or her self-perception of uniqueness. In conformity studies, when the research participants complied with the influences exerted by the group, they may have accepted the abandonment of their unique attitudes, beliefs, or behaviors as a *cost* in the immediate situation. As Homans (1961) put it, by conforming a person sacrifices the "maintenance of his personal integrity achieved by sticking to his own independent and publicly expressed opinion on the issue of the case" (p. 97).

Most studies of conformity focus only on conforming behavior in the immediate situation. They neglect residual aspects of behavior that develop with the passage of time. They also fail to recognize other potential responses that result from or occur subsequent to conformity. Yet, what becomes of these costs or the lost alternatives? Do we simply ignore or forget them? Can it be assumed that the deprived motives in any single exchange do not affect subsequent behavior? In spite of the vast literature that describes the effects of deprived motives upon behavior, most views of conformity pay relatively little or no attention to the subsequent dynamics of deprived motives, such as uniqueness deprivation, that occur as the result of a trade between an individual and a group. After such a transaction is concluded, it may be assumed that the costs and dissatisfactions that accrue to the individual as a result of deprived motives do affect his or her behavior. In this regard, it seems necessary to recognize that the process of profit maximization continues beyond the immediate situation, with a search for ways to increase our rewards and decrease our costs. In particular, when a person cannot secure both conformity and uniqueness outcomes in the same situation, he or she is likely to seek other modes of gaining some sense of uniqueness, while also showing some conformity to the norms that furnish him or her with protection, approval, and admission to groups. In this vein, Fromkin (1968, 1973) has suggested that in a society fraught with strong pressures toward deindividuation and conformity, individual needs for uniqueness are not foregone but merely manifested in more subtle and practical ways.

In spite of, or perhaps because of, the pressures that encourage public conformity and anonymity, people at times want to be different and seek socially acceptable symbols or anchors for their individuality. For example, there are a number of attributes (physical, material, informational, experiential, etc.) that are valued because they define the person as different from members of his or her reference group and that, at the same time, will not call down the forces of rejection and isolation for deviancy. Such attributes are referred to as *uniqueness attributes.* The following chapters survey some of these potential uniqueness attributes. It should be emphasized, however, that the attributes chosen for a detailed discussion in no way exhaust the potential list of such attributes. Rather, the uniqueness attributes discussed in this and the subsequent chapters in this section reflect selected interesting attributes that are prevalent in our society.

Introductory Comments on Commodities as Uniqueness Attributes

William James (1890), whose thinking set the stage for many psychological notions about the self (see Hall & Lindzey, 1957, pp. 467–502, for review), defined the "material self" as

> the total of all that he can call his, not only his body and his psychic powers, but his clothes and his house, his wife and his children, his ancestors and friends, his reputation and works, his land and horses, and yacht and bank account. All these things give him the same emotions. (p. 291)

It therefore follows that an expensive house and automobile may be used to define a "wealthy or successful self," canonical ornaments may be used to define a "religious self," and objets d'art may be used to define a "cultured self." Indeed, the widely observed tendency to augment and hoard material possessions may represent our search for separate identities. That is, it is possible that the possession of commodities that are rare, scarce, or unavailable to other persons may be used to define a "unique self." In this sense, commodities may serve as a uniqueness attribute.

"Hurry on Down While the Supply Lasts"

In order to understand the potential of commodities as uniqueness attributes, it may be useful to describe briefly what has come to be called *commodity theory* (Brock, 1968). Commodity theory, in contrast to economic theory (Fromkin, 1972), asserts that individuals value unavailable commodities because of scarcity, in and of itself, even when there is no demand or increased monetary reward associated with the scarcity. A commodity is any object (e.g., a piece of information, an experience, or a material) that a potential possessor perceives as useful. Also, the commodity is typically conceived of as being conveyable from person to person.

A number of different experiments have confirmed the notion that increased valuation accompanies the perception of scarcity. For instance, persuasive communications (Fromkin & Brock, 1971), simulated drug experiences (Fromkin, 1970), new products (Fromkin, 1971), leather boots (Fromkin, Williams, & Dipboye, 1974), nylon hosiery (Fromkin, Olson, Dipboye, & Barnaby, 1971), and pornographic books (Zellinger, Fromkin, Speller, & Kohn, 1974) have all been found to be associated with greater valuation when they were perceived as scarce relative to plentiful commodities. Many of these studies will be discussed further in the present chapter.

One possible explanation for the valuation of scarce commodities is that the possession of scarce commodities is in some way related to the self-perception of uniqueness. In the early 1890s, William James remarked that "the line between what is me and mine is very hard to draw." The economist Veblen (1934) also recognized a similar psychological meaning for the accumulation of possessions. If we are indeed defined partially in terms of our commodities, Fromkin (1968) reasoned that the possession of scarce commodities is one *socially acceptable* way to redefine the self as different in a society that is fraught with pressures toward conformity and deindividuation. That is, the tendency to prize scarce and unavailable objects may be a symbolic representation of a desire for uniqueness. Commonsense support for these ideas is seen in advertising campaigns that emphasize product scarcity. "Hurry on down while the supply lasts" has been invoked to sell such products as clothing, furniture, stereo records, automobiles, and even burial plots.

Who Pays Special Attention to the Scarcity of Products?

In the previous section we hypothesized that almost all of us respond to information regarding product scarcity. However, it is logical to speculate that certain people should be especially attentive to product scarcity information. For example, if products may serve as a means of obtaining a sense of uniqueness, then individuals with high as compared with a low need for uniqueness should perceptually accentuate the availability of products. Consistent with this prediction, it may be hypothesized that high as compared with low scorers on the uniqueness scale would perceive lesser availability in commodities when they are depicted as scarce; conversely, a high as compared with a low scorer on the uniqueness scale should perceive greater availability in commodities when they are depicted as not being scarce.

In order to test this hypothesis, people scoring either very high (top 20%) or very low (bottom 20%) on the Need for Uniqueness Scale (Snyder & Fromkin, 1977) were recruited to the experimental setting (Snyder & Atlas, 1978). Under the guise of a marketing study that purportedly related biographical data to product attitudes, the research participants were asked to "evaluate a product." For half of the research participants, the product was described as being scarce; for the other half of the research participants, the product was described as being plentiful. Prior to showing each of the research participants a picture of the product, the experimenter in the *scarce* condition noted that "it so happens that the manufacturer produced only a small quantity of this product. Therefore, this product will appear in only a very few stores scattered throughout the country." In the *nonscarce* condition, the experimenter noted that "it so happens that the manufacturer produced a large quantity of this product. Therefore, this product will appear in most stores scattered throughout the country." After hearing this scarce or nonscarce information about the product, the research participant looked at the picture of the product and was asked to fill out a series of filler questions that included the measure of interest, the availability dependent variable: "In how many stores do you feel the product will appear?" (1 = most stores; 3 = many stores; 7 = not very many stores; 9 = few stores).

Results showed that the scarce product was perceived as significantly less available than the nonscarce product. Thus, the scarcity manipulation proved to be effective. More importantly, however, the predicted interaction between product scarcity and the need-for-uniqueness score resulted. That is, the high-need-for-uniqueness research participants perceived the scarce product as being less available than did the low-need-for-uniqueness research participants; conversely, the high-need-for-uniqueness research participants perceived the nonscarce product as being more available than did the low-need-for-uniqueness research participants.

Overall, therefore, the interaction of product scarcity and need for uniqueness indicates that a high as compared with a low need for uniqueness may be associated with actual perceptual distortion of product availability information. That is, the high-need-for-uniqueness person may perceptually accentuate the product scarcity information so that a scarce product is perceived as *very* scarce and a plentiful product is perceived as *very* plentiful.

The Appeal to Uniqueness through Advertising

That advertisements for various products often appeal to a sense of uniqueness in the potential buyer is revealed in the examples in Figures 15 through 21. First, a travel agency notes the advantages of separating from the group in its "Birds of a feather need not flock together" theme. Second, the shoe company dramatically illustrates this appeal by noting that "each shoe wearing a Brass Boot label is unique; distinctive; set apart." Third, the pen ad notes: "in a world gone mad with mass production, this marches to a different drummer." In a similar vein, the fourth ad, for perfume, announces the opinion that "We know you don't want to look like the next girl." The fifth ad, for watches, links individuality and quality as it notes, "We create for individuals. Men of real quality are individuals." The sixth ad reveals that even a university business school can extol the uniqueness of their educational prod-

Birds of a feather need not flock together!

Icelandic Airlines' New Affinity Group Fares to Luxembourg

Now we can offer affinity groups,* the ultimate in flexibility. Icelandic's new affinity fare rules only require the group to fly to Europe together. Group members may fly home individually anytime they want.

Minimum group size is only 25 passengers as opposed to 40 on other airlines so chances of your group going are better.

Think of the possibilities and you'll agree with us that charters and IATA affinity fares are for the birds.

Chicago-Luxembourg-Chicago
$341   Nov.–March
$381   Apr., May, Sept., Oct.
$467   June–August

Send in the coupon for more details

✹Maupintour travel service

*affinity groups by definition, members of the same school, club or organization

Figure 15. Reprinted by permission of Maupintour Travel Service.

Figure 16. Reprinted by permission of Weyenberg Shoe Manufacturing Company, Milwaukee, Wisconsin.

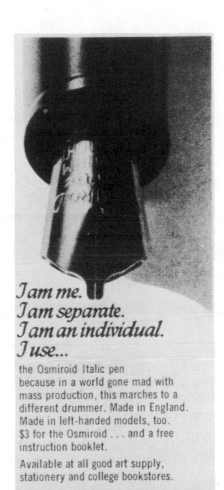

Figure 17. Reprinted by permission of Osmiroid Italic Pen, Hunt Manufacturing Company, Philadelphia, Pennsylvania.

Figure 18. Reprinted by permission of Cheseborough-Pond's, Inc., Greenwich, Connecticut.

Figure 19. Reprinted by permission of Norman M. Morris Corporation, New York, N.Y.

Figure 20. Reprinted by permission of the School of Management and Krannert Graduate School of Management, Purdue University, West Lafayette, Indiana.

Now Available

SYSTEMS AND THEORIES
IN PSYCHOLOGY 3/e

MELVIN H. MARX
University of Missouri, Columbia, and

W.A. HILLIX
San Diego State University

- The authors take advantage of the scholarship of writers such as Thomas Kuhn, Karl Popper, Herbert Feigl, and R.I. Watson;
- They clearly explain the transition between the various schools of psychology and current theoretical developments;
- They give thorough treatment to both classical systems and representative contemporary theories, including behaviorism, psychoanalysis, Third Force psychology, and information and detection theories.

Figure 21. Reprinted by permission of the McGraw Hill Book Company, New York, N.Y.

uct. Finally, the seventh ad implicitly assumes that a unique psychology book is a desirable one.

These advertisements, and many others like them, implicitly assume that uniqueness is a valued attribute. Furthermore, such ads assume that when a product is associated with uniqueness, the association increases the consumers' valuation of and desire to obtain the product. Thus, the assumption in such ads is that the uniqueness of a product will motivate us to buy it. The paradox is that as advertisements entreat us to become people of uniqueness by acquiring their products, through our compliance we may actually find our tastes becoming similar to those of others. In this circumstance, we may be prone to a state of pluralistic ignorance in that we never realize or believe that we are becoming similar to others by purchasing "unique" products.

Clothing as a Uniqueness Attribute

Clothing is one "commodity" that has special signal value as a uniqueness attribute. The intimate link between self-identity, clothing, and self-perceived uniqueness is recognized in many different disciplines. The sociologist Stone (1962) holds that the self is established, maintained, and altered in and through communication during social transactions. Stone identifies appearance as one important form of communication in symbolic interaction. Clothing is a primary dimension of appearance. For example, social announcements of the self are made by means of symbols such as uniforms (e.g., the policeman) or distinctive apparel (e.g., the pince-nez of Teddy Roosevelt). Indeed, "distinctive persistant dress may replace the name as well as establish it" (Stone, 1962, p. 95). Similarly, the French sociologist George Simmel (1957) observed how similarity in dress "unites" members of the same social class or group and, at the same time, "segregates" them from a larger number of members of other social classes or groups.

Although there often is a great deal of conformity in clothing styles (e.g., the length of women's skirts or the width of men's ties), the anxiety that occurs when two people wear the same piece of clothing at a social event is legendary. For example, when two people wear an identical suit or dress to the same social event, the resulting negative reactions provide anecdotal support for the important relationship between clothing and the self-perception of uniqueness. Seemingly, we may value our clothing in part because everyone else is not wearing the same thing. Two experiments that are described subsequently test this theorization. Each study demonstrates that enhanced valuation of clothing occurs when people become potential possessors of apparel that is unavailable to many other people.

In a first experiment (Fromkin, Olson, Dipboye, & Barnaby, 1971), female college students were recruited under the guise of a marketing research project. The project was purportedly a cooperative one between a French clothing manufacturer who was interested in testing the American market for his new hosiery products and a professor of marketing who was interested in studying attitudes toward new products. After a brief discussion of the quality, texture, price, and variety of hosiery, research participants viewed a 6-minute film that showed a series of laboratory tests (e.g., puncture resistance, tensile strength, and size/shape retention) performed on a number of different testing machines. The film, which was prepared for the experiment in the Department of Home Economics at Purdue University, showed the new French hosiery to be superior to American brands. Immediately after the film, the experimenter began the manipulation of the scarce–plentiful variable with the following explanation:

> The French manufacturer has provided us with some of these nylons to distribute in your area. Unfortunately (or fortunately), the number we have to distribute is (or is not) severely limited. We have been provided with only 1,000 (or 100,000) pairs to distribute to women in the United States. Since we are conducting this survey and demonstration in many cities, we can distribute 50 (or 5,000) pairs in your city.

Next, the research participants completed a postexperimental questionnaire that contained scales to measure the effectiveness of the manipulation and the valuation of the hosiery. Analysis of the questionnaire responses revealed that research participants in the scarce conditions perceived the nylons as more scarce than subjects in the plentiful conditions. Unexpectedly, however, both groups perceived the nylons as relatively scarce. Analysis of the research participants' responses to the questionnaire item "What price should we charge for these nylons?" revealed that people in the scarce condition tended to assign higher prices ($M = \$2.71$) to the nylons than people in the plentiful condition ($M = \$2.27$).

A second experiment more directly addressed the relationship between clothing and self-definitions of uniqueness. This experiment revealed that people who have a higher as compared with a lower need to be unique see scarce objects as more desirable. In this second experiment (Fromkin, Williams, & Dipboye, 1974), male and female research participants first responded to rating-scale items that seemed to reflect people's need to be unique. (The items in this scale were basically the same as those utilized in the uniqueness scale.) The results revealed that people who had a high need for uniqueness exhibited greater preferences for leather boots when the boots were perceived as available to only a few other persons than when they perceived the boots as being available to larger numbers of other persons. This preference was not shown by research participants who obtained low need-for-uniqueness scores. If people have a high desire to be unique, it follows that they should show a greater preference for scarce boots as compared with plentiful boots, especially if the commodities may represent a means of defining oneself as unique. Conversely, if a person has a low desire to be unique, it follows that a scarce commodity should not necessarily be significantly preferred over the plentiful commodity.

The role of fashion and clothing as uniqueness attributes is recognized by students in fashion distribution and clothing marketing–merchandising. Although "original" or limited editions in fashion are often confounded with high prices and perceptions of high quality, both high price and high quality may also be used to differentiate the self from large numbers of other persons. In a doctoral dissertation by Szybillo (1973), people participated in an alleged consumer psychology study of advertising and marketing. Research participants viewed slide photographs of ladies' pant suits. The pant suits varied in terms of their scarcity (scarce versus plentiful). Furthermore, research participants were also divided into two groups of high and low fashion-opinion leadership according to their scores on a scale that measured fashion leadership. The main dependent variables were ratings of the "overall desirability," "distinctiveness," "quality," and "likelihood of purchase" of each of the pant suits. The results showed that scarce pant suits were perceived as more desirable, more distinctive, of higher quality, and more likely to be purchased than plentiful pant suits. In addition, fashion leaders as compared to non-fashion leaders exhibited a stronger preference for the scarce pant suits over the plentiful pant suits. Thus, there appears to be some link between the tendency to be an innovator of new products and ideas and the valuation of commodities that are unavailable to other persons. Perhaps, those individuals who can be identified as "innovators" are expressing, at least in part, socially acceptable manifestations of the desire to see themselves as different from their peers (Fromkin, 1971).

Activities and Experiences as Uniqueness Attributes

A person's sense of uniqueness may also be reinforced by engaging in unusual or different activities, hobbies, vacations, etc. Fromkin (1970) performed the following experiment in order to test the link between uniqueness and the desirability of an experience. (This experiment was described previously in Chapter 3.) He did this by first varying the degree of self-perceived similarity that people felt and then assessing the magnitude of the research participants' preferences for scarce and plentiful experiences. Prior to the experimental session, the research participants completed an extensive battery of tests that allegedly measured a large number of their attitudes, values, aptitudes, and other related attributes. On arriving at the laboratory, the research participants received a bogus computer printout that contained approximately 60 pages. In one condition, the research participants were led to believe that they had responded very similarly to 10,000 other college students. This was the high-similarity condition. A second group of research participants were led to believe that they had responded differently than the other students. This was the slight-similarity condition.

Next, the instructions explained to research participants that a second experiment was examining the sensory effects of drugs. The effects of these drugs were being simulated technically with rooms that varied in their light and sound configurations. In addition, the instructions explained that two of the rooms were available on only a limited basis. Thus, only a small number of people would be able to experience them. The remaining two rooms were

DOONESBURY by Garry Trudeau

alleged to be available all of the time and a great many people would be able to experience them. Each person was told that, "Luckily, all four rooms are available at the present time." The people were then asked to choose which room they wanted and how much time they wanted to spend in it by completing rating scales. Analysis of the research participants' responses showed that under conditions of slight similarity, people did not prefer scarce over plentiful experiences. However, under conditions of high similarity, people preferred the scarce to the plentiful experiences. Thus, it seems reasonable to generalize from these findings that society's valuation of scarce experiences is enhanced in social climates that induce conformity and feelings of undistinctiveness.

In a similar vein, a book entitled *The Great Escape* (Yee, 1974) may have become popular, in part, because it offered people a catalog of potentially unique experiences. As described on the first

page, "This book is a window and a door. . . . A door to what is unique." By engaging in such activities as tubing down the Apple River (Kuralt, 1974), setting a world record (Allen, 1974), or acquiring the art of Jonathan Livingston Hang Glider (Cook, 1974), the cocktail party guest is "one up" on uniqueness relative to other people. Of course, sometimes the seeming uniqueness of our activities and experiences can be destroyed, as depicted by the three cartoons on pages 122 and 123. Here, the illusion of uniqueness is shattered by a dose of reality.

A Date or a Mate as a Uniqueness Attribute

Yet another "commodity" that may serve as a uniqueness attribute is one's mate. "The cliché that men prefer hard-to-get women misses the point. Men really adore women who are hard for other men to get" is offered by Walster, Piliavin, and Walster (1973, p. 80) as a conclusion derived from their findings in a series of experiments examining college men's perceptions of "hard-to-get" women. When research participants' perceptions of a "hard-to-get" woman were varied by representing her as a female who did not accept the date until a week after the research participant's request or a female who indicated a low probability for future dates, the results did not confirm the prediction of greater value for hard-to-get women. However, a final experiment contained three conditions: (1) a female who was reluctant to date either the research participant or the four other fictitious participants (uniformly hard-to-get); (2) a female who was willing to date the subject or any of the four fictitious participants (uniformly easy-to-get); and (3) a female who was willing to date the subject and reluctant to date the four other fictitious participants (selectively hard-to-get). Almost all of the research participants preferred the *selectively* hard-to-get female. According to the authors of the studies, "The reason for her popularity is evident. Men ascribe to her all the assets of the uniformly hard-to-get and the uniformly easy-to-get women, and none of their liabilities" (Walster, Walster, Piliavin, & Schmidt, 1973, p. 120).

One explanation of the Walster *et al.* research findings may be derived from commodity theory, that is, the valuation of commodities increases when a person perceives that he or she is a potential possessor of material objects, experiences, or information that is unavailable to other persons. As we have reasoned in the present chapter, scarce commodities enable a person to feel unique. In light of the findings of Walster and her colleagues, it is intriguing to speculate that dating women "who are hard for other men to get" may be an aspect of identity and appearance that satisfies a male's desire to see himself as different and/or to be seen as different from his peers. Although it may seem somewhat harsh to think of one's mate as a source of attaining a sense of uniqueness, this hypothesis appears to be not only intriguing but plausible.

Concluding Comments on Commodities

The present chapter has shown how commodities may symbolize a person's unique identity. Commodities such as one's clothing, activities, experiences, and even dates or mates may elicit a sense of identity and a commensurate unique position among other people. More and more in the past few decades, people in Western culture (which emphasizes production and material goods) have come to define themselves in terms of their possessions, their things. The attraction generated by the acquisition of commodities may stem from the signal value of these unique possessions. The question is not just to have *more*, then, but rather to have more things that enable us to perceive ourselves as being different from other people.

Perhaps the entire relationship between commodities and a sense of uniqueness is best characterized by a quote taken from the classic "children's" book *The Little Prince*, by Antoine de Saint-Exupéry (1971). In the story, the Little Prince happens upon a garden with many flowers that are like the only flower he has. The story notes:

> And he was overcome with sadness. His flower had told him that she was the only one of her kind in all the universe. And here were five thousand of them all alike, in a single garden!
>
> "She would be very much annoyed," he said to himself, "if she should see that . . . she would cough most dreadfully, and she would pretend that she was dying, to avoid being laughed at. . . ."
>
> Then he went on with his reflections: "I thought that I was rich, with a flower that was unique in all the world; and all I had was a common rose. A common rose. . . . That doesn't make me a very great prince. . . ."
>
> And he lay down in the grass and cried. (pp. 77–78)

References

Allen, W. How to set a world record. In M. S. Yee (Ed.), *The great escape.* New York: Bantam, 1974, pp. 224–225.

Becker, H. S. *Outsiders.* New York: Free Press, 1963.

Brock, T. C. Implications of commodity theory for value change. In A. G. Greenwald, T. C. Brock, & T. M. Ostrom (Eds.), *Psychological foundations of attitudes.* New York: Academic, 1968, pp. 243–275.

Clinard, M. B. *Sociology of deviant behavior* (3rd ed.). New York: Holt, Rinehart, & Winston, 1968.

Cook, W. J. The art of Jonathan Livingston Hang Glider. In M. S. Yee (Ed.), *The great escape*. New York: Bantam, 1974, pp. 98–100.

Freedman, J. L., & Doob, A. N. *Deviancy: The psychology of being different.* New York: Academic, 1968.

Fromkin, H. L. Affective and valuational consequences of self-perceived uniqueness deprivation. Unpublished doctoral dissertation, Ohio State University, 1968.

Fromkin, H. L. The effects of experimentally aroused feelings of indistinctiveness upon valuation of scarce and novel experiences. *Journal of Personality and Social Psychology*, 1970, *16*, 521–529.

Fromkin, H. L. A social psychological analysis of diffusion and adoption of new products from a uniqueness motivation perspective. Paper presented at the Association for Consumer Research, University of Maryland, College Park, September 1971.

Fromkin, H. L. The "irrationality" of "economic man": A psychological view of scarcity. Paper presented at the American Psychological Association, Honolulu, September 1972.

Fromkin, H. L. The psychology of uniqueness: Avoidance of similarity and seeking of differentness. *Institute for Research in the Behavioral, Economic, and Management Sciences.* Paper No. 438, Purdue University, 1973.

Fromkin, H. L., & Brock, T. C. A commodity theory analysis of persuasion. *Representative Research in Social Psychology*, 1971, *2*, 47–57.

Fromkin, H. L., Olson, J. C., Dipboye, R. L., & Barnaby, D. A commodity theory analysis of consumer preferences for scarce products. Paper presented at the American Psychological Association Convention, Washington, September 1971.

Fromkin, H. L., & Snyder, C. R. The search for uniqueness and valuation of scarcity: A neglected dimension of value in exchange theory. In K. Gergen, M. S. Greenberg, & R. H. Willis (Eds.), *Social exchange: Advances in theory and research.* New York: Plenum, 1980.

Fromkin, H. L., Williams, J. J., & Dipboye, R. L. Birth order, responses to need for uniqueness scale items, and valuation of scarce commodities. Unpublished manuscript, Purdue University, 1974.

Goffman, I. *Stigma: Notes on the management of spoiled identity.* Englewood Cliffs, N.J.: Prentice-Hall, 1963.

Hall, C. S., & Lindzey, G. *Theories of personality.* New York: Wiley, 1957.

Homans, G. C. *Social behavior: Its elementary forms.* New York: Harcourt, Brace, & World, 1961.

James, W. The principles of psychology, vol. 1. New York: H. Holt & Company, 1890.

Kiesler, C. A., & Kiesler, S. B. *Conformity.* Reading, Mass.: Addison-Wesley, 1969.

Kuralt, C. Tubing on the Apple. In M. S. Yee (Ed.), *The great escape.* New York: Bantam, 1974, p. 63.

Lofland, J. *Deviance and identity.* Englewood Cliffs, N.J.: Prentice-Hall, 1969.

Matza, D. *Becoming deviant.* Englewood Cliffs, N.J.: Prentice-Hall, 1969.

Nord, W. R. Social exchange theory: An integrative approach to social conformity. *Psychological Bulletin,* 1969, *71,* 174–208.

Palmer, S. *Deviance and conformity: Roles, situations, and reciprocity.* New Haven, Conn.: College and University Press, 1970.

Saint-Exupéry, A. de *The little prince.* New York: Harcourt Brace & Jovanovich, 1971.

Schachter, S. Deviation, rejection, and communication. *Journal of Abnormal and Social Psychology,* 1951, *46,* 190–207.

Schur, E. M. *Crimes without victims; deviant behavior and public policy: Abortion, homosexuality, drug addiction.* Englewood Cliffs, N.J.: Prentice-Hall, 1965.

Schur, E. M. Reactions to deviance: A critical assessment. *American Journal of Sociology,* 1969, *75,* 309–322.

Simmel, G. Fashion. *American Journal of Sociology,* 1957, *62,* 541–558.

Snyder, C. R., & Atlas, M. Need for uniqueness and perceived product scarcity. Unpublished manuscript, University of Kansas, 1978.

Snyder, C. R., & Fromkin, H. L. Abnormality as a positive characteristic: The development and validation of a scale measuring need for uniqueness. *Journal of Abnormal Psychology,* 1977, *86,* 518–527.

Stone, G. P. Appearance and the self. In A. M. Rose (Ed.), *Human behavior and social processes.* Boston: Houghton-Mifflin, 1962, pp. 86–118.

Szybillo, G. J. The effects of price and scarcity on the valuation of fashions by fashion opinion leaders and nonopinion leaders. Doctoral dissertation, Purdue University, 1973.

Veblen, T. *The theory of the leisure class: An economic study of institutions.* New York: The Modern Library, 1934.

Walster, E., Piliavin, J., & Walster, G. W. The hard-to-get woman. *Psychology Today,* 1973, *7,* 80–83.

Walster, E., Walster, G. W., Piliavin, J., & Schmidt, L. "Playing hard to get": Understanding an elusive phenomenon. *Journal of Personality and Social Psychology,* 1973, *26,* 113–121.

Yee, M. S. (Ed.) *The great escape.* New York: Bantam, 1974.

Zellinger, D. A., Fromkin, H. L., Speller, D. E., & Kohn, C. A. A commodity theory analysis of the effects of age restrictions upon pornographic materials. *Institute for Research in the Behavioral, Economic, and Management Sciences.* Paper No. 440, Purdue University, 1974.

Names as Uniqueness Attributes

Drawing by C.R. Snyder.

Names: A Source of Identity

A second uniqueness attribute to be considered in this section is one's name, which may be the "most important anchorage of our self identity" (Allport, 1961, p. 117). The special psychological significance of a person's name is revealed by the dismay and anger that are frequently evoked when someone forgets, misspells, or mispronounces it. The reader can perform a very reliable "field" experiment to check out this phenomenon. When introduced to a new person, just mispronounce the person's name. Typically, and with some impatience, the person will correct you. If you mispronounce the name a second time, the person will become even more annoyed. (It is usually best to stop this experiment at this point!)

We often find names and initials on peoples' possessions, including such items as clothing (monograms) and luggage. For example, Fromm (1941) commented, "We are informed of the individual names of the railroad clerk we buy our tickets from;

handbags, playing cards, and portable radios are also personal-ized'' (p. 255). Why do people do this?

Perhaps it is not only the material possession but the *individual* who is being singled out by his or her initials or name. Our name represents who we are. A direct link between names and self-identity is found in a study by Bugental and Zelen (1950), who examined self-perceptions by asking the question, ''Who are you?'' When people's responses were analyzed against 17 different dimensions, names were given as the most prevalent response to this question. Thus, at a very simple level of analysis, one's name is an important link to one's identity.

In relation to the topic of names as a source of identity, it is revealing to explore recent developments in what happens to a woman's family name after marriage. The retention of maiden names or the hyphen form of maiden–married name has become a more common custom in our society. For instance, the journalist Ruth Hale refused to concede to the social dictum that she adopt her husband's name after marriage. Among other instances of re-sistance, she insisted that both her maiden name and her husband's name be on their mailbox, and she answered phone requests for *Mrs.* with the phone number of her husband's mother (Stannard, 1973a). The Lucy Stone League, whose motto is ''My Name Is the Symbol of My Identity Which Must Not Be Lost,'' was established in 1921 to further the legal right of a married woman to use her own name. Similarly, the recently established Center for a Woman's Own Name provides descriptions of personal experiences, helpful advice, and state-by-state listings of attorneys experienced in the legal and personal aspects of retaining one's maiden name. Also, two works, ''Married Women's Common Law Rights to Their Own Surnames'' (MacDougall, 1973–1974) and *Married Women v. Husbands' Names: The Case for Wives Who Keep Their Own Names* (Stannard, 1973b), provide comprehensive treatment of the histori-cal and legal issues surrounding the subject of name change.

That one's name is related to one's identity is seen in the recent emergence of adopted persons' desire to learn their ''real'' names and their biological parents. UCLA psychiatrist Arthur Sor-rosky has reported that adopted people tend to have special iden-tity problems. One hypothesis in this regard is that for many adopted people, finding one's "real" name and "roots" may play an important role in defining one's individuality and uniqueness. That is, in learning about his or her lineage, the person may be able to differentiate him- or herself more fully from all the other people in the world. To date, there have been thousands of members of the Adoptee's Liberty Movement Association, an organization that helps the adopted locate their biological parents. Likewise, a recent popular book entitled *The Search for Anna Fisher* (Fisher, 1974) depicts a New York woman's hunt for her natural parents. Again, this movement may reflect people's desire to find a unique identity, and "the welling up of a natural human desire to answer the question: who am I?" ("Unsealing the records," 1974). Obviously, the phenomenal popularity of Alex Haley's best-selling novel *Roots* is a further indication of the importance of one's unique ancestry.

That's My Name

Since one's name is an important source of identity, it may be implicitly assumed that a person's name belongs to him or her. The fallacy of this thinking was vividly portrayed to one of the authors recently. In the second quarter of a professional football game with 70,000 fans in attendance, the loudspeaker instructed Rick Snyder to go to the emergency room. Feeling quite singled out by this message, he arrived at the first aid room only to find another Rick Snyder there! In a similar fashion, the uniqueness of one's name is the focal point of the two cartoons on pages 132 and 133.

The positive response that may accompany the receipt of a personal letter, addressed especially to our name, may also reflect our desire to be unique "among the masses." In fact, one fairly common response among developing adolescents is to view a personal letter as an indication that they are entites separate from their parents—young people with unique identities. In this same vein, Rich (1974) has noted, "Most people are delighted—some are overjoyed—to open their mailboxes and find something unexpected and personal there; some poor souls even scan junk mail in hopes of finding some vague reference to themselves" (p. 32).

The "Show" of Names

Names become symbols of our unique identity among many other people. Our names are frequently associated with recognition for success and the material and psychological rewards that accompany success. Names are displayed in schools and various organizations for athletic, academic, and other kinds of performance achievements. This display occurs through honor rolls, trophies, and certificates. Presumably, these avenues of recognition

"Gracious! Not the John Doe?"

FRED BASSET by Alex Graham. © 1974 Field Newspaper Syndicate™® Associated Newspapers Group, Ltd.

serve to distinguish us from others for the approval of significant persons such as parents, teachers, coaches, and supervisors. Thus, our names are reinforced as an important element of our self-identity because they enable us to be singled out in competition with our neighbors and to receive social rewards for our achievements. (Competition as a uniqueness-motivated behavior is treated in greater detail in Chapter 9.) Eventually, names may acquire value, in and of themselves, through their prior continuous association with the attainment of social rewards. Certainly, such prominent names such as Roosevelt, Kennedy, and Nixon elicit definite associative connotations.

Names as labels may, of course, convey positive or negative connotations. Often, nicknames reflect a special set of behaviors, characteristics, or feelings that a group of people see in another person. Therefore, the nickname serves to differentiate a person from the rest of the group. Typically, a nickname has positive connotations upon which both the person and the group agree. Sometimes, however, the nickname can convey negative sentiment. For example, children give other kids such negatively toned nicknames as "Fatty," "Crybaby," and "Four-eyes." Likewise, there are other labels that differentiate the person from the group and almost always convey negative connotations. Society utilizes such labels as *crazy, insane, senile, ex-con,* and *queer* to stigmatize particular behaviors.

A label that is *applied by a person to himself or herself* may –

reflect a desire to be unique from others. It is important to emphasize, therefore, the difference between a self-generated and a
group-generated label. That is, a self-generated nickname may re-
 ↞ flect a desire to establish oneself as positively unique among others, while a nickname generated by others may have more of a
negative uniqueness or stigma. In this regard, it is noteworthy that
graffiti consisting of nicknames has recently proliferated in big-city
environments that are extremely anonymous and deindividuating.
For example, Kurlansky, Naar, and Mailer (1974) have noted:

> As we lose our senses in the static of the ongoing universal
> machine, so does our need to exercise the ego take on elephan-
> tiastical proportions. Graffiti is the expression of a ghetto. . . .
> In the ghetto it is almost impossible to find some quiet location
> for your identity. (last page, Chapter 5)

The comments of graffiti artist "Japan I" reveal some of the
subtle linkages among nicknames, graffiti, and the search for
uniqueness:

> Japan says with full appreciation of his work, "You have to put
> in the hours to add up the names. You have to get your name
> around!" Since he is small and could hardly oppose too many
> who might choose to borrow his own immortal Japan I, he
> merely snorts in answer to the question of what he would do if
> someone else took up his name and used it. "I would still get
> the class," he remarks. (Kurlansky, Naar, & Mailer, 1974, third
> page, Chapter 1)

Among the hundreds of such names that are depicted in Kurlansky, Naar, and Mailer's *The Faith of Graffiti* (1974), the following 40 graffiti names are illustrative (the numbers opposite the
names are just further "identifiers" that particular graffiti artists
added to their names):

Magic 156	Queen Sexy 62
Magician 120	R. L. M. II
Malo 175	Rafi 179
Mark 169	Rap 135
Marty 193	Ray B 154
Mikey III	Ree 136
Miko 170	Reno 170
Mink 66	Satern 1
Mouse 152	Sexy Sun

Mr Big 120	Shaft 112
Mr Breeze	Shorty 135
Mr Cool 138	Shotgun 164
Mr Nice	Sisco Lad
Mr Sex 2237	Sky 3
Pollo 136	Slo 135
Pook 149	Smooth 159
Popeye I	Snake 131
Punghie	Snub I
Python 120	Soh 135
Queen Eva 62	Sotern 161

In considering many of the aforementioned graffiti nicknames, it should be emphasized that such names may take on enormous physical proportions. For example, an entire side of a subway car may bear one such name. One logical inference to be drawn from such gigantic name graffiti is that the authors had a strong desire to show their uniqueness.

A recent article in the *Jerusalem Post* reveals that the use of signatures in graffiti is not restricted to the American culture. The *Post* writer admonishes the graffiti artists in Israel for the desecration of public buildings and historical sites:

> The autograph has proliferated and many regretable examples of this horrible art to be seen at Massada and other historical sites in Israel. . . . I was horrified to see some large Hebrew signatures prominently displayed on ancient stones. . . . Though not yet finished, the new building next to Jerusalem's Central bus station is already covered with a rash of graffiti. Nearly all of these barbarous scrawls are simply names, pathetic bids for an immortality which, judging by the atrocious writing is undeserved. (Wednesday, April 23, 1975, p. 6)

These recent trends in American and Israeli graffiti may relate to the rapid population growth of the 1960s, the subsequent enlargement of primary and secondary groups, and the resulting enhancement of our need to distinguish ourselves from our contemporaries. While many people would assert that they need not "show" their name publicly through such a vulgar medium as graffiti, it is interesting to note that a great number of Americans are showing their names in a more respectable way. That is, the skyrocketing sales of family coats of arms may represent a desire to display one's name. As Dennis Hashinger, the president of one of the largest manufacturers of heraldry, put it, "People get their shields because they are turned off by being a social security number. They want to remind themselves that they are something special" ("Arms and the mail," 1975).

Before leaving the present subsection, it is appropriate to describe one other means of "showing" one's name. Within the last several years, researchers have examined the social significance of names by exploring the physical size of signatures (e.g., Zweigenhaft, 1970; Zweigenhaft & Marlowe, 1973). Snyder, Omens, and Bloom (1977) performed the following experiment in order to investigate the relationship between need for uniqueness and one's name as measured by signature size. Initially, people scoring either very high (top 20%) or very low (bottom 20%) in their need for uniqueness (as measured by the uniqueness scale [Snyder & Fromkin, 1977]) were recruited to an experiment. Research participants' signature size was gained unobtrusively as they signed the experimental consent form. Much to the research participants' delight, the experimenters told them that the experiment was over at that point! Statistical analysis showed that the signature areas (height multiplied by length of signature) of the high-need-for-uniqueness research participants were significantly larger than that of the low-need-for-uniqueness research participants (M centimeters squared = 10.45, 7.21, respectively). From these results, Snyder, Omens, and Bloom (1977) concluded, "the individual who has a strong desire to be different and unique may evidently express this need by leaving his or her mark in a large signature size" (p. 6 in manuscript).[1] Interestingly, Figure 22, an advertisement for a fountain pen, illustrates the appeal of making one's signature uniquely.

[1]Based on the present correlational research, it cannot be determined whether a higher need for uniqueness results in larger signatures or larger signatures influence a person to have a higher need for uniqueness. Additionally, a third variable (e.g., self-concept) may serve a mediating role in regard to the relationship between need for uniqueness and signature size. Further research is warranted on this issue.

Figure 22. Reprinted by permission of Becker and Becker, Inc., Westport, Connecticut.

Unusually Named People: What Are They Like?

Are Americans giving their children more unusual names than was the case several years ago? What characterizes the person with an unusual name as compared with someone who has a more common name? Is it "good" to have an unusual name? Should we give our children unusual names? We will address these questions in this subsection.

A survey of birth records in New York hospitals by Beadle (1974) reveals a tendency for people to select more uncommon or unusual names in the 1970s than in the 1930s. Perhaps, therefore, we are witnessing a growth of uniquely named people. One interpretation of this trend is that the recent population growth and the accompanying forces of deindividuation may generate an increased need to distinguish ourselves from other people.

Generally, it appears that females may possess more uncommon first names than males. For example, Allen, Brown, Dickinson, and Pratt (1941) investigated the relationship between frequency of occurrence of first names and preferences for first names among college students. The findings showed that males possessed and preferred the more common or more frequently occurring first names and were more dissatisfied if they had unusual or less common first names. Females did not exhibit either preferences or dissatisfaction related to the degree of commonness of their first names. It should be noted, however, that this finding is somewhat confounded because females possessed less common first names than males. This appears to be especially true of black females as compared with black males (Zweigenhaft, 1977). In investigating 11,246 high school students from North Carolina, Zweigenhaft (1977) operationally defined an unusual first name as being a name that appeared only once in his sample. In using this procedure, 15. 4% of the blacks had unusual first names, while only 5.5% of the whites did. It should be emphasized, however, that this higher percentage of unusual first names for blacks evidently resulted because of a strong tendency for black females as compared with males to have unique names.

Is it good to have an unusual name? The early literature on this question suggested that unusual names are potentially bad. Researchers warned parents against giving their children first names that are unique (Hartman, Nicolay, & Hurley, 1968; Schonberg & Murphy, 1974), rare or unusual (Harari & McDavid, 1973), uncommon (Houston & Sumner, 1948; West & Shults, 1976), peculiar (Ellis & Beechley, 1954), or singular (Savage & Wells, 1948). Unfortunately, these assertions about unusual names may not be accurate because of methodological problems in this research (see Zweigenhaft, 1977; Zweigenhaft, Hayes, & Haagen, 1978). For example, several studies explored the commonsense hypothesis that people did not like their unusual names, but such studies did not go on to study the actual overall self-concept and behavior of the unusually named person as compared with the person with a more common name.

Zweigenhaft and his colleagues have conducted a recent series of studies aimed at giving more clear-cut information about the impact of unusual names. Several of the Zweigenhaft studies are described in this chapter in order to give a better understanding of the characteristics of people with unusual names. In a first study, Zweigenhaft (1977) argued against the previous literature by reasoning that "Some individuals with unusual first names may come to look upon themselves as rare in a good way rather than a bad one—a rare gem as opposed to a rare disease—and thus, as both special and privileged" (p. 293). Zweigenhaft further reasoned that unusual first names may be especially positive for those individuals who are members of the upper class. This entire hypothesis is best described in the author's own words:

> It was hypothesized that the unusual first names among the upper class would not have the negative ramifications suggested by the literature. Such an unusually named child might indeed think he is different from the other children with the common names, but he also would come to realize that he is different in desirable ways—as a result of birth, he is economically, educationally, and culturally privileged, and his difference is one of "specialness." In this situation, having an unusual name might simply emphasize one of the advantageous qualities of his life: that he is different from (and he might assume, "above") the rest of the herd. Along the same lines, it was presumed that an upper-class child with an unusual name might be encouraged to do unusual and exceptional things, rather than to behave in ways that would necessarily make him "popular." Therefore, it was predicted that unusually named members of the upper class

would demonstrate greater achievement than a matched group
of common named peers. (p. 294)

In order to test this hypothesis, Zweigenhaft randomly selected 2,000 adult male names from *The Social Register* (a book
that contains members of the upper class). He then compared the
achievement of the individuals whose names appeared only once in
the sample with a comparison control group of individuals with
names that were not unusual. The achievement of the unusually
and common named men was examined by seeing how many of
each appeared in the book *Who's Who* (a book that lists men and
women who have shown "conspicuous achievement"). Results
showed that a significantly higher number of those individuals with
unusual names appeared in *Who's Who* than those individuals with
common names. Are these results surprising? Perhaps not, if we
consider our name as one important characteristic that allows a
sense of uniqueness.

Another study, by Zweigenhaft, Hayes, and Haagen (1978),
suggested that unusual names may not be associated with negative
consequences but may actually relate to greater psychological adjustment. To examine this question, Zweigenhaft *et al.* reviewed
the psychological profiles (as measured by the California Psychological Inventory—CPI) of 2,603 freshmen who entered Wesleyan
University between 1966 and 1973. Unusual names were defined as
those that appeared only once in the sample. The CPI profiles of
the unusually named students were compared with those of students with more common names. Results again ran counter to the
older notion that unusual names are associated with negative consequences for people. On the contrary, the unusually named females showed *greater* psychological stability than the control group
of female peers with common names. For males, there were generally no differences in the psychological profiles of those students
with unusual as compared with usual names. Because Zweigenhaft
has replicated these results, a fairly reliable conclusion appears to
be that, at least for females, unusual names are associated with
greater adjustment.

In a recent country song, singer Johnny Cash described the
negative side of giving a boy a girl's name. "A Boy Named Sue"
has to fight his way through life and doesn't like his unique female

name. But what does the relevant research on names suggest regarding the "boy named Sue" phenomenon? In comparing the psychological profiles of people with sexually misleading names and a control comparison group of people with sexually accurate names, *no* differences in psychological adjustment have appeared (Zweigenhaft, Hayes & Haagen, 1978). Thus, while the "boy named Sue" apparently didn't like his name (at least in the song), he and others like him may not suffer any great psychological damage.

In order to explore directly the relation between unusual names and uniqueness, Zweigenhaft (personal communication, November 1978) performed the following study. Initially, the uniqueness scale (Snyder & Fromkin, 1977) was given to a large number of female college students. When the desire-for-uniqueness scores of unusually first-named people (names occurring only once in the entire college population) were compared with common first-named people, the unusually first-named individuals evidenced a significantly higher need for uniqueness. This study reveals the special signal value that an unusual name may have for a person who is high in the need for uniqueness. Likewise, this study serves to further support the role of one's name as a uniqueness attribute.

The recent series of studies by Zweigenhaft and his colleagues suggests that there is no evidence to support the rather common belief that people with unusual names are at a psychological disadvantage. If anything, this recent body of research suggests that at times there may be distinct advantages associated with an unusual name. Furthermore, the unusual name appears to characterize the individual who has a strong desire to be unique. Thus, an unusual name is a socially acceptable manifestation of uniqueness.

Concluding Comment on Names

The present chapter has developed the thesis that the name serves as a source of identity by which one is differentiated from others. Both laboratory studies and applied examples that are consistent with this hypothesis have been reviewed. Anyone whose name has been forgotten, or who has been called "what's-his-name" or "hey, you" can verify this phenomenon: one's name and the accompanying sense of uniqueness are important to one's identity.

Drawing by C. R. Snyder.

References

Allen, L., Brown, V., Dickinson, L., & Pratt, K. C. The relations of first name preferences to their frequency in the culture. *Journal of Social Psychology*, 1941, *14*, 279–293.

Allport, G. W. *Pattern and growth in personality.* New York: Holt, Rinehart, & Winston, 1961.

Arms and the mail. *Time*, January 27, 1975, 71.

Beadle, M. The name of the game. *New York Times Magazine*, October 21, 1974, 38.

Bugental, J. F., & Zelen, S. L. Investigations into the "self-concept": The W-A-Y technique. *Journal of Personality*, 1950, *18*, 483–498.

Ellis, A., & Beechley, R. M. Emotional disturbances in children with peculiar given names. *Journal of Genetic Psychology*, 1954, *85*, 337–339.

Fisher, F. *The search for Anna Fisher.* Greenwich, Conn.: Fawcett Publishers, 1974.

Fromm, E. *Escape from freedom.* New York: Farrar & Rinehart, 1941.

Harari, H., & McDavid, J. W. Name stereotypes and teachers' expectations. *Journal of Educational Psychology*, 1973, *65*, 222–225.

Hartman, A. A., Nicolay, R. C., & Hurley, J. Unique personal names as a social adjustment factor. *Journal of Social Psychology*, 1968, *75*, 107–110.

Houston, T. J., & Sumner, F. C. Measurement of neurotic tendency in women with uncommon given names. *Journal of General Psychology*, 1948, *39*, 289–292.

Kurlansky, M., Naar, J., & Mailer, N. *The faith of graffiti.* New York: Praeger, 1974.

MacDougall, P. R. Married women's common law right to their own surnames. *Women's Rights Law Reporter*, 1973–1974 (Fall–Winter).

Rich, R. Letter writing: The return winds will keep you flying. In M. S. Yee (Ed.), *The great escape.* New York: Bantam, 1974, p. 32.

Savage, B. M., & Wells, F. L. A note on singularity in given names. *Journal of Social Psychology*, 1948, *27*, 271–272.

Schonberg, W., & Murphy, D. M. The relationship between the uniqueness of a given name and personality. *Journal of Social Psychology*, 1974, *93*, 147–148.

Snyder, C. R., & Fromkin, H. L. Abnormality as a positive characteristic. The development and validation of a scale measuring need for uniqueness. *Journal of Abnormal Psychology*, 1977, *86*, 518–527.

Snyder, C. R., Omens, A. E., & Bloom, L. J. Signature size and personality: Some truth in graphology? Paper presented at the Southwestern Psychological Association, Fort Worth, Texas, 1977.

Stannard, U. Lucy Stone et al. *Ms. Magazine*, 1973, *11*(6), 100. (a)

Stannard, U. *Married women v. husbands' names: The case for wives who keep their own names.* San Francisco: Germainbooks, 1973. (b)

Unsealing the records. *Time*, June 24, 1974, 81.

West, S. G., & Shults, T. Liking for common and uncommon first names. *Personality and Social Psychology Bulletin*, 1976, *2*, 299–302.

Zweigenhaft, R. L. Signature size: A key to status awareness. *Journal of Social Psychology*, 1970, *81*, 49–54.

Zweigenhaft, R. L. The other side of unusual first names. *Journal of Social Psychology*, 1977, *103*, 291–302.

Zweigenhaft, R. L., Hayes, K. N., & Haagen, C. H. The psychological impact of names: Another look. Unpublished manuscript. Wesleyan University, 1978.

Zweigenhaft, R. L., & Marlowe, D. Signature size: Studies in expressive movement. *Journal of Consulting and Clinical Psychology*, 1973, *40*, 469–473.

Attitudes and Beliefs as Uniqueness Attributes

"...And now we will hear the dissenting opinion."

Source: Samuel H. Gross; © Copyright 1973, Dell Publishing Co. *"How Gross."*

All individuals develop a set of attitudes and beliefs about their world and about themselves. These beliefs are a result of the prior and current experiences of each person. Our beliefs can serve as another important source whereby we may derive a sense of difference relative to other people. The present chapter investigates the role of attitudes and beliefs in generating a sense of difference.

Before examining the role of attitudes and beliefs as uniqueness attributes, it first may be useful to understand the nature of attitudes more generally. One perspective on attitudes and beliefs is that they serve as expressions of a person's values. According to this value-expressive function, "the individual derives satisfaction from expressing attitudes appropriate to his personal values and to his concept of himself" (Katz, 1960, p. 170). The value-expressive functioning is central to the doctrines of ego psychology, where the importance of self-expression, self-importance, self-development, and self-realization are emphasized. Katz (1960, p. 173) has suggested that attitudes may give "positive expression" to the type of person that one believes himself or herself to be. However, the "reward to the person in these instances is not so much a matter of gaining social recognition or monetary rewards as of establishing his self identity and confirming his notion of the sort of person he sees himself to be." Overall, therefore, our attitudes about external events, as well as our attitudes about ourselves, enable us to maintain a particular self-perception. In the process of expressing our beliefs about external events or ourselves, we may also achieve a sense of difference.

Beliefs about Our World in General

Important Unique Attitudes

A survey by Fromkin and Demming (1967) revealed that college students perceived their attitudes, beliefs, and values as most unique about themselves and their behavior as least unique about themselves. Thus, it seems reasonable to assume that individuals covet a small set of beliefs that are conceptualized as being highly idiosyncratic to themselves. It is important to highlight at this point, however, the rather obvious fact that the beliefs that a person holds in public may or may not match that person's private attitudes. This distinction has been made with regard to conformity behavior (see Kiesler & Kiesler, 1969) and clarifies how a person may publicly express attitudes similar to those of others but may privately hold divergent or unique attitudes. The subsequent discussion shows, however, that at times even a person's public attitudes differ from the attitudes of others in order for him or her to achieve a sense of uniqueness.

If we believe that it is important to have a particular attitude or set of attitudes that are different from those of other people, then we certainly should perceive these attitudes as being very different from those held by the majority of people. The more that we want our attitudes to be different, the more we should actually perceive these attitudes as being different from those of other people. This conclusion was supported in a study by Weir (1971), which was described in Chapter 3. In this study, Weir had each of 20 male research participants respond to a 20-item attitude questionnaire by rating (1) his own attitude position on each item; (2) his perception of the average college student's position on each item; and (3) how important it was for him to maintain the difference between his position and the position of the average college student. Research participants' rating of the importance of the difference on the items correlated positively ($r = +.50$), with the magnitude of the *actual difference* between the person's own position and the person's *perception* of the position of the average student on the items. However, whether or not, these important "unique" attitudes were actually different from those of the average person was not examined. Therefore, on the basis of these data, we cannot answer the question of whether people's important unique attitudes are *really* any different from the "average" person's attitudes.

Are Unique Attitudes Really Unique?

The best conclusion from the Weir study is that people think that some of their attitudes are "unique." Brandt and Fromkin (1974) took this question one step further by examining whether a person's "unique" attitudes really are all that different from those actually held by most other people. In this survey study, 200 male and 200 female college students at Purdue University were asked to give their beliefs on a questionnaire containing 200 items. These items included beliefs in different categories such as religion, politics, sex, academics, economics, social activities, moral issues, and drugs. The research participants responded to each item by rating the same questions asked in the initial Weir study. Again, the results showed that the participants perceived that they were different from the average person on those attitudes where they felt it was important that they be different. Females rated their *sexual* beliefs as most different, and males rated their *religious* beliefs as most different. *Interestingly, however, it was surprising to find that there actually was very little variation either among female responses to the sexual items or among male responses to the religious items.* That is, attitude positions that people believed to be different were, in fact, not very different from those of their peers. The sexually liberal attitudes of females were rather similar, as were the unreligious attitudes of the males. While these people believed that these important attitudes were quite different from those of the average person, they were not!

In the aforementioned survey study, the research participants must *not* have been totally aware of the attitudes of their peers. This is analogous to the state of "pluralistic ignorance" (Katz & Schanck, 1938), where the person mistakenly believes that he or she has a set of nonconformist beliefs. This phenomenon is most likely to occur for specific beliefs that are not publicly expressed; therefore, the uniqueness of these beliefs is rarely, if ever, tested. For example, it is likely that the males in the previous study rarely talked about their religious beliefs and that the females rarely talked about their beliefs related to sex.

Drawing by C. R. Snyder.

Consequences of Finding Out That Unique Attitudes Are Not Unique

What would happen if we were to find out that an attitude that we previously believed to be very different was shared by many other people? In other words, what will a person do when the state of pluralistic ignorance is shattered? If we want to maintain some sense of uniqueness, we should then deviate from others in some other acceptable way. Weir (1971) studied this question by telling each member of one group of research participants that his or her peers had selected the same attitude position that the person had previously rated as different from that of his or her peers. (The subsequent Weir studies were described in Chapter 3.) A second comparison group of research participants was told that their peers had selected the same attitude position that the participants had previously rated as similar to that of their peers. All research participants then heard a series of aesthetic preferences supposedly made by two peers and were also asked to report their own aesthetic preference. The group of people who were told that their previous "unique" attitude was not different deviated more in their subsequent aesthetic preferences than the comparison group of research participants. It was as if these people had to reestablish their sense of difference because their previous "unique" attitude had been negated.

Another study by Weir (1971) is again worthy of consideration regarding our attempts to hold different attitudes. Initially, males and females were asked to rate their own attitudes on several dimensions as well as the attitudes of the average college student. At a second meeting, these people were led to believe that they, along with two other research participants would again respond to five of the attitude items. The two other "research participants" were confederates. After the two confederates reported their attitude, the real research participant responded with his or her attitude. The dependent variable was how much the real research participant changed his or her attitude on each of the five items from the first to the second session. However, unknown to the real research participants, the confederates in one condition responded to each item with the same attitudinal position that the participant had initially taken. This was called the *uniqueness-deprived* condition. In the second condition, the research participant heard the two confederates agree with the person's original estimate of the average college student's response to each of the five items. This was called the *uniqueness-not-deprived* condition. Which group changed their attitudes more?

Results showed that males and females responded similarly. On the first and second attitude items, it didn't appear to make a difference whether the person was in the uniqueness-deprived or the not-deprived condition. But by the third item, the research participants in the uniqueness-deprived condition were evidently beginning to feel that their "unique" attitudes were very similar to those of the average other person, and they then began to change their original attitudes. This trend generally continued through the fifth item. What is going on here? In all likelihood, we are seeing attitudes changing so that people can maintain the belief that they are different.

Reactions When Forced to Hold the Same Attitude as Other People

To this point, we have explored how people sometimes believe that their attitudes are different from those of other people. Likewise, we have seen that people tend to change their attitudes in order to reestablish their sense of uniqueness. Now, suppose that we try to force another person to change his or her attitude? Implicitly, we are saying to a person, "Hold this attitude!" By publicly adopting an attitude we are told to have, we are giving up the potential difference of our own attitude. In this regard, Brehm's (1966, 1972) theory of psychological reactance predicts that a person will want to express attitudes that are different when that person feels coerced. More specifically, Brehm postulated that reactance is aroused when a person feels that a freedom has been threatened or eliminated. In response to the threat, the person becomes motivationally aroused and attempts to restore his or her freedom by regaining the lost alternative.

An experimental example of reactance may be useful at this point. Sensenig and Brehm (1968) studied reactance within an attitude-change paradigm. Initially, pairs of research participants completed attitude questionnaires and expected to write essays supporting one side or the other of selected items on the questionnaire. Each participant was told that his or her partner would decide which side of the issue he or she would support and *might* ask for the participant's preference in this decision. For a first one-third of the research participants, the preference was solicited (i.e., a control condition). The second one-third of the research participants were told which side to support on the first issue but were also told that the partner would not tell them on subsequent issues (i.e., the low-implied-threat condition). The final one-third of the research participants were told which side to support on the first issue and were also instructed that they would be told on all the other issues (i.e., the high-threat condition). The research participants' attitudes toward the first issue were measured again prior to writing the essay.

Results showed that the participants' attitudes in the control condition did not change, while in both the low- and the high-threat condition, the participants *changed their attitudes away from the side of the issue they were told to support.* Further, the amount of reactance increased when the research participants felt that their freedom would be repeatedly controlled (i.e., the high-threat-condition people evidenced more reactance than the low-threat-condition people). In short, then, people may regain their sense of choice by publicly stating the opposite of what is expected when they feel that their freedom has been threatened.

In this Sensenig and Brehm experiment, the research participants especially chose dissimilarity of attitudes relative to their partners in the high-threat conditions. In this high-threat condition, the individual was told that he or she would hold the same attitude on several subsequent attitude dimensions, and it follows from uniqueness theory that under such circumstances, the person should attempt to maintain the difference of his or her attitudes. In this regard, the high-threat condition may have implicitly conveyed many of the properties of the high or very high degrees of similarity conditions cited in Chapter 2. That is, phenomenologically, the person *told* that he or she will have to hold the same attitudes on a great number of subsequent issues may experience such information as meaning he or she is to be *very highly* similar to another person.

It should be emphasized that Brehm would regard the maintenance of freedom of choice as being the force that motivates people to change their attitudes away from the attitudes of other people (Brehm, personal communication, 1977). However, when the individual is told that he or she will be told what opinions to hold on many subsequent issues, this lack of freedom is also reflective of a state in which the person is made to feel highly similar to another person. Thus, from the perspective of uniqueness theory, we would argue that people are maintaining their freedom to be different when they express a different attitude.[1] Therefore, attitudes about external events in our world serve to define us as unique

---

[1]To date, there is no reported study that simultaneously tests the predictions of uniqueness and reactance theories. Thus, the nature of the relation between the two theories remains an open question that awaits empirically based answers.

people. That people may fight to reestablish such attitudinal freedom is a recurring lesson of American history.

Beliefs about Ourselves

Personality Feedback: "It's Just for You"

Beliefs about our personality offer another example of pluralistic ignorance. Research has consistently shown that people will-
ingly give their approval and acceptance of personality interpretations purportedly derived from the results of assessment
procedures (see Snyder, 1976; Snyder & Shenkel, 1975; and Snyder, Shenkel, & Lowery, 1977, for reviews of this literature). This
acceptance has occurred in spite of the fact that the personality
interpretations are nonspecific in nature. In this regard, Forer
(1949) was the first to hypothesize that most individuals see the
characteristics stated in the general personality description in
themselves *while failing to recognize their existence in others*. This
is analogous to pluralistic ignorance in that the individual believes
that he or she has a set of personality characteristics that are not
equally shared by others. Snyder and his colleagues (Snyder,
1974a,b; Snyder & Handelsman, 1978; Snyder, Handelsman, &
Endelman, 1979; Snyder, Larsen, & Bloom, 1976; Snyder & Larson, 1972; Snyder & Shenkel, 1975, 1976) have explored the acceptance of personality interpretations as it may relate to a state of
pluralistic ignorance.

In an initial study, Snyder and Larson (1972) gave female research participants paper-and-pencil personality tests and then instructed the persons to wait in the lobby. When the person returned after a 10-minute period, she was delivered the following
personality interpretation, which has been utilized extensively in
this research area:

> Some of your aspirations tend to be pretty unrealistic. At times
> you are extroverted, affable, and sociable, while at other times
> you are introverted, wary, and reserved. You have found it
> unwise to be too frank in revealing yourself to others. You
> pride yourself on being an independent thinker and do not accept
> others' opinions without satisfactory proof. You prefer a cer-
> tain amount of change and variety and become dissatisfied
> when hemmed in by restrictions and limitations. At times you

> have serious doubts as to whether you have made the right decision or done the right thing. Disciplined and controlled on the outside, you tend to be worrisome and insecure on the inside. Your sexual adjustment has presented some problems for you. While you have some personality weaknesses, you are generally able to compensate for them. You have a great deal of unused capacity which you have not turned to your advantage. You have a tendency to be critical of yourself. You have a strong need for other people to like you and for them to admire you.

Depending on the relevance condition to which the research participant was randomly assigned, she was told that the personality interpretation was (1) derived specifically "for her" based on her test results or (2) derived by psychologists as being "generally true for people." In both conditions, the research participants received the same general interpretation. The person then rated the extent to which the personality interpretation described her own personality on a five-point scale (5 = excellent, 4 = good, 3 = average, 2 = poor, 1 = very poor).

The results of this experiment showed that the research participants who believed that the interpretation was derived specifically "for you" rated the interpretation significantly higher than persons told that the interpretation was "generally true of people." Similar results have been found in three subsequent studies using a design in which one group of people believed that the feedback was "just for them" and a second group of people believed that this feedback is true of most people (this is known as a *between-subject design*) (Snyder, 1974a,b; Snyder, Larsen, & Bloom, 1976). These results suggest the consistency with which people see positively toned interpretations as describing themselves to a greater degree than they describe others.

The previously mentioned acceptance studies utilized between-subject designs in which only positively toned interpretations were utilized. Snyder and Shenkel (1976) utilized a slightly different experimental design in order to more precisely examine the pluralistic ignorance phenomenon. In this study, the research participants took personality tests, waited in the lobby for 15 minutes, and upon returning were delivered a personality interpretation that was purportedly derived specifically for the person on the basis of the test results. In actuality, the research participants were randomly assigned to receive a favorably worded interpretation (the same utilized in the previous research) or a negatively worded interpretation. This constituted the variable of favorability. The research participants then rated the interpretation on a 5-point scale (5 = excellent, to 1 = very poor). Finally, the participants were asked to rate the extent to which "their" interpretation fit "other people generally" on the same 5-point scale. The results are shown in Figure 23. The results revealed that the favorable interpretation was significantly more accepted for oneself than for other people in general; moreover, the unfavorable interpretation was seen as equally accurate for oneself and for other people in general. Similar results have been obtained in other studies employing similar experimental procedures (Snyder & Handelsman, 1978; Ziv & Nevenhaus, 1972).

The aforementioned results generate the interesting specula-

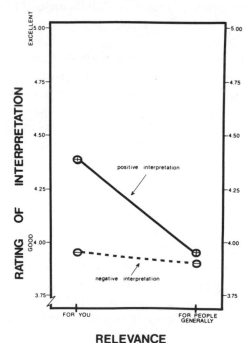

RELEVANCE

Figure 23. An illusion of uniqueness: The effects of relevance and favorability on acceptance of feedback (taken from Snyder & Shenkel, 1976).

tion that people are especially prone to perceive uniqueness in their personality when positive feedback is involved. Therefore, an illusion of uniqueness may be occurring in these experiments in that persons readily accept positive information as being more applicable to them than it is to other people. In actuality of course, the positive feedback should be as applicable to other people in general as it is to oneself. The revealing point may be that we tend to see the positive information as being especially true of us.

An Experiment for the Reader

The reader may be interested in performing short "experiments" similar to those just mentioned. Not only are such experiments fun to run, but they also highlight the pervasiveness of the illusion-of-uniqueness phenomenon. As a first step, it will be necessary to recruit someone to serve as the research participant in your demonstration. Tell your research participant that you have been doing some reading and have learned how to make personality diagnoses from inkblots. Hand your research participant a homemade inkblot (the pattern doesn't matter) and ask the person to tell you everything he or she sees in the inkblot. As the experimenter, you should busily write down everything the person sees. Next, tell the research participant to wait for 15 minutes while you come up with an interpretation based on his or her inkblot responses. In longhand, write out the positive personality description printed earlier in this chapter. Then, have your research participant read the interpretation that you have "specifically derived for him or her." Using a 5-point scale (5 = excellent, 4 = good, 3 = fair, 2 = poor, 1 = very poor), have the person rate the accuracy of the interpretation. Finally, in a casual manner, you may ask the person to rate how accurately "his" or "her" interpretation fits "other people generally" (use the same 5-point scale). At this point, you should carefully explain that you were merely performing a demonstration and that you did not specifically derive the feedback for your research participant. Further, explain to your research participant that you performed the demonstration in order to investigate the illusion of uniqueness.

If your research participant behaves like hundreds of previous people, he or she will have rated this positive feedback as more accurate for him or her than for people generally. Likewise, you probably will have been praised for your exceptional diagnostic skills! Don't be swayed by such praise, however, for the feedback you gave is true of most people and does not reflect either your diagnostic skill or the veracity of your assessment techniques. A comment on this latter phenomenon notes that "One is aptly reminded of P. T. Barnum's alleged statement, 'There's a sucker born every minute.' This may especially be true of clinicians who misinterpret clientele praise of personality feedback" (Snyder, Shenkel, & Lowery, 1977, p. 113).

The Illusion of Uniqueness

It has been theorized that an opposite kind of "illusion" of uniqueness occurs for one's beliefs about very negative consequences (Snyder, 1978). In this vein, it has been argued that a person will often ascribe negative consequences to others but not to himself or herself. In this regard, Snyder (1978) wrote:

> This speculation is supported by two class demonstrations that I typically perform in my undergraduate courses. In the first demonstration, students are delivered "insurance company longevity" data. Based on the projected death rates for people of various ages, each student's age of death is predicted on the basis of actuarial data. When students report their estimated age of death, however, they typically state they will live ten years longer than the age predicted actuarially. Second, a class demonstration on obedience also reveals the illusion of uniqueness for negative feedback. Students view Stanley Milgram's film in which the majority of subjects are shown to deliver "damaging" electric shocks to other subjects within the context of an experiment [Milgram, 1974]. When students in my class are asked whether they would administer such shocks to another person in the same circumstances, only 2% believe that they would do so. In these two cases, people are confronted with the base-rate statistics regarding extremely negative activities (one's age of death, and administering punishment to another), and yet "deny" that these data apply to them.
>
> The class demonstration data suggest that people feel unique in that negative behavior or consequences are seen to be more applicable to other people. This results in the "it won't happen to me" illusion of uniqueness. Other real-life examples also support this idea; e.g., smokers' attitudes about getting cancer. The actuarial statistics show that the heavy smoker has

a greater probability of having cancer than the non-smoker. Nevertheless, heavy smokers may say that such statistics are not applicable to them. Likewise, people who reject the use of automobile seatbelts may invoke the argument that they don't need to use them because they are not going to have an accident. (pp. 37–38)

A person may believe, according to the aforementioned research, that positive information is more applicable to himself or herself, while negative information is more applicable to others. In short, a person believes that he or she has more of the "good" and less of the "bad" than others. These results highlight the importance of considering the value attached to a potential attitude or belief. A person may especially want to be unique in situations where he or she perceives that there are advantages to uniqueness (e.g., more of the "good" or less of the "bad" than for the average person). This notion forms the premise of the cartoon on this page.

The attributional literature adds further evidence supporting

THE BETTER HALF.

"According to a survey, nine husbands out of 10 are rated as lousy lovers. I really feel sorry for those guys."

Source: The Register and Tribune Syndicate.

the contention that one's attitudes and beliefs are defined as being uniquely different from those of others. Jones and Nisbett (1971; see also Nisbett, Caputo, Legant, & Maracek, 1973; Storms, 1973) have noted a tendency for people to attribute their own behaviors, attitudes, and beliefs to situational factors and to attribute other peoples' behaviors, attitudes, and beliefs to dispositional characteristics. Restated, this means that we see our own beliefs in terms of the discrete situations that elicited these beliefs; conversely, we see others' beliefs as reflecting enduring personality characteristics or traits. Thus, in comparing one's beliefs and attitudes with those of another, a person emphasizes the "unique" specific situations that make him or her have a particular attitude, while not focusing on the situational precursors in describing another's attitudes. Therefore, a person may perpetuate the illusion of uniqueness by ascribing individualistic specific situational factors for himself or herself and general and global personality trait factors or labels for others.

"Dating Game" Studies

Although it is probably more frequent for an individual to achieve a sense of uniqueness in the inner state of his or her private beliefs, there are instances where the public expression of deviant attitudes and beliefs about oneself may result in desired outcomes in specific kinds of situations. For instance, two experiments by Dipboye, Boss, and Fromkin (1974) illustrate the potential for attitudes to operate as uniqueness attributes. The following experiments were based on the television show "Dating Game." In a first study, under the guise of "examining first impressions," the research participants expected an attractive (or an unattractive) female to select one of them for a "Coke date" based on their answers to her questions. The questions asked by the female were taken from the Marlowe–Crowne Social Desirability Scale (Crowne & Marlowe, 1964). The research participant responded second (or fourth) in a group of five males. The responses of the other four "research participants" (who were actually trained confederates) were always identical to one another. The results showed that deviations from the other person(s)' responses were greatest when there were an attractive female and four other research participants, and that deviations from the other person(s) were smallest when there were an unattractive female and one other research participant.

In the second study, Dipboye, Boss, and Fromkin (1974) again employed the "Dating Game" format to examine the effects of the same independent variable upon self-descriptions. Male research participants stated their attitude positions and then wrote short descriptions of themselves. Content analysis of the self-descriptions was performed by three female judges who were naive about the experiment and the research participants' experimental conditions. The judges independently rated each protocol for the number and kinds of attributes, the degree of differentness of each attribute, and so forth. The judges' ratings were combined to form a "uniqueness score" for each research participant. Analyses of these scores yielded findings that are similar to the previous attitude-change results. That is, uniqueness scores were highest in the condition with an attractive female and four other persons and lowest in the condition with an unattractive female and one other person.

The content analysis of this second "Dating Game" study also revealed some interesting tactics of self-presentation. Beliefs received higher uniqueness scores than any other attributes. Beliefs were more frequently used for self-descriptions in the condition with an attractive female and four other persons. Demographic and physical attributes (e.g., college major, college year, height, and weight) were most frequently used in the condition with an unattractive female and one other person. For example, the physical characteristics in the unattractive-female-and-one-other-person condition were similar to the norms for the male college population in general: brown hair, height 5 feet 9 inches, and a weight of 165 pounds.

Overall, the "Dating Game" studies reveal a particular situation in which beliefs serve to help the public presentation of oneself as different. Presumably, a person is more difficult to recognize as distinct from *four* other persons and he is therefore *less* likely to be chosen by the attractive female. In this situation, the public expression of unusual attitudes helps in obtaining a valued outcome, that is, being chosen for a date with an attractive female. It is also interesting to note that these "Dating Game" findings demonstrate a situation in which beliefs are *not* employed as uniqueness attributes. When the female is unattractive, the male research participants evidently made their attitudes and beliefs similar to those of the other research participant(s). These males may not have wanted their attitudes) or beliefs to become too differentiated for this might make them more attractive to the ugly princess!

Concluding Comment on Attitudes and Beliefs

The present chapter has focused on the role that attitudes and beliefs may play in developing a sense of difference relative to other people. One's attitudes appear to be intimately linked to the self-concept, and individuals may actually change their attitudes in order to maintain some sense of difference. Thus, people may publicly express different attitudes—sometimes to gain a favorable outcome for their distinctiveness, sometimes to achieve a sense of freedom, or sometimes simply to avoid feeling that their attitudes lack uniqueness. Additionally, people often maintain a state of pluralistic ignorance or an illusion of uniqueness regarding their beliefs about themselves and other people. That is, we often *believe* that our beliefs and attitudes are more different than they actually are. The studies concerning beliefs about our personalities, when taken together, strongly suggest that we acquire and maintain a set of beliefs about ourselves (e.g., our personality) that enhance our self-perceptions of difference relative to other people. Overall, therefore, our attitudes and beliefs seem to serve as an important vehicle for achieving and maintaining a sense of uniqueness.

References

Brandt, J. M., & Fromkin, H. L. A survey of unique attitudes among college students: A state of pluralistic ignorance. Unpublished manuscript, Purdue University, 1974.

Brehm, J. W. *A theory of psychological reactance.* New York: Academic, 1966.

Brehm, J. W. *Responses to loss of freedom: A theory of psychological reactance.* Morristown, N. J.: General Learning Corporation, 1972.

Crowne, D. P., & Marlowe, D. *The approval motive.* New York: Wiley, 1964.

Dipboye, R. L., Boss, D., & Fromkin, H. L. The effects of interpersonal indistinctiveness upon disclosure of distinct self attributes in the dating game. Unpublished manuscript, Purdue University, 1974.

Forer, B. R. The fallacy of personal validation: A classroom demonstration of gullibility. *Journal of Abnormal and Social Psychology*, 1949, *44*, 118–123.

Fromkin, H. L., & Demming, B. A survey of retrospective reports of feelings of uniqueness. Unpublished manuscript, Ohio State University, 1967.

Jones, E. E., & Nisbett, R. E. The actor and observer: Divergent perceptions of the causes of behavior. In E. E. Jones, D. E. Kanouse, H. H. Kelley, R. E. Nisbett, S. Valins, & B. Weiner (Eds.), *Attribution: Perceiving the causes of behavior.* New York: General Learning Press, 1971, pp. 79–94.

Katz, D. The functional approach to the study of attitudes. *Public Opinion Quarterly,* 1960, *24,* 163–204.

Katz, D., & Schanck, R. L. *Social psychology.* New York: Wiley, 1938.

Kiesler, C. A., & Kiesler, S. B. *Conformity.* Reading, Mass.: Addison-Wesley, 1969.

Milgram, S. *Obedience to authority.* New York: Harper & Row, 1974.

Nisbett, R. D., Caputo, C., Legant, P., & Maracek, J. Behavior as seen by the actor and as seen by the observer. *Journal of Personality and Social Psychology,* 1973, *27,* 154–164.

Sensenig, J., & Brehm, J. W. Attitude change from an implied threat to attitudinal freedom. *Journal of Personality and Social Psychology,* 1968, *8,* 324–330.

Snyder, C. R. Acceptance of personality interpretations as a function of assessment procedures. *Journal of Consulting and Clinical Psychology,* 1974, *42,* 150. (a)

Snyder, C. R. Why horoscopes are true: The effects of specificity on acceptance of astrological interpretations. *Journal of Clinical Psychology,* 1974, *30,* 577–580. (b)

Snyder, C. R. Ways to generate "accurate" personality interpretations: The "P. T. Barnum effect." In I. K. Goldberg (Ed.), *Behavioral Science Tape Library.* Leonia, N.J.: Sigma Information, 1976.

Snyder, C. R. The "illusion" of uniqueness. *Journal of Humanistic Psychology,* 1978, *18,* 33–41.

Snyder, C. R., & Handelsman, M. Desire for and acceptance of positive and negative feedback. Paper presented at the Western Psychological Association, San Francisco, 1978.

Snyder, C. R., & Larson, G. R. A further look at student acceptance of general personality interpretations. *Journal of Consulting and Clinical Psychology,* 1972, *38,* 384–388.

Snyder, C. R., & Shenkel, R. J. Astrologers, handwriting analysts, and sometimes psychologists use the P. T. Barnum effect. *Psychology Today,* 1975, *8* (10), 52–54.

Snyder, C. R., & Shenkel, R. J. Effects of "favorability," modality, and relevance upon acceptance of general personality interpretations prior to and after receiving diagnostic feedback. *Journal of Consulting and Clinical Psychology,* 1976, *44,* 34–41.

Snyder, C. R., Larsen, D., & Bloom. L. J. Acceptance of personality interpretations prior to and after receiving diagnostic feedback supposedly based on psychological, graphological, and astrological assessment procedures. *Journal of Clinical Psychology,* 1976, *32,* 258–265.

Snyder, C. R., Shenkel, R. J., & Lowery, C. R. Acceptance of personality interpretations: The "Barnum effect" and beyond. *Journal of Consulting and Clinical Psychology*, 1977, *45*, 104–114.

Snyder, C. R., Handelsman, M., & Endelman, J. R. Can clients provide valuable feedback and personality interpretations? A reply to Greene. *Journal of Consulting and Clinical Psychology*, 1979, *46*, 1493–1495.

Storms, M. Video-tape and the attribution process: Reversing actors' and observers' point of view. *Journal of Personality and Social Psychology*, 1973, *27*, 165–175.

Weir, H. B. Deprivation of the need for uniqueness and some variables moderating its effects. Unpublished doctoral dissertation, the University of Georgia, 1971.

Ziv, A., & Nevenhaus, S. Acceptance of personality diagnoses and perceived uniqueness. *Abstract Guide of XXth International Congress of Psychology*, 1972, 605.

Performance as Uniqueness-Motivated Behavior

The previous chapters on uniqueness attributes reveal that commodities, names, and attitudes and beliefs may serve to define a person as different from other people. The present chapter examines another potential uniqueness attribute, namely, unique performance in competitive situations. The subsequent discussion explores the role of performance as a means of deriving various kinds of uniqueness relative to others.

Normal Competition: "Playing the Game . . ."

In the most typical case, competition carefully defines the performance outcome that will be rewarded. That is, authorities (bosses, administrators, referees, judges, teachers, etc.) establish the criteria for good or desirable performance outcomes. Rewards such as plaques, prizes, high grades, recognition, money, and promotion are bestowed on the performer judged to be the "best." As shown in Figure 24, in normal competition one person emerges from the crowd because that person has most successfully met the performance criteria established and becomes the "winner." The postulated link between uniqueness and winning occurs in situations where there is only one winner from a larger group of competitors or perhaps only a very few winners from a larger group of competitors.

Striving for success is well documented in the achievement motivation literature (see Atkinson & Raynor, 1974; and McClelland, 1961, for reviews). Indeed, to win has become an extremely

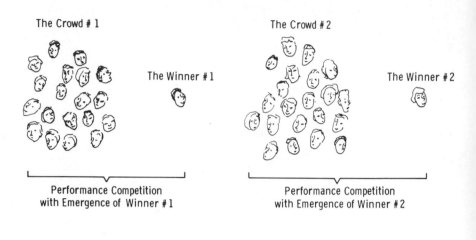

Figure 24. Normal competition: "Playing the game . . . ."

important goal in Western culture. This sentiment was succinctly expressed by the late Vince Lombardi, former coach of the Green Bay Packers professional football team, as he asserted, "Winning isn't everything, it's the *only* thing" (cited in Aronson, 1972, p. 154). Additionally, however, when only one person has been designated as a winner by the authorities, that person experiences a sense of achievement, recognition, and monetary reward *and* a sense of uniqueness, or difference from his or her competitors. It is this sense of difference resulting from winning that is the focus of the present discussion.

The attainment of a sense of difference through winning carries positive connotations in that authorities (society) have agreed that the performance outcome is desirable (whether it be more touchdowns scored, automobiles sold, etc.). Over time, the winner finds himself or herself in competition with other winners and may continue to strive and to excel according to the established criteria. To win through "normal" competition thus may be a principal avenue through which a sense of uniqueness is achieved and rewarded in our society. In this sense, winning truly fits the definition of a uniqueness attribute in that it represents a socially acceptable characteristic by which a person may achieve a difference relative to other people.

The effect of a sense of uniqueness on one's performance in a competitive situation has received some empirical investigation (see Snyder, 1972, 1975; Snyder & Katahn, 1970, 1973). In a series of experiments, students were placed in the competitive context of an experimental verbal learning task and either were or were not given feedback regarding the performance of previous research participants on the same task. The feedback consisted of a level of performance attained by previous people who had taken the same verbal learning task. Thus, a particular research participant was or was not allowed to see how previous people had performed on the same task. For those research participants who did receive feedback, individuals in a first group were given feedback as to how the best previous research participants had performed (the high-comparison feedback); individuals in a second group were given feedback as to how the poorest previous participants had performed (the low-comparison feedback). In a third condition, individuals were given no feedback regarding how previous research participants had performed (the no-comparison feedback).

It should be noted that the research participants who did receive comparison feedback in the aforementioned studies could readily tell how they were performing relative to their respective comparison feedback group. This was the case because a person could see how many items he or she was getting correct relative to the comparison group (the top or poorest of previous research participants). Of the people receiving the low comparison feedback, 90% were exceeding their comparison standard (i.e., were getting more items correct than their comparison group); 90% of the people receiving the high-comparison feedback were falling below their comparison standard (i.e., were getting less items correct than their comparison group). Therefore, in these experiments, individuals in two groups were perceiving their performance outcomes as being different relative to their comparison feedback (the group receiving the low feedback were different in that they were exceeding the feedback through their performance, while the group receiving the high feedback were different in that they were falling below the feedback in their performance), and one group was not receiving any comparison feedback information.

When the actual performance of individuals in each of these

three feedback conditions (low, high, or no) was analyzed in three separate experiments, similar patterns of findings resulted. The people receiving the low-comparison feedback (i.e., the "winners," or the individuals who were different in that they were seemingly *exceeding* a low-comparison standard) actually performed best on the verbal learning task; the people receiving no comparison feedback performed second best; and the people receiving the high-comparison feedback (i.e., the "losers," or the individuals who were unique in that they were seemingly *falling below* the high-comparison standard) performed most poorly. The research participants also self-reported their emotions in these experiments. These emotional results showed that the individuals who received the low-comparison feedback (the "winners") reported the most positive and the least negative affect, and the individuals who received the high-comparison feedback (the "losers") reported the least positive and the most negative affect.

These comparison-level results potentially offer an important clarification regarding the effects of a sense of uniqueness on performance. The "winners," who were made to feel different by means of surpassing a low standard, *not only reported the most positive emotional state but also performed the best.* Conversely, the "losers," who were made to feel different by means of falling below a high standard, *not only reported the least positive emotional state but also performed the worst.*

Evidently, then, the most rewarding sense of uniqueness, in terms of motivation and subsequent learning, occurs when a person perceives that his or her "outcomes" are exceeding those of other people. This state of difference is similar to having won a competitive activity. The participant has "played the game" and derived a sense of satisfaction and continued motivation by seemingly having excelled the performance of some segment of people ("the crowd").

Unfortunately, a more pessimistic projection results for the person who falls below his or her comparison group in the competitive context. These people who "fall behind" according to some performance criterion that is rewarded by society may be motivationally "turned off," frustrated, and unwilling to "play the game." Indeed, people who continually fail to succeed in their "crowd" are often labeled "losers" by society. Having repeatedly failed to "win," the person may stop trying, and a revolving cycle may develop. Thus, "In the words of Jacques Brel, we are on a carousel" (Clair & Snyder, 1979, p. 57).

Interestingly, people may engage in "normal" competitive activities and *achieve the same outcome but utilize different approaches to achieve the same outcome.* As a case in point, consider an example from the area of sports. Black and white athletes are equally concerned about their outcomes (e.g., touchdowns or baskets scored), but the black athlete may be more concerned about the style or form he or she employs (Jones, 1972, 1973). Perhaps it is not just getting the basketball in the basket but how one goes about doing this that elicits a unique style or identity for a black performer. Thus, the means as well as the end (winning) in a competitive endeavor have potential uniqueness properties.

Successful Differentiation: "Changing the Game . . ."

As has been noted, competition typically defines the desired performance outcome. Sometimes, however, a person may seek to establish new performance goals or outcomes and consequently may also open up many new approaches to achieve the new performance outcomes. The individual *differentiates* himself or herself from "the crowd" and confronts the traditional performance outcomes (beliefs, attitudes, ideas, traditions, behaviors, appearances, etc.) with a new viewpoint or perspective (Lemaine, 1974). Elizabeth Ashley, in her recent popular book *Actress: Postcards from the Road* (1978), describes her differentiating process in the following manner:

> I had always known that my only chance in anything was to emphasize the difference between myself and everyone else. I never got anywhere trying to be the same. So as flat-chested as I was, I made myself look even more flat-chested. I went totally against the stereotyped sexuality of the girls in the movies, which had never been my kind of sexuality to begin with. . . . To be sure, the minute I went on other people's turf I couldn't get to first base. (p. 36)

A person who adopts a unique position often must then prepare for a heated competition with the traditional viewpoint (see Figure 25). If the differentiation is to be successful in establishing a

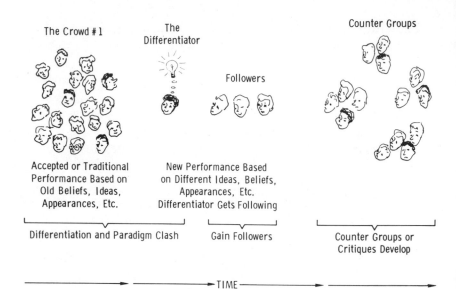

The Crowd #1   The Differentiator   Counter Groups

Followers

Accepted or Traditional   New Performance Based
Performance Based on   on Different Ideas, Beliefs,
Old Beliefs, Ideas,   Appearances, Etc.
Appearances, Etc.   Differentiator Gets Following

Differentiation and Paradigm Clash   Gain Followers   Counter Groups or
                                                            Critiques Develop

TIME

Figure 25. Successful differentiation: "Changing the game . . . ."

unique position for a person, a confrontation (see Kuhn, 1970, for a description of paradigm clashes) of sorts occurs. This phase of differentiation has been characterized as getting the authorities in a system to recognize the legitimacy of a new activity or idea. Once recognition for one's unique position is advanced, the person seeks to get followers. The followers help the person to handle the criticism of those people who have been impugned in the differentiation process (Lemaine, 1974). Countergroups may even form in opposition to the new viewpoint. If the "unique" person and his or her followers become sufficiently established, they may form "the crowd" or traditional stance from which others may differentiate themselves. That is, the successfully differentiating person may influence the traditional group or the societal position so much that the group changes so as to incorporate the differentiator's idea, belief, or behavior. When this happens, the new perspective of the differentiator becomes socially acceptable and thus may be considered a uniqueness attribute.[1]

[1]Once the differentiator has achieved success in getting his or her perspective adopted by society, that person still attains a sense of uniqueness as the person who initiated the change.

The entire sequence of successful differentiation is concisely summarized by Suran (1978) in the following nine steps:

> 1. Individuals come together to share and conserve a cultural frame of reference or set of social values and conventions. Many aspects of this frame of reference are implicit and unarticulated.
> 2. An individual rejects some aspect of the accepted frame of reference in preference for some innovative behavior or idea. Implicit aspects of the cultural frame of reference are brought more clearly into focus, and explicit aspects of the conventional value system are directly challenged.
> 3. Public conflict takes place between the social group that seeks to conserve the traditional values and the deviant individual.
> 4. The reaction of conserving individuals is to reaffirm and refine the traditional values and conventional wisdom.
> 5. The reaction of the oddball is to pursue further and with increased vigor the unique nature of the innovative idea or behavior.
> 6. A latency period takes place in which the oddball innovation begins to acquire social support. This newly acquired social support system tends to modify or make acceptable some of the outlandish aspects of the oddball's individuality.
> 7. The distinction between the traditional values and the innovation becomes somewhat blurred.
> 8. The cultural frame of reference gradually adjusts to the extent that the less outlandish aspects of the oddball idea or behavior are integrated into the conventional mainstream.
> 9. With the passing of generations, the oddball is canonized as a father of cultural traditions. (p. 207)

Lemaine and his co-workers have performed several experiments that relate to this differentiation strategy of "changing the game" in order to achieve a sense of unique identity. It should be noted in these examples that as the person "changes the game," he or she is also decreasing the perception of having lost and is enhancing the perception of having won. For example, Lemaine and his colleagues (Lemaine, 1966; Jamous & Lemaine, 1962) studied the competitive behavior of children in the naturalistic setting of summer camps. Children in separate groups were given the task of building a hut in the woods, with a reward going to the producers of the best hut. One group, chosen at random, was not given sufficient supplies to build the hut. The reaction of this group was eventually to admit the superiority of the other groups' huts, but this "hand-icapped" group also sought to change the game so that perform-ance in other activities in which they were engaging (e.g., garden growing) would be rewarded. It was as if the handicapped group needed to make sure that they were perceived as unique (and supe-rior) according to some performance criteria upon which others could concur. They thus sought to change the rules.

The extreme competition that occurs within the scientific com-munity is common knowledge among scientists, although it is rarely described in Western culture (a notable exception is the *Double Helix*, 1968, by J. B. Watson). The French psychologist Gerard Lemaine and his colleagues (Lemaine & Kasteraztein, 1972; Lemaine, Lecuyer, Gomis, & Barthelemy, 1972; Lemaine, Matalon, & Provansal, 1969), however, have written of the reward system in the scientific community that fosters the production of original works and ideas whereby a scientist gains "visibility" (i.e., positive uniqueness). How many energetic graduate students have been told by their advisers that success in the science game results from a person's capacity to "carve out a place of your own"? These students are imbued with a desire to differentiate a place for themselves in their particular academic field.

The point of the present section is that people often compete through their performance and that one potential strategy for this endeavor is to propose a unique viewpoint that will hopefully gen-erate an accompanying sense of positive difference relative to other people. In these instances, it should be emphasized that self-perceived difference is not necessarily an end state in and of itself, especially since there may be considerable rewards (recognition, praise, or money) for the person who successfully differentiates from the group.

While the person may initiate the differentiation from "the crowd," there is no certainty that a sense of positive uniqueness will result. In fact, the self-differentiating individual may often find that his or her difference is viewed as deviancy and results in his or her being made an outcast. This process is explored next.

Unsuccessful Differentiation (Deviance): "You Can't Play . . ."

Any person who performs acts or has ideas that violate the norms of a particular group runs the risk of being labeled a deviant.

Becker (1963) noted that a behavior is not necessarily deviant because it violates a norm. Rather, he reasoned that the label of *deviant* was a result of both rule breaking and a reaction from others ("the crowd"). Thus, "whether a given act is deviant or not depends in part on the nature of the act (that is, whether or not it violates some rule) and in part in what other people do about it" (Becker, 1963, p. 14). The difference between the differentiated and the deviant individual, then, is that the deviant is not successful in getting the group's acceptance of his or her behavior.[2] In this case, the deviant may or may not have initiated the differentiation by his or her particular behavior, but it is the group that *enforces* the split. It is as if the group tells the deviant "You can't play in our game."

One of the variable aspects of deviance is that what is defined as different may differ according to the reference group and time in which it occurs. For example, running nude in public would historically be seen as negative uniqueness and would generate the pejorative label of *deviant*. In recent years, however, streaking has become a more common occurrence and is therefore considered less negatively deviant.

Once a person is labeled as deviant, that individual (as shown in Figure 26) may attempt to gather other deviants who have been outcast from society. Over time, the labeled deviant may actually begin to act according to "his" or "her" label, and others may treat him or her so as to elicit the expected behavior. This process may create a self-fulfilling prophecy (see Rosenthal & Jacobson, 1969; and Rosenthal & Rubin, 1978, for reviews) in which the "negative" deviant behavior is perpetuated.

The distinction between differentiation and deviance in the present context is that the latter, while sometimes self-initiated, is always characterized by group ostracization. The deviant is then forced to stay apart from the group, whether or not he or she likes it. The successfully differentiated person, on the other hand, stays

[2]In the present context, a deviant is considered an unsuccessful differentiator if his or her behavior is not accepted during that person's lifetime. Obviously, however, there are many people who were considered deviants during their lifetime, but subsequent generations have adopted their "deviant" viewpoints, ideas, or behaviors. In this latter sense, a person who may be a deviant within his or her lifetime may come to be seen as a successful differentiator in the eyes of subsequent generations.

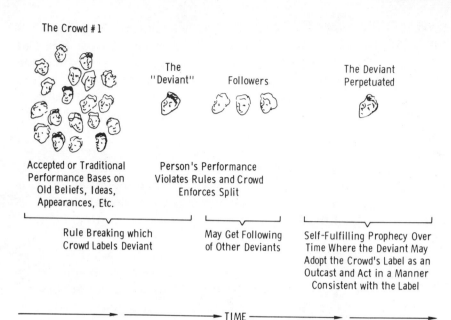

Figure 26. Unsuccessful differentiation (Deviance): "You can't play . . . ."

apart from the group because that is the way he or she wants it. In the initial stages, then, both deviation and differentiation may reflect a self-generated separation from the group.[3] When the person is able to achieve positive reinforcement and acceptance of his or her different position and/or accompanying unique performance, successful differentiation has occurred. However, when the person is unable to get the group to accept the different performance, then the negative connotations of deviance are invoked. In this latter case, therefore, unsuccessful differentiation illustrates an instance in which performance fails to generate the social acceptance that is characteristic of a uniqueness attribute.

Overall, the importance of the differentiating uniqueness maneuvers is amplified by the fact that they emerge in a context in which ostracization is probable. In other words, people continue to

---

[3]At times, a deviant may never have explicitly chosen to separate from the group, and yet the group will ostracize the person for some purported unusual idea or behavior. Often, however, there is some idea or behavior on the part of the person that serves as an indication that the person has differentiated himself or herself from the group in some particular area.

generate different ideas and behaviors even though the chances are fairly high that they may be labeled as deviant and ostracized. The perseverance of differentiating behaviors under such circumstances indicates that the risk is not overwhelming. In this sense, then, performance through ideas and behavior remains a viable means of attaining some sense of uniqueness.

Review of Performance

The present chapter has sought to establish the potential for uniqueness that is inherent in performance in most competitive situations. Since competition through performance is such a pervasive phenomenon in our society, one is naturally prompted to examine why people compete. As has been noted in previous chapters, individuals have a desire to compare themselves with other people, and this comparison process may contribute to a competitive performance atmosphere. In the comparison process and the consequent competition, we often want our performance outcomes to be better than the performance outcomes of our competitors. To be "better than" another person or persons often elicits a sense of esteem, status, satisfaction, recognition, *and a sense of uniqueness.* Thus, to win (whether in the normal competitive process or in the differentiation process) means to stand out from "the crowd," to be different. It should be emphasized, therefore, that standing out in a crowd because of an outstanding performance may not be solely a function of an achievement motive (see McClelland, 1961). Instead, winning or singular achievement in part may represent another socially acceptable avenue for reaffirming a sense of uniqueness for those individuals with the requisite skills in such activities as sports, science, art, or business.

References

Aronson, E. *The social animal.* San Francisco: W. H. Freeman, 1972.

Ashley, E. *Actress: Postcards from the road.* New York: M. Evans & Company, 1978.

Atkinson, J. W., & Raynor, J. O. *Motivation and achievement.* Washington, D.C.: V. H. Winston, 1974.

Becker, H. S. *Outsiders.* New York: Free Press, 1963.

Clair, M. S., & Snyder, C. R. The effects of sequential evaluative feedback upon classroom-related performance and instructor evaluations. *Journal of Educational Psychology*, 1979, *71*, 50–57.

Jamous, H., & Lemaine, G. Compétition entre group d'inégale resources: Expérience dans un cadre naturel. *French Psychologie*, 1962, *7*, 216–222.

Jones, J. M. Some personality correlates of sports attitudes and performance. Colloquium presented at Psychology Department, Princeton University, 1972.

Jones, J. M. Racial differences in sports activities: A look at the self-paced versus reactive hypothesis. *Journal of Personality and Social Psychology*, 1973, *27*, 86–95.

Kuhn, T. S. *The structure of scientific revolutions* (2nd ed.). Chicago: University of Chicago Press, 1970.

Lemaine, G. Inégalité, comparaison et imcomparabilité: Esquise d'une théorie de l'originalité sociale. *Bulletin Psychologie*, 1966, *20*, 24–32.

Lemaine, G. Social differentiation and social conformity. *European Journal of Social Psychology*, 1974, *4*, 17–52.

Lemaine, G., & Kasteraztein, J. Recherches sur l'originalité sociale: La différenciation et l'incomparabilité. *Bulletin Psychologie*, 1972, *25*, 673–693.

Lemaine, G., Matalon, B., & Provansal, B. La lutte pour la vie dans la cité scientifique. *Review of French Sociologie*, 1969, *10*, 139–165.

Lemaine, G., Lecuyer, B. P., Gomis, A., & Barthelemy, C. *Les voies de socces. Sur quelques factèurs de la réussite des laboratoire de recherche fondamentale en France*. Paris: Group d'Etudes et recherches sur la science, 1972.

McClelland, D.C. *The achieving society*. Princeton, N.J.: Van Nostrand, 1961.

Rosenthal, R., & Jacobson, L. *Pygmalion in the classroom: Teacher expectation and pupils intellectual development*. New York: Holt, Rinehart, & Winston, 1969.

Rosenthal, R., & Rubin, D. B. Interpersonal expectancy effects: The first 345 studies. *The Behavioral and Brain Sciences*, 1978, *3*, 377–415.

Snyder, C. R. Effects of comparison level feedback on classroom-related verbal learning performance. *Journal of Educational Psychology*, 1972, *63*, 493–499.

Snyder, C. R. The comparison process and "classroom" performance. In I. K. Goldberg (Ed.), *Audio seminars in education*. Fort Lee, N.J.: Sigma Information, 1975.

Snyder, C. R., & Katahn, M. The relationship of state anxiety, feedback, and ongoing self-reported affect to performance in complex verbal learning. *American Journal of Psychology*, 1970, *83*, 237–247.

Snyder, C. R., & Katahn, M. Comparison levels, test anxiety, ongoing affect, and complex verbal learning. *American Journal of Psychology*, 1973, *86*, 555–565.

Suran, B. G. *Oddballs: The social maverick and the dynamics of individuality*. Chicago: Nelson-Hall, 1978.

Watson, J. B. *The double helix*. New York: Atheneum, 1968.

IV

Uniqueness Seeking in Perspective

To be nobody-but-yourself in a world which is doing its best, night and day, to make you everybody else—means to fight the hardest battle which any human being can fight; and never stop fighting.

—E. E. Cummings, "Letter," 1955

Deindividuation: Loss of Uniqueness

This final section is aimed at drawing conclusions about the role of uniqueness motivation in our society. The present chapter examines how people may lose their sense of uniqueness in our "mass" societal contexts, which tend to deindividuate people. In this vein, it is important to note that existential philosophers, psychologists, political scientists, and sociologists alike have often portrayed the loss of uniqueness and individualism as one of the central problems in American society. As expressed by Gross and Osterman (1971):

> Much of the contemporary American social and political thought can be seen as a continuing debate over problems and prospects of individualism in our national life . . . so basic is the concept of individualism to American society that every major issue which faces us as a nation invariably poses itself in these terms. (p. xi)

From his perspective as a psychologist, William James (1890) described the personal relevance of individuality:

> No more fiendish punishment could be devised, were such a thing physically possible, than that one should be turned loose in society and remain absolutely unnoticed by all members thereof. If no one turned round when we entered, answered when we spoke, or minded what we did, but if every person we met "cut us dead," and acted as if we were nonexistent things, a kind of rage and impotent despair would ere long well up in us, from which the cruelest bodily tortures would be a relief; for these would make us feel that, however bad might be our plight, we had not sunk to a depth as to be unworthy of attention at all. (pp. 293–294)

The noted political historian, Alexis de Tocqueville, also spoke of these concerns:

> As men grow alike, each man feels himself weaker in regard to all the rest; as he discerns nothing by which he is considerably raised above them, he mistrusts himself as soon as they assail him. (Quoted in Davis, 1971, p. xvi)

With these thoughts in mind, we will now discuss the phenomena of deindividuation in terms of their meaning, causes, and repercussions.

A Society That Does Away with Differences

Imagine, for a moment, a society in which one could not evidence any uniqueness relative to other people. This seemingly absurd premise is the basis of the satirical short story entitled "Harrison Bergeron" by Kurt Vonnegut (1971). In the introduction (pp. 7–8) to this story, we are told:

> The year was 2081, and everybody was finally equal. They weren't only equal before God and the law. They were equal every which way. Nobody was smarter than anybody else. Nobody was better looking than anybody else. Nobody was stronger or quicker than anybody else. All this equality was due to the 211th, 212th, and 213th Amendments to the Constitution, and to the unceasing vigilance of agents of the United States Handicapper General.
>
> Some things about living still weren't quite right, though. April, for instance, still drove people crazy by not being Springtime. And it was that clammy month that the H-G men took George and Hazel Bergeron's fourteen-year-old son, Harrison, away.
>
> It was tragic, all right, but George and Hazel couldn't think about it very hard. Hazel had a perfectly average intelligence, which meant she couldn't think about anything except in short bursts. And George, while his intelligence was way above normal, had a little mental handicap radio in his ear. He was required by law to wear it at all times. It was turned to a government transmitter. Every twenty seconds or so, the transmitter would send out some sharp noise to keep people like George from taking unfair advantage of their brains.
>
> George and Hazel were watching television. There were tears on Hazel's cheeks, but she'd forgotten for the moment what they were about.

On the television screen were ballerinas.

A buzzer sounded in George's head. His thoughts fled in panic, like bandits from a burglar alarm.

"That was a real pretty dance, that dance they just did," said Hazel.

"Huh?" said George.

"That dance it was nice," said Hazel.

"Yup," said George. He tried to think a little about the ballerinas. They weren't really very good—no better than anybody else would have been, anyway. They were burdened with sashweights and bags of birdshot, and their faces were masked, so that no one, seeing a free and graceful gesture or a pretty face, would feel like something the cat drug in. George was toying with the vague notion that maybe dancers shouldn't be handicapped. But he didn't get very far with it before another noise in his ear radio scattered his thoughts.

George winced. So did two out of the eight ballerinas.

Hazel saw him wince. Having no mental handicap herself, she had to ask George what the latest sound had been.

"Sounded like somebody hitting a milk bottle with a ball peen hammer," said George.

"I'd think it would be real interesting, hearing all the different sounds," said Hazel, a little envious. "All the things they think up."

"Um," said George.

"Only, if I was Handicapper General, you know what I would do?" said Hazel. Hazel, as a matter of fact, bore a strong resemblance to the Handicapper General, a woman named Diana Moon Glampers. "If I was Diana Moon Glampers," said Hazel, "I'd have chimes on Sunday—just chimes. Kind of in honor of religion."

"I could think, if it was just chimes, "said George.

"Well—maybe make 'em real loud," said Hazel. "I think I'd make a good Handicapper General."

"Good as anybody else," said George.

While Vonnegut's story may seem farfetched, it should be readily apparent that there are already places in the world where the display of unique behavior—whether in dress, ideas, or beliefs—is tightly controlled. In China, for example, people are trained to dress and think alike. Likewise, the average Russian citizen would not dare to express a political view that is different from the doctrine expressed by the government. In fact, Russian political dissidents may be labeled insane and sent to asylums for the mentally incompetent (Suran, 1978). But what about our own country? Are there constraints on uniqueness in our American society?

Some have argued that, indeed, many of our society's contemporary social structures arouse forces alien to the expression of uniqueness. For instance:

> Man hasn't won many battles lately in his constant fight against anonymity. To his bosses rewarding his work, he has become just a number. To TV announcers staring him in the eye and telling him what to buy, he is a decimal in the rating. To the polster soliciting his opinion, he is no more than just a yes or no or, most impersonal of all, a quavering don't know. (*Life*, October 16, 1970, p. 79)

Goffman (1961) has suggested that many of the *total institutions* in the American society, as well as in other societies, tend to strip the person of a sense of uniqueness. Included in such total institutions are such places as (1) homes for the aged, the orphaned, and blind; (2) mental hospitals; (3) jails and penitentiaries; (4) army barracks, boarding schools, and work camps; and (5) abbeys, monasteries, and convents. In these institutions, "each phase of the member's daily activity is carried on in the immediate company of a large batch of others, all of whom are treated alike and required to do the same thing together" (Goffman, 1961, p. 6). For example, upon arriving at such total institutions, the inhabitants are initiated into the deindividuation process through similar rituals. Again, Goffman notes:

> The process of entrance typically brings other kinds of loss and mortification as well. We very generally find staff employing what are called admission procedures, such as taking a life history, photographing, weighing, fingerprinting, assigning numbers, searching, listing personal possessions for storage, undressing, bathing, disinfecting, haircutting, issuing institutional clothing, instructing as to rules, and assigning to quarters. Admission procedures might better be called "trimming" or "programming" because in thus being squared away the new arrival allows himself to be shaped and coded into an object that can be fed into the administrative machinery of the establishment, to be worked on smoothly by routine operations. Many of these procedures depend upon attributes such as weight or fingerprints that the individual possesses merely because he is a member of the largest and most abstract of social categories, that of human being. Action taken on the basis of

such attributes necessarily ignores most of his previous bases
of self-identification. (p. 16)

The notion of total institutions suggests that there are large
bureaucracies within our society, as well as in other societies, that
may seriously constrain people's differences. If this is the case, it
is logical to address the possible reactions to the loss of a sense of
uniqueness within such societal contexts. The concept of deindividuation offers a starting point.

Forces against Uniqueness: Deindividuation

Deindividuation has captured the interest of psychologists in
the last few years. Conceptualizations of deindividuation typically
refer to undistinctiveness of self, nonidentifiability of self to others, anonymity, and loss of self-consciousness. Social scientists
have operationally manipulated deindividuation by varying a person's identifiability relative to other people. For example, researchers have employed (1) some form of name tags versus no
name tags, (2) lab coats, and/or (3) large hoods or costumes (Cannavale, Scarr, & Pepitone, 1970; Diener, Westford, Diener, & Beaman, 1973; Diener, Westford, Dineen, & Fraser, 1973; Festinger,
Pepitone, & Newcomb, 1952; Singer, Brush, & Lublin, 1965; Watson, 1973; Zabrack & Miller, 1972; Zimbardo, 1969). Once one of
these deindividuating manipulations has been performed, investi-
gators have been especially interested in individuals' reactions. As
we will see in subsequent discussions, these reactions to deindividuation are often rather unpleasant.

Most social scientists adhere to the view of deindividuation as
a hypothetical construct with specific antecedent and consequent
conditions, such as nonidentifiability and/or anonymity on one side
and the potential for antisocial acts on the other side (see Zimbardo, 1969). Although there are many subtle points of divergence,
it is generally agreed that the principal precursor of deindividuation
is an attack on ego identity, that is, a person's "loss of self-consciousness" or the subjective feelings of nonidentifiability (Duval
& Wicklund, 1972; Singer, Brush, & Lublin, 1965; Ziller, 1964;
Zimbardo, 1969). For instance, "operations which would heighten
the salience of distinctiveness of the person's clothing would serve
to produce individuation; and operations which would minimize

distinctiveness would serve to create deindividuation" (Singer, Brush, & Lublin, 1965, p. 357). Similarly, "Loss of identity can be conferred by being submerged in a crowd, disguised, masked, or dressed in uniform like everyone else, or by darkness" (Zimbardo, 1969, p. 255). Thus, most conceptualizations of deindividuation contain at least two principal components: *uniformity* or similarity in appearance and *anonymity* or nonidentifiability by observers.

Anonymity and Antisocial Acts

There is a need to clarify some of the conceptual confusion surrounding the concept of deindividuation. In this regard, an experiment by Baron (1971) reveals a difference in the magnitude of antisocial behavior between conditions of undistinctiveness as (1) uniformity or similarity in appearance and (2) anonymity or nonidentifiability of the research participant by the victim. Baron's experiment independently varied uniformity (lab coats and hoods versus name tags and own clothing) and anonymity (the research participant was or was not viewed by the victim). An aggression measure consisted of the latency of electric shock that the research participants believed they were administering to the victim (in actuality, no shock was administered). The results revealed that under the nonanonymous conditions, people in the high-uniformity condition (lab coats and hoods) aggressed less against the victim than people in the low-uniformity condition. However, under the anonymous conditions, the high-uniformity people aggressed more against the victim than the low-uniformity people.

The Baron experiment suggests that the high degrees of interpersonal similarity that threaten self-perceived uniqueness may be more closely allied with the uniformity than the anonymity component of deindividuation (or undistinctiveness). This follows because the responses to similarity-induced undistinctiveness, described in the previous chapters, are directed largely toward socially acceptable modes of redefining the person as having a sense of uniqueness. However, according to most definitions, the consequences of deindividuation are restricted only to antisocial behavior. Considering these issues, it is plausible to propose a reconciliation that encompasses both the uniqueness and the deindividuation views. That is, hypothetically one may expect more socially acceptable responses when the threats to self-perceived uniqueness involve *only* the uniformity component. However, when the threats involve *both* the uniformity and the anonymity components, the anonymity component may operate to release restraints and responses will tend to be more asocial or antisocial. On this issue, Couch (1970) notes:

> Normal social control is effective largely because the individual is known and identified and held responsible for his actions. The so-called irresponsibility of crowds probably results in part from the lack of differentiation. Those who cannot be held accountable are more likely to commit irresponsible acts; to be held accountable, persons must be differentiated and identified. (p. 466)

The importance of the anonymity component of deindividuation in relation to the release of aggression is also shown in experiments reported by Zimbardo (1969). In a controlled laboratory study, female college students were made to feel either anonymous or individuated. In order to achieve the set for the anonymity condition, research participants were required to wear a hood over their head and the experimenter did not address them by their names (see Chapter 7 for a discussion of the uniqueness properties of names). On the contrary, the research participants in the individuation condition wore large name tags. The dependent variable in this study was aggressive behavior toward another person. This was measured by examining the strength of electric shocks that the students would deliver to another student. (In actuality, of course, no such shocks were delivered.) Results showed that the students in the anonymous condition delivered shocks that were about twice as high as students in the individuation condition.

Zimbardo (1969) followed this first laboratory study of the effects of anonymity on aggression against people with a naturalistic or field study of aggression against property. He reasoned that large urban settings offer environments of extreme anonymity. In smaller towns, however, the inhabitants often know each other (by sight and/or name). In order to explore the effects of anonymity on aggressive behavior in a real-life setting, Zimbardo left an unattended car parked in New York City (the large urban setting) and in Palo Alto, California (the small community setting). Observers watched the cars from nearby windows. Ten minutes after he left the car in New York City, a band of car strippers (a mother, a father, and a son!) descended on the car. In the same three-day period in Palo Alto, all that transpired was that a person put the hood down on the car when it began to rain. Based on these two studies by Zimbardo and others like them, one must conclude that the anonymity associated with deindividuation may foster anti-social acts. Indeed, the hoods of Klu Klux Klan members bring to mind the individual's potential for violence when sheltered by anonymity.

Yet another example of how anonymity may serve as a stimulus for the release of restraints on antisocial behavior is shown in legitimate or socially recognized groups in which uniforms are worn. That is, antisocial acts may result in group contexts when uniforms or dress standards prohibit distinctive clothing and thereby reduce the amount of identifying information conveyed to observers. Uniformity of appearance may thus prevent the individual from mustering the "apparent symbols" (Gross & Stone, 1964) or "front" (Goffman, 1955) that attract the attention of others and allow the person to be distinct from others. Antisocial inhibitions are most likely to be liberated when the individual perceives that he or she cannot be identified with his or her acts and therefore cannot be held accountable for any negative consequences of these acts. For instance, under tense conditions of arousal and excitement, the uniforms that did not distinguish one policeman from another during the 1968 Democratic National Convention in Chicago or one National Guardsman from another at Kent State University may have reduced their restraints against violent acts.

Observations of other examples of antisocial acts are obviously possible. Most if not all of these observations refer to phenomena that involve both uniformity and anonymity and resulting acts that are typically aggressive and destructive to other people and sometimes to the actor. For example, the violence that erupted on American college campuses during the decade of the 1960s has been linked to the impersonal modes of instruction and the resulting denial of the uniqueness of each student that accompanied the rapid growth of modern universities (Keniston, 1968; Reich, 1970). Similarly, the heavy use of drugs has been attributed to the deindividuating nature of a collective society (Tyran, 1967). Finally, the substantial increase in the number of senseless and apparently motiveless acts of violence in major metropolitan areas has been linked to the anonymity produced by rapid urbanization (Zimbardo, 1969).

Deindividuation in Work Environments

(Given the fact that deindividuation seems to result in a variety of environments in which many people interact, it should not be surprising to learn that deindividuation may affect many of us in our work environments.) In this vein, it may be reasoned that the metamorphosis of earlier craft guilds to the gigantic corporation of today has yielded work environments that inhibit identification of self and one's unique contributions. Consistent with this argument, a classic book in the area of organizational psychology, the *Organization Man* (Whyte, 1956), graphically portrays the person as an anonymous cog in the wheel of technological society. The cartoon on this page echoes this sentiment.

"Now then, what makes you feel that we're dehumanizing you, 624078?"

From the *Wall Street Journal*, with permission of Eli Stein.

Modern organizations often attempt to maintain order and control over large numbers of human resources by reducing the variability in their members' behavior (Katz & Kahn, 1966) Therefore, such organizations may erect social structures and employ strategies of control that create conditions of deindividuation and nonidentifiability (Campbell, Dunnette, Lawler, & Weick, 1970; Dipboye, 1973; Ziller, 1964). The process may begin with psychological testing as the basis of selection and may continue with testing as the basis of appraisal or promotion. These testing procedures pose a threat to self-identity by virtue of the implication that a person is being forced to *fit* himself or herself and his or her behavior to match some standardized general profile. In the first few weeks on the job, the new employee is shaped into the organizational mold. For example, Schein (1968, 1971) traces the process of organizational "socialization" whereby new members are integrated into an organization. Frequently, there are demands for conformity to new rules, codes of dress, etc., that are already shared by other members of the large organization. An employee is strongly encouraged to "fit into" the organization as a whole. The cartoon on this page addresses the deindividuating nature of large organizations.

The attention of the job architect is directed toward the discovery of important aspects of job design. In this regard, however, traditional management models follow a blueprint of "people-as-machines." This model views the variability in the way different people perform a task as an undesirable cost that is to be eliminated. For instance, the assembly-line method of production may in the short-run enhance efficiency, but it also produces dissatisfac-

© 1976 United Feature Syndicate, Inc.

tion among those who must work on it. The negative aspects of the assembly line are commonly attributed to boredom and tedious routine (Scott, 1966). There is reason to suspect, however, that the absence of variability and the nonidentifiability of any one person's unique contribution may also be responsible for the dissatisfaction. In this regard, Walker and Guest (1952) asserted:

> Any production worker can, and sometimes does say: "There are hundreds of jobs like mine, not much better, not much worse. The differences are so slight to management that I am interchangeable." To escape this impersonality quite as much perhaps, as to escape monotony, the average worker does not aspire to climb into another, slightly better, production job, but into a utilityman's or repairman's where he can be recognized and where also he can recognize himself as an individual. We suggest that the sense of becoming de-personalized, or becoming anonymous . . . is a psychologically more disturbing result of the work environment than either the boredom or the tension that arises from repetitive and mechanically paced work. (p. 169)

As noted previously in the chapter on competition through performance (Chapter 9), rules are another mode of organizational control used to reduce interpersonal variability. Deviations from group standards of task performance and failure to cooperate with or disrespect for standardized company policies are met with disciplinary actions (Booker, 1969). Given the emphasis on rules in organizations, as well as the potential punishments for violating these rules, one might expect that workers may increasingly adhere to such rules. However, this does not appear to be the case. For example, during the post-World War II years, the frequency of norm violation in the industrial world increased (Sinha & Wherry, 1965).

In regard to norm violations, leadership style and group characteristics seem to be important determinants of such behavior (Mulder, 1971). Two leadership styles may be briefly noted for their potential deindividuating effects. First, White and Lippitt (1960) have drawn attention to the loss of individuality that accompanies authoritarian leaders. Second, Fiedler's (1967) scale to measure leadership style, the "assumed similarity of opposites" (ASO), requires the supervisor to rate his or her most and least preferred co-worker on a number of dimensions. A high ASO score

BIRTH

Here I come!

Here I am!

I am different!

I'm the one with my name on
my bracelet...

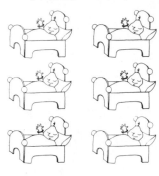

The one in the upper right corner
is me...there are a lot of us
these days.

My parents know who I am...
I'm the one with my name on
my bracelet.

From *Comparisons* by C. R. Snyder. Copyright © 1974 by Celestial Arts. Reprinted with permission of
the publisher.

depicts a leader who sees the least and most preferred co-worker
as very similar, that is, who discriminates very little among his or
her subordinates. Ziller (1964) interpreted the ASO as a measure of
deindividuating styles of leadership, that is, "a measure of the
extent to which the leader is aware of each member as an individual and is capable of noting or remembering the characteristics of
individual performance" (p. 352). Similarly, research on incentive
systems reveals that motivation and satisfaction increase when
rewards are public rather than anonymous (Patchen, 1961) and
when rewards are made contingent on *individual* performance
(Galbraith & Cummings, 1967; Georgopolous, Mahoney, & Jones,
1957; Graen, 1969; Lawler, 1971). One interpretation of these findings is that individual incentive plans provide greater identifiability
of the individual and his or her products—a process of *individuation* that is motivating. Consistent with this interpretation, research
reveals that job satisfaction and motivation may actually increase
as the size of work group and the organization decreases (Barker &
Gump, 1964; Indik, 1965; Shaw, 1960; Warner & Hilander, 1964;
Wilken, 1971).

While the organization often strains to reduce variability

DEATH

Finally, I'm getting sick, tired, and beginning to suffer... there are a lot of us at the hospital... still no private room.

I'm in the wing on the right... you can't see me.

Death is no big deal... here I am in my casket... I'm the one with the name on my bracelet...

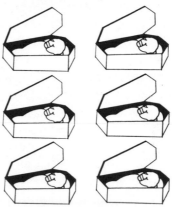

OK, the one in the lower right corner... the mortician knows who I am... I'm the one with my name on my bracelet.

Here I am at the cemetery...

I am different!

among its membership, there are other data that suggest that individuality is a significant factor in the success of management personnel (Alvarez, 1968; Ghiselli, 1960). Perhaps the loss of creativity and spontaneity due to imposed deindividuation may be too costly a tribute for the organization to pay in the interests of control and efficiency. Indeed, some costs may reach into the very foundations of the organization's structure, that is, decision making. For example, the tendency of individuals to take greater risks in their decision making after a group discussion is referred to as the *risky-shift phenomenon* (Brown, 1965; Dion, Baron, & Miller, 1970). Increases in the degree of risk in decision making tend to be associated with increases in (1) group size (Teger & Pruitt, 1967) and (2) the nonidentifiability of the participants (Pincus, 1969). In fact, only partial nonidentifiability is required to produce a tendency for individuals to make more extreme decisions (Argyle, 1969). Such extreme decisions may reflect the individual's attempt to recapture a sense of uniqueness within the large group or organizational structure.

Concluding Remarks on Deindividuation

The present chapter has surveyed the potential societal repercussions of environments that deprive a person of a sense of uniqueness. Even in democratic societies such as ours, there are forces inherent in the sheer mass of people that contribute to deindividuation. While there sometimes may be temporary positive effects of deindividuation—for example, the joy of becoming free from "small-town" gossip—the more prevalent picture that emerges regarding deindividuation is a rather negative one.

As the forces of society seemingly continue to deprive people of a sense of uniqueness, there may be successively stronger attempts to establish some degree of impact, worth, or identity among the multitude of other people. Unfortunately, in an environment where we perceive ourselves as lacking a unique identity, we may also treat others rather impersonally and callously. A society in which the members cannot achieve some sense of uniqueness may therefore engender self-dissatisfaction. Equally important, however, the resulting lack of self-respect may generalize to losing respect for another's identity. As other people become objects, one might expect steady increases in violent crimes against others. This may be especially the case when people come to perceive that they are relatively anonymous among the masses.)

In summary, then, deindividuation in Western culture may be associated with negative consequences for both the individual and society as a whole. It is not surprising, therefore, that philosophers and social scientists from many disciplines decry the process and the effects of deindividuation, dehumanization, and depersonalization as being among the primary underlying causes of many current social problems. Indeed, a citizen of modern mass environments may cry out against such deindividuating forces. An ironical plea against deindividuation and mass anonymity (see Snyder, 1974) is vividly portrayed in the illustrations on pages 188 and 189.

References

Alvarez, R. Informal reactions to deviance in simulated work organizations: A laboratory experiment. *American Sociological Review*, 1968, *33*, 895–912.

Argyle, M. (Ed.). *Social interaction*. London: Methuen, 1969.

Barker, R. G., & Gump, P. V. *Big school, small school: High school size and student behavior*. Stanford, Calif.: Stanford University Press, 1964.

Baron, R. S. Anonymity, deindividuation and aggression. Paper presented at the Western Psychological Association, 1971.

Booker, G. S. Behavioral aspects of disciplinary action. *Personnel Psychology*, 1969, *15*, 525–529.

Brown, R. *Social psychology*. New York: Free Press, 1965.

Campbell, J. P., Dunnette, M. D., Lawler, E. E., III., & Weick, K. E. *Managerial behavior performance, and effectiveness*. New York: McGraw-Hill, 1970.

Cannavale, F. J., Scarr, H. A., & Pepitone, A. Deindividuation in the small group: Further evidence. *Journal of Personality and Social Psychology*, 1970, *16*, 141–147.

Couch, C. J. Dimensions of association in collective behavior episodes. *Sociometry*, 1970, *33*, 457–471.

Davis, D. B. *The fear of conspiracy: Images of un-American subversion from the revolution to the present*. Ithaca, N.Y.: Cornell University Press, 1971.

Diener, E., Westford, K. L., Diener, C., & Beaman, A. L. Deindividuating effects of group presence and arousal on stealing by halloween trick-or-treaters. *Proceedings of the 81st Annual Convention of the American Psychological Association*, 1973, *8*, 219–220.

Diener, E., Westford, K. L., Dineen, J., & Fraser, S. Beat the pacifist: The deindividuating effects of anomymity and group presence. *Proceedings of the*

81st Annual Convention of the American Psychological Association, 1973, *8*, 221–222.

Dion, K. L., Baron, R. S., & Miller, N. Why do groups make riskier decisions than individuals? In L. Berkowitz (Ed.), *Advances in experimental social psychology*, vol. 5. New York: Academic, 1970, pp. 305–377.

Dipboye, R. L. Unrestrained behavior, identity seeking, and overcontrolled behaviors as responses to deindividuating environments. Unpublished manuscript. Purdue University, 1973.

Duval, S., & Wicklund, R. A. *A theory of objective self awareness*. New York: Academic, 1972.

Festinger, L., Pepitone, A., & Newcomb, T. Some consequences of deindividuation in a group. *Journal of Abnormal and Social Psychology*, 1952, *47*, 382–389.

Fiedler, F. E. *A theory of leadership effectiveness*. New York: McGraw-Hill, 1967.

Galbraith, J., & Cummings, L. L. An empirical investigation of the motivational determinants of task performance: Interactive effects between instrumentality valence and motivation–ability. *Organizational Behavior and Human Performance*, 1967, *2*, 237–257.

Georgopolous, B. S., Mahoney, G. M., & Jones, N. W. A path-goal approach to productivity. *Journal of Applied Psychology*, 1957, *41*, 345–353.

Ghiselli, E. E. Individuality as a factor in the success of management personnel. *Personnel Psychology*, 1960, *13*, 1–10.

Goffman, E. On face-work: An analysis of ritual elements in social interactions. *Psychiatry*, 1955, *18*, 213–231.

Goffman, E. *Asylums*. Garden City, N. Y.: Doubleday Anchor, 1961.

Graen, G. Instrumentality theory of work motivation: Some experimental results and suggested modifications. *Journal of Applied Psychology*, 1969, *53* (Whole No. 2, part 2), 1–25.

Gross, E., & Stone, G. P. Embarrassment and the analysis of role requirements. *American Journal of Sociology*, 1964, *70*, 1–15.

Gross, R., & Osleman, P. *Individualism: Man in modern society*. New York: Dell, 1971.

Indik, B. P. Organization size and member participation: Some empirical tests of alternative explanations. *Human Relations*, 1965, *18*, 339–350.

James, W. *The principles of psychology*, vol. 1. New York: Holt & Co., 1890.

Katz, D., & Kahn, R. L. *The social psychology of organizations*. New York: Wiley, 1966.

Keniston, K. *Young radicals: Notes on committed youth*. New York: Harcourt, Brace, & World, 1968.

Lawler, E. E. III. *Pay and organizational effectiveness: A psychological view*. New York: McGraw-Hill, 1971.

Mulder, F. Characteristics of violators of formal company rules. *Journal of Applied Psychology*, 1971, *55*, 500–502.

Patchen, M. *The choice of wage comparisons*. Englewood Cliffs, N.J.: Prentice-Hall, 1961.

Pincus, F. L. Risky and conservative group shifts: Conformity, leadership, or responsibility diffusion. Unpublished doctoral dissertation, University of California, Los Angeles, 1969.

Reich, C. A. *The greening of America.* New York: Random House, 1970.

Schein, E. H. Organizational socialization and the profession of management. *Industrial Management Review*, 1968, *9*, 1–6.

Schein, E. H. The individual, the organization, and the career: A conceptual scheme. *Journal of Applied Behavioral Science*, 1971, *7*, 401–426.

Scott, W. E. Activation theory and task design. *Organizational Behavior and Human Performance*, 1966, *1*, 3–30.

Shaw, D. M. Size of share in task motivation and work group. *Sociometry*, 1960, *23*, 203–208.

Singer, J. E., Brush, C. A., & Lublin, S. C. Some aspects of deindividuation: Identification and conformity. *Journal of Experimental Social Psychology*, 1965, *1*, 356–378.

Sinha, J. B. P., & Wherry, R. J., Jr. Determinants of norm violating behavior in a simulated industrial setting. *Personnel Psychology*, 1965, *18*, 403–412.

Snyder, C. R. *Comparisons.* Milbrae, Calif.: Celestial Arts, 1974.

Suran, B. *Oddballs: The social maverick and the dynamics of individuality.* Chicago: Nelson-Hall, 1978.

Teger, A. I., & Pruitt, D. G. Components of group risk taking. *Journal of Experimental Social Psychology*, 1967, *3*, 189–205.

Tyran, K. Orson Welles. *Playboy*, 1967, *14*, 53–64.

Vonnegut, K. Harrison Bergeron. In K. Vonnegut, *Welcome to the monkey house.* New York: Dell, 1971, pp. 7–13.

Walker, C. R., & Guest, R. H. *The man on the assembly line.* Cambridge, Mass.: Harvard University Press, 1952.

Warner, W. K., & Hilander, J. S. The relationship between size of organization and membership participation. *Rural Sociology*, 1964, *29*, 30–39.

Watson, R. I., Jr. Investigation into deindividuation using a cross-cultural survey technique. *Journal of Personality and Social Psychology*, 1973, *25*, 342–345.

White, R. K., & Lippitt, R. *Autocracy and democracy: An experimental inquiry.* New York: Harper & Row, 1960.

Whyte, W. H. *The organization man.* New York: Simon & Schuster, 1956.

Wilken, P. H. Size of organization and member participation in church congregations. *Administrative Sciences Quarterly*, 1971, *16*, 173–180.

Zabrack, M., & Miller, N. Group aggression: The effects of friendship ties and anonymity. *Proceedings of the 80th Annual Convention of the American Psychological Association*, 1972, *7*, 211–212.

Ziller, R. C. Individuation and socialization: A theory of assimilation in large organizations. *Human Relations*, 1964, *17*, 341–360.

Zimbardo, P. G. The human choice: Individuation, reason, and order vs. deindividuation, impulse, and chaos. In W. Arnold & D. Levine (Eds.), *Nebraska Symposium on Motivation*, vol. xvii. Lincoln: University of Nebraska Press, 1969, pp. 237–307.

Individuation: The Pursuit of Difference

Are People Unique?

With regard to the question of actual human uniqueness, Gordon Allport (1961) has asserted:

> *the outstanding characteristic of man is his individuality*. He is a unique creation of the forces of nature. There was never a person just like him, and there never will be again. Remember the fingerprint, even it is unique. All sciences, including psychology, tend to neglect this paramount fact of individuality. . . . In daily life, on the other hand, we are in no danger of forgetting that individuality is the supreme mark of human nature. All during our waking life, and even in our dreams, we recognize and deal with people as separate, distinct, and unique individuals. . . . In view of the uniqueness of each person's inheritance and environment it could not be otherwise. (p. 4)

In a similar vein, Leona Tyler (1965) stated that "The uniqueness of individuals is one of the most fundamental characteristics of life" (p. 1).

Indeed, an examination of the study of genetic inheritance reveals that people are equipped with distinct physical attributes. The mating and sexual reproduction processes explain the origins of our uniqueness. Of the approximately 4 billion people on earth, each with his or her particular genetic pool, two individuals mate and form a unique genetic combination. The uniqueness of genetic composition is highlighted by an analysis of the probability of any ovum and sperm's uniting. The female has approximately 400,000 primordial follicles, and in a given month, one mature follicle generates an ovum that is capable of impregration. During intercourse, an average male deposits 240 million sperm in the female uterus (Langley & Cheraskin, 1954). As a result, the chance of union between any ovum and sperm is infinitesimally small. The proba- bilities become even more staggering to the imagination when one considers that each sperm and egg cell contains 23 chromosomes and that each of these chromosomes contains a multitude of genes that serve as the basic hereditary units (Tyler, 1978). In fact, the number of human genotypes has been estimated as being some- where in the magnitude of *70 trillion* (Tyler, 1978). For these rea- sons, the biologist Dobzhansky (1956) has asserted that "Every human being is, then, the carrier of a unique genotype" (p. 56). Therefore, from the point of conception, differences between indi- viduals seem guaranteed (Good, 1974).

Given that genetic inheritances vary greatly between individu- als, variability should naturally occur in the physical and the phy- siological characteristics of adults (Williams, 1956). As medical students can attest, organs may not be "where they are supposed to be," nerve tracts may be missing, and so on. The variation of the human body is also the focus of such "practitioners" as manu- facturers of shoes, brassieres, hats, pants, and other items of clothing. In short (or long!), each human being is composed of a highly idiosyncratic physical makeup. This physical distinctiveness is revealed in the college professor's (Hunt, 1962) perception of his class shown in the cartoon on page 197.

The extreme genetic differences between individuals may be further amplified by environmental factors. While it is beyond the scope of the present discussion to explore in any detail the effects of environment on behavior, it is useful to imagine the possible diversifying effects of environments on already genetically differ- ent individuals. The classic study by John B. Watson and Rosalie Rayner (1920) illustrates how various behaviors can be learned through simple conditioning. A 9-month-old infant, Albert, was simultaneously exposed to a rat and a loud noise (the clang of a hammer on a steel bar). The noise caused Albert to cry, and after seven pairings of the noise and the rat, the rat alone came to elicit crying and avoidance by "little Albert." Furthermore, Albert's fear response generalized to other fur objects (e.g., a rabbit, a dog, a sealskin coat, and Watson's hair) that had physical characteris- tics similar to those of the original rat fur.

This is what I see at eight o'clock in the morning. Many people are worried about conformity. I am not.

While this "little Albert" experiment is typically invoked to exemplify conditioning principles (Harris, 1979), the important point for the present discussion is that a variety of conditioning histories may be associated with circumstances like those described above. For example, Albert learned to cry at fur objects, but Child X may have learned to laugh at fur objects, and Child Y may have learned to ignore fur objects. Moreover, not only may people vary in their past experiences with a given stimulus, but they may also vary in the amount of generalization they exhibit toward that stimulus. And finally, if one considers the enormous amount of different kinds of behavior that are conditioned for any particular individual, it becomes even more evident that each person's background contributes specifically to his or her unique psychological identity. Although one can only estimate the combined effects of heredity and environment on a person, it is, nevertheless, reasonable to speculate that hereditary and environmental factors interact to produce a truly unique identity for each person.

Do We Seek Uniqueness?

No doubt, the above evidence about the genetic and physical uniqueness of every individual does not come as a surprise. However, the *actual* uniqueness of each person has *not* been the focus of our attention throughout this book. Instead, our major hypothesis has been that individuals *want to perceive* themselves as having some differences and are constantly struggling with cultural and social forces that inhibit the expression and self-perception of uniqueness. It is the cultural and social forces that seek to deprive us of our uniqueness and the resulting overt and covert attempts to reestablish our self-perceptions of uniqueness that have been the focus of the theory and research in this volume.

The previous chapter reveals that there are strong societal forces that may foster deindividuation. Therefore, a meaningful question to readdress at this point is whether uniqueness seeking is possible within such an overall societal context. Like actual uniqueness, uniqueness seeking appears to be not only possible but very probable. The present book has generated anecdotal and research evidence to document the existence of the uniqueness-seeking phenomenon. Data from several experiments in different laboratories show the avoidance of high degrees of similarity and the seeking of differentness in many diverse response domains. Individual differences in need for uniqueness have been illustrated, and uniqueness attributes have been introduced as a socially acceptable means of attaining a sense of uniqueness. While the findings in any single experiment may be challenged as providing the "critical" test of the theory, the full portfolio of studies supports the viability of uniqueness-seeking behaviors in particular and uniqueness theory more generally.

The reader can answer the questions regarding the existence and operation of uniqueness seeking at another level. This can be accomplished by simply asking whether you *feel* a sense of uniqueness. As one recalls his or her particular background, experiences, attitudes, achievements, and so forth (see Part III for review of the various uniqueness attributes), he or she may be convinced of having some degree of difference. In fact, it would be the rare individual who would not perceive that he or she has differences relative to other people. Interestingly, however, the attainment of a sense of uniqueness is possible at both the behavioral and the phenomenological levels. While people engage in extensive, observable, public uniqueness-seeking activities, it is also likely that an even greater sense of uniqueness is achieved in the private phenomenological sphere of each individual. This is analogous to the distinction made with regard to conformity (see Kiesler & Kiesler, 1969), whereby, a person may exhibit varying degrees of publicly observable conformity, while maintaining a private state that is nonconforming. In the case of uniqueness behavior, the private phenomenological level may enable the person to achieve a sense of uniqueness even though uniqueness may seemingly be lacking at the behavioral or observable levels.

What Environments Foster a Sense of Uniqueness?

A third question to be considered in this chapter is where people acquire a sense of uniqueness in our society. The previous section on uniqueness attributes has given several specific examples of socially acceptable means by which a person may seek and obtain a sense of uniqueness. Now, we would like to explore a few basic environmental arenas for the development and maintenance of a sense of uniqueness. Each of the following environments is best conceptualized as a *potential* arena for the pursuit of difference. In some cases, these environments may actually serve to decrease a person's sense of uniqueness and uniqueness-seeking behavior. Nevertheless, these environmental contexts are important to consider because they *may* imbue a person with a sense of uniqueness and foster uniqueness-seeking behavior.

The Family Context

A first source through which uniqueness may evolve is the family context. Imagine the development of the infant within the family setting. At birth, the infant and the environment are nothing more than a single "apperceptive mass"; moreover, the infant is unable to separate the "me" from the "not-me." During this stage, the infant frequently feels pleasant and unpleasant pressure on the body or skin and struggles to make appropriate coping responses. This early stage is characterized by complete dependence of the infant on the parents for the gratification of needs; this has been described as "unilateral dependence" (Harvey, Hunt, & Schroder, 1961). Indeed, for the first four months, the infant is merged with the mother through dependence (Kaplan, 1978). At this point, obviously, only the stage of uniqueness perception and motivation is being set.

Beginning around the age of 5 months, the infant's total merger with the mother in particular and the rest of the family more generally begins to decrease. The infant begins what Kaplan (1978) has called the conflict between "oneness and separateness." Slowly, the infant acquires a sense of its separate identity (see also Mahler, Pine, & Bergman, 1975). The child eventually learns to distinguish himself or herself as different from objects and other organisms in the environment. This realization of one's uniqueness from others in the family and the home environment may originate, at least in part, as an extension of the competence motive system (White, 1959, 1960). During infancy, for example, parents may begin to encourage and reward independent and autonomous behaviors that require the child to perceive himself or herself and external objects as discriminable stimuli in the family environment. During this stage of development, parents encourage and reward the child for making appropriate labeling responses, such as "mama" or "dada." Furthermore, in the process of making the correct "labeling" response, which leads to a reward, the child must perceive himself or herself and the other family members as discriminably different stimuli in the environment.

By the age of 18 months, the child has achieved a "psychological birth" in which he or she begins to use the word *I*. This truly signals the child's awareness of his or her separateness, although the child may continue to struggle with this issue until the age of 36 months (Kaplan, 1978). This psychological birth, or self-revelation of uniqueness is portrayed by a young girl, Emily, in Hughes's *A High Wind in Jamaica* (1929):

> And then an event did occur, to Emily, of considerable importance. She suddenly realized who she was.
>
> She had been playing house when it suddenly flashed into her mind that she was *she . . .*
>
> Each time she moved an arm or leg in this simple action, however, it struck her with amazement to find them obeying her so readily. Memory told her, of course, that they had always done so before: but before, she had never realized how surprising this was. (pp. 134–135)

One intriguing possibility is that the self-perceptions of uniqueness may acquire functionally autonomous "drive properties" as a result of their occurrence in contiguity with successful coping responses and social rewards. In this regard, any parent (or person who has worked with young children) can testify to the prevalence of "the terrible two's." It is as if the 2-year-old child deliberately does the opposite of what he or she is told. While such oppositional behavior may cause enormous inconveniences for a parent, *this behavior is normal.* Perhaps our 2-year-old, fresh from the "psychological birth," is further establishing his or her sense of uniqueness by engaging in oppositional behavior. Oppositional behavior in children was described (Allport, 1924; MacDougall, 1911–1912) and documented (Levy & Tulchin, 1925; Mayers, 1935) by psychologists over 50 years ago. However, recent research on oppositional behavior in children has generated inconsistent results (e.g., Brehm, 1977; Brehm & Weinraub, 1977). Therefore, there is currently no clear-cut explanation of the underlying motivation for "the terrible two's." Lacking a definitive explanation of oppositional behavior in children, however, one plausible hypothesis is that such behavior partly reflects early manifestations of uniqueness seeking.

More elaborate distinctions between the child and other people within the family context develop in the period following psychological birth (Sarbin, 1962; Sawrey & Telford, 1971). For example, one of the child's first family experiences with competitive social interaction, sibling rivalry, may be an important factor in the development of uniqueness seeking. Bossard and Boll (1955) observed that children in large families exhibit tendencies to assume roles that differ from the roles previously assumed by their brothers and sisters, for example, "the responsible type," "the studious type," and "the popular type." This assumption of specialized roles that have not be preempted by other siblings may be an attempt to establish some sense of uniqueness within the family setting. In a similar vein, Schachter (1959) and others have discussed the relationship between birth order and identity. Presumably firstborn and only children are "individuated" more than those born later. Their identity is specific ("our son" or "our daughter"). Likewise, Ziller (1964) hypothesized that firstborn and only children will continue to strive to maintain high visibility and differentiation from the group.

It seems reasonable, given the aforementioned examples, to conclude that the family context may foster a sense of uniqueness on the part of the developing child. It should be emphasized, however, that the family also serves as an arena for socialization and training to "fit into" society. In fact, some theorists have even gone so far as to assert that parents and families usually squelch the sense of uniqueness in children. In this regard, Berne (1970) wrote:

> Man is born free, but one of the first things he learns is to do as he is told, and spends the rest of his life doing that. Thus his first enslavement is to his parents. He follows their instructions forevermore, retaining only in some cases the right to choose his own methods and consoling himself with an illusion of autonomy. (p. 194)

We do not hold this pessimistic view of the family. Nevertheless, Berne's point is well taken in that much of what a child learns in a family setting is when *not* to evidence uniqueness. Likewise, there are many family settings that undoubtedly overtly or covertly inhibit uniqueness-seeking behavior.

Contrary to Berne's suggestion, we believe that the family

may foster uniqueness seeking on the part of children. A child may be taught the basic rules and values of society and a respect of others' rights; moreover, that child *also* may be imbued with a sense of uniqueness and rewarded for manifesting this uniqueness. A critical factor for parents is not to imprison the child in their stereotypes (Hart, Pogrebin, Rodgers, & Thomas, 1974). This point forms the concluding theme to James and Jongeward's (1975) best-selling book for parents entitled *Born to Win*. James and Jongeward suggested to parents and their children:

> It takes courage to experience the freedom that comes with autonomy, courage to accept intimacy and directly encounter other persons, courage to stand in an unpopular cause, courage to choose authenticity over approval and to choose it again and again, courage to accept the responsibility for your own choices, and, indeed, courage to be the very unique person you really are. (p. 274)

Interestingly, most family system theorists assert that a psychologically healthy family context is one that allows the child to achieve a sense of differentiation *and* some sense of merger with the parents. Minuchin (1974) identified this as an individuation–merger process. On this topic, he noted:

> Human experience of identity has two elements: a sense of belonging and a sense of being separate. The laboratory in which these ingredients are mixed and dispersed is the family, the matrix of identity. (p. 47)

Likewise, Ackerman (1959) asserted:

> A healthy separation of the child's individual self is contingent on the maintenance of a healthy emotional togetherness of child and mother. If the togetherness is impaired, the process of separation is distorted. If the separation experience is impaired, the sense of togetherness is impaired. . . . The relations of individual identity and family identity are characterized by the delicate interplay of processes of merging and differentiation. (p. 21)

Finally, it is noteworthy that one of the touchstones of Virginia Satir's (1967) theorization about a healthy family context is the notion of "different-ness." According to Satir, this "different-ness" involves the ability of the child to engage in the individuation process in the context of a supportive, merged family. In essence, therefore, the various descriptions of well-functioning family systems all acknowledge the importance of fostering the child's sense of uniqueness within the supportive and cohesive framework of the family.

Neighborhood Context

A second source of uniqueness may come through one's living environment. As noted in the previous chapter on deindividuation, the living environments generated by mass groups of people in close proximity often promote anonymity and stifle a sense of uniqueness. One solution to the deindividuating nature of urban apartment living was most creative. Peter Nemetschek, a photographer in Munich, Germany, took pictures of apartment dwellers and placed poster-sized reproductions in their windows. Because of this bold maneuver, the occupants felt less anonymous. In fact, the ambience of the building was changed so that people were warmer and friendlier and talked to each other more frequently (*Life*, Oct. 16, 1970, p. 80).

Whether one lives in the suburbs or in the inner city, similar people often live near each other in similar circumstances. Such need not be the case, however. For example, community planners recognize the many personal satisfactions served by religious, ethnic, and regional diversity among neighbors in Levittown (Gans, 1967). Dissatisfied with the smothering of creativity in the middle-class suburbs in the mid-1950s, social change has been advocated to establish neighborhoods of people with a heterogeneous mixture of differences in races, religions, ages, and socioeconomic backgrounds. For example, a community made up of people with diverse backgrounds, talents, and interests may be livelier and more productive than a homogeneous community (Allen, 1954).

Rubin (1973) recognized the delicate balance between people's needs for similar and dissimilar other persons by noting that "For a human being to adapt to a rapidly changing world, he needs the companionship and support of others with whom he may sometimes disagree, but nevertheless feels a fundamental bond of like-mindedness" (p. 154). Gans (1967) also recognized the need to moderate differentness. He recommended that neighborhoods designed with homogeneous subblocks of persons with similar age and economic backgrounds be embedded in more heterogeneous larger communities. The larger community also provides the opportunity for a sense of uniqueness through contacts in other neighborhood facilities, including schools. The role of schools and education in relation to uniqueness is addressed next.

Educational Context

A third major potential source for acquiring a sense of uniqueness is through education. Philosophically, educational systems can be conceptualized on a continuum in which socialization represents one extreme and individuation represents the other. This continuum is described by Minuchin, Biber, Shapiro, and Zimiles (1969) in the following manner:

> If the goal is adaptation to an existing world and the acquisition of competence so as to reap the greatest rewards in that world, a kind of school will take shape that lays great emphasis on the process of socialization. Another view, that the world needs constant remaking by individuals who can make an impact, dictates another kind of school, one that considers the nurturing of individuality and concern for the child's identity a major part of its responsibility. (p. 41)

Education has at times been criticized for an overemphasis on the socialization philosophy. That is, schools may actually serve to delimit individuality rather than foster the individual student's unique identity, talents, and aptitudes (see Silberman, 1970). The following characteristics shared by most schools certainly contribute to an accentuation of socialization as compared with individuation. First, one must be in school because it is either a legal requirement or a requirement of one's parents. Second, school is a collective experience. This means that the individual is put into a crowd. Third, school is evaluative; one's verbal and physical actions are usually under the scrutiny of the teacher. Often, therefore, the student is placed in the position of doing and saying exactly what the teacher expects in order to obtain the reward of a high grade.

Even if a potential educational system philosophically endorses an individuation model of education, the actual school arena may *not* produce an atmosphere that fosters the student's unique identity and performance. There are at least two major reasons for this. The first reason is based on economic reality: schools can afford only a certain number of teachers for the total number of students. Therefore, the most usual classroom scene is characterized by *one teacher* and approximately *30 students*. How, given such a teacher–student ratio, can there be any full-scale attention and nourishment of the unique talents of each student? Second, even if teachers did want to embark on programs to enhance student uniqueness, they would find it difficult because they are often not rewarded for such actions. That is to say, teachers are commonly rewarded (and punished) if they can or cannot maintain order and control in their classrooms. In this vein, Silberman (1970) wrote:

> If teachers are obsessed with silence and lack of movement, therefore, it is in large part because it is the chief means by which their competence is judged. A teacher will rarely, if ever, be called on the carpet or denied tenure because his students have not learned anything; he most certainly will be rebuked if his students are talking or roaming about the classroom. (p. 144)

Given the aforementioned realistic constraints in the educational system, it is easy to see why it is often difficult to operationalize the individuation philosophy in educational arenas. There are, however, at least two emerging educational trends that indicate that the role of the unique student may be receiving more attention. First, special education programs for exceptional children are flourishing (Dunn, 1973) because school systems have made the economic decision to allocate some of their resources to unique or exceptional students. Included in this exceptional-children category are the gifted, the educable mentally retarded, the trainable mentally retarded, the emotionally disturbed, the socially maladjusted, the speech-impaired, the deaf, the hard of hearing, the blind, the partially seeing, the crippled, and chronic health cases (Dunn, 1973). Likewise, special educational programs are emerging for those students who may have specific learning disabilities (see Levy, 1973). Another potential individuation trend is the increased use of programmed instruction (sometimes computer-assisted). Here, the individual student moves through a prearranged set of materials *at his or her own pace*. After acquiring the programmed information, the individual student may be allowed to embark on a specialized set of readings and experiments in a particular area.[1]

Psychotherapy Context

A fourth possible arena for gaining a sense of uniqueness may be the psychotherapeutic context. Many writers would strongly disagree with this statement, however, because the psychotherapist sometimes plays the role of making a person "fit into" a societal context (see Halleck, 1971; Lowe, 1970; Tennov, 1976). In fact, some writers have asserted that our legal system fosters the employment of therapy as a means of "helping" deviants to "fit in." For example, Kittrie (1973) observed that our legal system acts "in a parental role *(parens patriae)*—seeking not to punish, but to change or socialize the nonconformist through treatment and therapy" (p. 3). Psychotherapy thus has the possibility of becoming a coercive arena in which the client's manifestation of unusual or abnormal behavior is to be lessened or stopped.

While psychotherapy undoubtedly at times has diminished the uniqueness of clients, it has also offered a haven for many people to explore their uniqueness. "Fitting in," in other words, is probably not a goal *per se* that many psychotherapists would hold for their clients. As one psychotherapist noted:

> It seems to me, rightly or wrongly, that psychotherapy is one of the last bastions for the individual *qua* individual. A therapist may well wear many hats and function in a variety of ways for a particular client, but I cannot help but believe that psychotherapy is for the individual as an individual. When a therapist becomes a moralist, an arbiter of social values and societal

---

[1]The reader should be apprised of the fact that programmed learning has been criticized because the student cannot (1) specify his or her own goals; (2) reach his or her goals in an individual way; and (3) express his or her own concept as an answer (Silberman, 1970). If programmed learning enables the student to acquire the traditional "facts" more quickly, however, this then frees time for the development of unique talents.

> expectations, then that unique idiosyncratic side of the individual self will inevitably be insufficiently explored and supported. (Suran, 1978, p. 3)

A client seeking help is at some level asking recognition of the fact that he or she is a unique person, of worth to someone. As Raimy (1978) observed:

> Many, if not most, persons coming for treatment feel unhappy, unwanted, frightened, depressed, and rejected. They are miserable at least in part because they are unable to obtain even their normal share of what the analysts refer to as "narcissistic supplies." The therapist . . . is providing such persons with evidence that at least to the therapist they are valued members of society, they are worth talking and listening to, they are important. . . . The therapist may, at least temporarily, be the only person who supplies the client with some of his narcissistic supplies. (p. 6, in manuscript)

The empathy and warmth of the psychotherapist are often considered critical components in a positive therapy context (Carkhuff, 1969). For the person with sufficient troubles to prompt him or her to seek help, this may mean that the helper (therapist) is willing to listen and understand the client's unique circumstances. Whether experiencing psychological problems or not, people cannot attain the gratifications of a positive sense of uniqueness *unless some person or persons are paying attention to them*. For most of us, there are individuals who will listen to our ideas, aspirations, and problems. It is through this feedback process that we can attain a sense of worth *and* uniqueness. The person with profound psychological problems, however, often has lost the normal channels of feedback with other people.

The person in therapy typically has intensive problems with which to deal. As the client interacts with a psychotherapist who truly listens to the problems, the client may achieve some sense of uniqueness because he or she is at least being recognized in a supportive manner. The client may then become energized to work on the problems, and with some successful management of these problems, the person may feel more positively about himself or herself. Concurrent with this acquisition of self-esteem and worth, then, therapy may enable the person to gain a more enduring sense of uniqueness.

Those familiar with psychotherapy may at this point question the uniqueness proposition, since a common clinical bromide is that "misery loves company." Time and again, people who describe their problems may be told by the therapist that their problems are very similar to those of other people. This may occur in either individual or group psychotherapy. In this regard, some theorists have suggested that such consensus information may alleviate the client's perceptions of negative abnormality, incompetence, and inadequacy (Storms & McCaul, 1976; Valins & Nisbett, 1971). But is this supposed actuarial information about the similarity of the client's problems to the problems of many others actually of any therapeutic use? The current data on this point suggest that it may not be. Nisbett and his colleagues have provided research evidence that is relevant to this question.

Nisbett, Borgida, Crandall, and Reed (1976) examined the effects of "uniqueness" manipulations on depression. In three separate studies, these experimenters sought to lessen depression by informing people that their feelings were common to most people in their particular situation. Nisbett *et al.* (1976) reasoned that people would not feel so bad about themselves if they knew that others in similar circumstances felt the same way they did. In getting such a message, the person supposedly would not feel as negatively unique or abnormal relative to other people. This knowledge hypothetically may then reduce the depressed person's worry and concern about his or her ability to cope, and in turn, the person's depression may lift.

In a first study, Nisbett *et al.* (1976) sought to alleviate the "Sunday blues," which purportedly are the psychological letdown that many college students experience on Sundays. By informing one group of students "that dormitories around you are full of people in the same stale state," it was reasoned that the student's blues might be lessened if "misery does love company." In order to test this hypothesis, students at Yale university filled out mood scales on a Sunday prior to the experimental manipulations. Members of three separate groups were then given an experimental manipulation during the week and their moods were measured again on the next Sunday. For the first group, the students were merely told that the experimenters were studying moods on Sundays. In a second group, the "Sunday blues" were described rather specifically, including statistics about the high incidence of the "Sunday blues" in college students. A third group were given the same "Sunday blues" data but additionally were given a theory about why these blues set in. Contrary to predictions, there were *no* differences in the mood states (the second Sunday as compared to the first Sunday) of the students in the three groups.

Two subsequent studies by Nisbett *et al.* (1976) have also failed to find any positive effects in telling people that their depressive states were not unique to them. In a first study with depressed male college students, a manipulation was performed on half of the students in order to convince them that many other college males had or would undergo depressive states similar to theirs (this was called a *consensus manipulation*). The self-reported mood of the experimental (consensus) group did not differ over a two-week period from that reported by a group of depressed college males who did not receive the nonuniqueness (consensus) manipulation. In a second study of hundreds of first-year faculty members, Nisbett *et al.* (1976) gave half of the sample information about how widespread the sense of depression and worry was among first-year faculty. These faculty were told, in essence, that any stress they might feel was not unique but was rather widely experienced (again, this is a consensus manipulation). The other half of the sample were not given this nonuniqueness (consensus) manipulation but were merely informed that the researchers were studying the adjustment of first-year faculty. At the end of the year, the first-year faculty were asked to fill out a questionnaire about their moods over the year, as well as information about number of grant applications, research papers, and even cigarettes smoked and alcohol consumed. Overall, there were *fewer* differences between the nonuniqueness (consensus) manipulation and the control group than would be expected by chance. Again, therefore, telling a person that he or she was not unique did not appear to help. Although the authors cautioned that depressive states are very difficult to change through any manipulation, the three studies by Nisbett *et al.* do indicate that the value of nonuniqueness or consensual information may be questionable. This conclusion is also supported by subsequent research that reveals that consensus information does not help people to cope effectively with stress (McCaul, 1978).

Why does the commonsense notion of telling the troubled person that many others have also experienced similar troubles fail? One possibility is that people with problems do not really believe or "hear" such nonuniqueness feedback. As we have argued previously in this section, a troubled client may want to believe that the therapist is listening and cares. Perhaps the therapist's statement that many other people have had the same problems is interpreted by the client as a lack of caring and attention to *his* or *her* problem. Simply put, it may be necessary for the psychotherapist to refrain from making statements about "most" people or the "typical" client, since the client may be most receptive to information especially specific to him or her. This latter point is consistent with research that has consistently shown that people are most accepting of personality feedback from diagnosticians and therapists when they believe the feedback is specific to them (see Snyder, Shenkel, & Lowery, 1977). A second possibility is that the client may "hear" the information that his or her problems are very similar to the problems of other people, but this nonuniqueness feedback may lack positive therapeutic effects. Indeed, it may be quite unproductive to give the troubled client feedback that he or she is "no different from anyone else." The world may look just as (or more) bleak to the troubled person given such a message.

Political Context

In the broadest sense, the political context may provide an environment that influences people's uniqueness. Any political system is by necessity concerned with the interplay between social control and the individual unique behavior. How a political system defines this interplay provides a good insight into that system's fundamental structure. Obviously, many political systems emphasize social control, with external constraints on uniqueness seeking evidenced in the citizens' ideas, attitudes, and behaviors. Whether the system is totalitarian, communistic, or socialistic in emphasis, a common thread emphasizing social control can be seen. Democratic societies, on the other hand, seek to maximize the individual uniqueness of the citizenry and to minimize the necessity of external social control. This is not to suggest that democracies do not have social control, however, but rather that democracies attempt to engender individual freedom within the structure of society.

The Constitution of the United States and the Bill of Rights expressly seek to establish an orderly societal framework in which the individual's potential for uniqueness is protected. From the inception, the United States has been the melting pot of people with diverse ethnic and social backgrounds. Likewise, the attitudes and behaviors of the American people have been rather heterogeneous since the beginning. How has the uniqueness of this diverse group fared over the last 200 years of American history? At times, our democratic system has allowed travesties against individually unique people. We all have probably heard of, witnessed, or perhaps even perpetrated injustices against individuals of a particular ethnic, ideological, or religious background. However, we must in fairness also acknowledge that the uniqueness of particular individuals has been carefully protected in many instances. In such cases, the Bill of Rights has evidently nurtured Americans' rights to individual freedom of ideas, thoughts, and behavior. That is, the right to evidence uniqueness has been preserved.

The manifestation of uniqueness is undoubtedly influenced by citizens' perceptions of the government's attitudes about such behavior. The founding fathers developed a system that sought to foster tolerance of the individual uniqueness of the citizenry. The Constitution and the Bill of Rights stand as the "paper backbone" that legitimized the uniqueness of individual behavior. But like any document, our Constitution and Bill of Rights will be only as effective as the populace wants them to be. Tolerance of individual uniqueness was bequeathed to Americans, but how do we really feel in our present democratic society about such tolerance?

Large-scale survey studies on Americans' tolerance in 1954 (Stouffer, 1955) and 1973 (Nunn, Crockett, & Williams, 1978) addressed the aforementioned question. Generally, the findings of these studies indicate that Americans have become *more* tolerant toward nonconformists during this period. Whether the nonconformity is that of a communist, a socialist, an atheist, or a homosexual, Americans report that they are more tolerant of such uniqueness.

What contributes to this increase in tolerance? Nunn, Crockett, and Williams (1978) hypothesized that education has a strong influence on the development of increased tolerance. This reasoning is supported by the fact that level of education was found to be the best predictor of tolerance in the 1973 survey. Evidently, education serves to increase general knowledge and cultural sophistication, as well as enhancing a flexible cognitive style.

Whatever the exact reasons for this increased tolerance, it is encouraging that the citizens of the American democratic system are becoming increasingly tolerant of others' uniqueness. Perhaps our democratic system—and more importantly, the citizens who make this system function—will increasingly provide an atmosphere conducive to the manifestation of individuals' unique ideas, thoughts, and actions. In this regard, Nunn, Crockett and Williams (1978), in their concluding comments about their survey results, asserted:

> The post-World War II decades, as we have seen, brought revolutionary changes in American society. Changes of such magnitude bring with them social disruption, value confusion, uncertainties, and other strains on the social fabric. Both because of the changes and in spite of the strains, Bill of Rights' principles as guidelines for citizen relationships have advanced, not collapsed. More and more Americans, particularly better informed and active citizens, show signs of greater willingness to extend civil liberties even to those who are considered extreme ideological nonconformists. (pp. 172–173)

Although there are other environmental arenas in addition to the family, the neighborhood, education, psychotherapy, and the political context mentioned in this section, these examples should suffice in that they convey the common elements associated with environments that foster a sense of uniqueness. In whatever place the person acquires an adaptive sense of uniqueness, it appears that the environment fosters a sense of freedom and exploration on the part of the person. Likewise, a sense of uniqueness may flourish in an atmosphere in which the individual feels that his or her ideas, beliefs, and behaviors are recognized and valued. In the aforementioned contexts, however, it should be emphasized that the environments do not foster a boundless sense of difference. This is the case because these environments also at times impart the necessity and advantage of socialization or fitting in.

Is There Value in Comparing Oneself with Others in Order to Derive a Sense of Uniqueness?

If at this point the reader grants that the data do seem to support the fact that in many situations a person has a need to feel unique, and that there are several environments where a sense of uniqueness is potentially fostered, then a final question logically follows. This question is whether there is value in comparing oneself with others in order to derive a sense of uniqueness? The following quote represents an initial answer to this question:

> I spend a lot of time comparing myself with others. Frankly, it doesn't seem to do me much good. But I still keep doing it. Sometimes I feel good when I seem to be like others; sometimes I feel good when I feel different from others. It's all a bit of a folly, though, I mean, spending all this time comparing. Maybe if I stop, I can be me. (Snyder, 1974, p. 1)

What this quote seems to be suggesting is that comparison process, *when taken to an extreme*, may cultivate a reactive stance in which a person is constantly trying to be unique (or similar) relative to others. Also implicit in this statement is the sentiment that extensive or pervasive uniqueness-motivated or similarity-motivated behavior is maladaptive. Too much uniqueness-seeking behavior is bound to cause a person problems. Indeed, the clinical psychologist or psychiatrist may at times have to treat clients who engage in a never-ending search for uniqueness relative to other people. This syndrome is similar to Raimy's (1975) characterization of the client with special person problems:

> The psychological core of the special person cluster of misconceptions is exaggerated self-importance, which has various names—superiority complex, arrogance, vanity, conceit, egotism, and many others. . . . Its principal manifestation is found in compulsive attempts to wrest from others confirmation of one's superiority. If that superiority is threatened, vigorous efforts are made to defend it; if it is shattered, serious psychological problems occur. Reducing anyone's self-esteem is usually a hazard to his mental health; reducing the exaggerated self-esteem of the special person is often disastrous. (p. 109)

While the aforementioned narcissistic client may appear extreme in his or her "pursuit of differences," it should be pointed out that there are many modern writers who are concerned because our society as a whole is evidencing an increase in individual self-absorption (see Campbell, 1975; Hogan, 1975; Milgram, 1974). In fact, the late 1970s have been characterized as the "Me Generation" (Kanfer, 1979). For example, the very popularity of such books as *Looking Out for Number One* and *The Art of Being Selfish* reveals that a segment of our society may embrace extreme appeals to uniqueness. A major criticism of this trend is that people may spend more and more of their time establishing their own uniqueness but that they may not pause to consider the repercussions of their behavior on others in their societal context (Schur, 1976). Furthermore, such continuous uniqueness-seeking may lessen the individual's willingness to pursue common social objectives (Kanfer, 1979).

Based on the foregoing discussion, we would conclude that a first answer to the value of uniqueness-motivated behavior is that it may be rather unproductive and self-defeating when taken to an extreme. There are at least two factors, however, that indicate the importance of spending some time in the comparison process and deriving a subsequent sense of uniqueness. First, many theorists hold that a person attains a sense of identity by comparing himself or herself with others. That is, a person finds out about himself or herself through comparison with peers. This is a very natural and adaptive process *when not taken to an extreme*. Second, a person derives self-esteem feelings by comparing himself or herself with others. To feel a sense of uniqueness is in many cases (although there are important exceptions) a positive state. We are *not* talking here about the narcissistic uniqueness-seeking person described in the previous paragraphs but about the individual who has developed a solid identity that enables him or her to feel some sense of difference. If one's self-concept is relatively secure, then he or she may be expected to engage in occasional behaviors or phenomenological maneuvers to enhance the sense of uniqueness. Some uniqueness seeking, or at least the perception of uniqueness, is probably an integral and necessary part of existence within our Western culture, which emphasizes the individual. In fact, in light of the negative consequences of deindividuating urban environments (see the previous chapter), it may be very important to develop and foster those environmental contexts through which we can achieve some sense of uniqueness.

Concluding Statement

In closing, it should be emphasized that the pursuit of difference is tempered by the fact that in many situations, people want not to be unique but to be similar to others. A desire to be similar to others in many situations has been widely documented (see Chapter 2), and to be around similar others and to "fit in" at times are undeniably adaptive and desirable. In fact, it is the authors' hope that the present book has not lessened the reader's belief in the importance of being similar to others. Rather, it is our hope that the role of uniqueness-seeking behavior has attained recognition in concert with the interpersonal attraction and conformity literature.

At this point, it is appropriate to consider the themes of two popular children's books. In a first picture book entitled *Tootle* (Crampton & Gergely, 1969), the reader is told the story of a train engine who learns the rewards of "fitting in" (e.g., "staying on the rails no matter what"). In a second picture book entitled *Why Am I Different?* (Simon & Leder, 1976), the reader is told a story of children who are happy with the fact that they are different (e.g., "I am different. And so are you. That's good!"). In our estimation, both of these stories are worth hearing. That is, we applaud the person who sometimes strives to participate and cooperate in the traditions and conventions of society, just as we applaud the person who sometimes seeks to transcend societal customs of thought and action. Indeed, both of these processes may be found in the same person at different times. On occasion, a person seeks the comfort and shelter of the crowd, and at other times, the person seeks to establish a unique stance in society. This give-and-take process is the essence of the "human pursuit of difference."

An environment in which the inhabitants are constantly seeking uniqueness is as deplorable as one in which people are incessantly trying to be similar to each other. Any environment, however, that enables the individual to achieve the gratifications stemming from a sense of uniqueness *and* a sense of similarity deserves careful nurturing. This book is dedicated to such a possibility.

References

Ackerman, N. W. *The psychodynamics of family life.* New York: Basic, 1959.

Allen, F. L. The big change in suburbia. *Harper's Magazine*, June–July, 1954.

Allport, F. *Social psychology.* Boston: Houghton Mifflin, 1924.

Allport, G. W. *Pattern and growth in personality.* New York: Holt, Rinehart, & Winston, 1961.

Berne, E. *Sex in human loving.* New York: Simon & Schuster, 1970.

Bossard, J. H. S., & Boll, E. S. Personality roles in the large family. *Child Development*, 1955, *26*, 71–78.

Brehm, S. S. The effect of adult influence on children's preferences: Conformity versus opposition. *Journal of Abnormal Child Psychology*, 1977, *5*, 31–41.

Brehm, S. S., & Weinraub, M. Physical barriers and psychological reactance: 2-year olds' responses to threats to freedom. *Journal of Personality and Social Psychology*, 1977, *35*, 830–836.

Campbell, D. T. On the conflicts between biological and social evolution and between psychology and moral tradition. *American Psychologist*, 1975, *30*, 1103–1126.

Carkhuff, R. R. *Helping and human relations: A primer for lay and professional helpers.* New York: Holt, Rinehart, & Winston, 1969.

Crampton, G., & Gergely, T. *Tootle.* New York: Golden, 1969.

Dobzhansky, T. *The biological basis of human freedom.* New York: Columbia University Press, 1956.

Dunn, L. M. (Ed.). *Exceptional children in the schools.* New York: Holt, Rinehart, & Winston, 1973.

Gans, H. J. *The Levittowners: Ways of life and politics in a new suburban community.* New York: Pantheon, 1967.

Good, P. *The individual.* New York: Time-Life, 1974.

Halleck, S. L. *The politics of therapy.* New York: Science House, 1971.

Harris, B. What happened to Little Albert? *American Psychologist*, 1979, *34*, 151–160.

Hart, C., Pogrebin, L. C., Rodgers, M., & Thomas, M. (Eds.). *Free to be . . . you and me.* New York: McGraw-Hill, 1974.

Harvey, O. J., Hunt, D. E., & Schroder, H. M. *Conceptual systems and personality organization.* New York: Wiley, 1961.

Hogan, R. Theoretical egocentrism and the problem of compliance. *American Psychologist*, 1975, *30*, 533–540.

Hughes, R. *A high wind in Jamaica.* London: Chatto & Windus, 1929.

Hunt, J. R. *An illustrated primer for professionals.* Topeka, Kansas: J. M. Hart Co., Inc. 1962.

James, M., & Jongeward, J. *Born to win: Transactional analysis with gestalt experiments.* Reading, Mass.: Addison-Wesley, 1975.

Kanfer, F. H. Personal control, social control, and altruism: Can society survive the age of individualism. *American Psychologist*, 1979, *34*, 231–239.

Kaplan, L. *Oneness and separateness.* New York: Simon & Schuster, 1978.

Kiesler, C. A., & Kiesler, S. B. *Conformity.* Reading, Mass.: Addison-Wesley, 1969.

Kittrie, N. N. *The right to be different: Deviance and enforced therapy.* Baltimore: Penguin, 1973.

Langley, L. L., & Cheraskin, E. *The physiology of man.* New York: McGraw-Hill, 1954.

Levy, H. B. *Square pegs, round holes: The learning disabled child in the classroom and at home.* Boston : Little, Brown, 1973.

Levy, D. M., & Tulchin, S. H. The resistant behavior of infants and children. *Journal of Experimental Psychology,* 1925, *8,* 209–224.

Lowe, C. M. *Value orientations in counseling and psychotherapy.* San Francisco: Chandler, 1970.

MacDougall, R. Contrary suggestion. *Journal of Abnormal Psychology,* 1911–1912, *6,* 368–391.

Mahler, M. S., Pine, F., & Bergman, A. *The psychological birth of the human infant: Symbiosis and individuation.* New York: Basic, 1975.

Mayer, B. A. Negativistic reactions of preschool children on the new revision of the Stanford-Binet. *Journal of Genetic Psychology,* 1935, *46,* 311–334.

McCaul, K. D. Symptom information consensus and emotional responses to stress. Unpublished doctoral dissertation, University of Kansas, 1978.

Milgram, S. *Obedience to authority.* New York: Harper & Row, 1974.

Minuchin, S. *Families and family therapy.* Cambridge, Mass.: Harvard University Press, 1974.

Minuchin, P., Biber, B., Shapiro, E., & Zimiles, H. *The psychological impact of school experience.* New York: Basic, 1969.

Nisbett, R. E., Borgida, E., Crandall, R., & Reed, H. Popular induction: Information is not always informative. In J. S. Carroll & J. W. Payne (Eds.), *Cognition and social behavior.* Hillsdale, N.J.: Lawrence Erlbaum Associates, 1976, pp. 113–134.

Nunn, C. Z., Crockett, H. J., & Williams, J. A. *Tolerance for nonconformity.* San Francisco: Jossey-Bass, 1978.

Raimy, V. *Misunderstandings of the self.* San Francisco: Jossey-Bass, 1975.

Raimy, V. Appeals to the special person in psychotherapy. Unpublished manuscript, University of Colorado, 1978.

Rubin, Z. *Liking and loving: An invitation to social psychology.* New York: Holt, Rinehart, & Winston, 1973.

Sarbin, T. R. A preface to a psychological analysis of the self. *Psychological Review,* 1962, *59,* 11–22.

Satir, V. *Conjoint family therapy: A guide to theory and technique* (revised ed.). Palo Alto, Calif.: Science and Behavior Books, 1967.

Sawrey, J. M., & Telford, C. W. *Psychology of adjustment.* (3rd ed.) Boston: Allyn & Bacon, 1971.

Schachter, S. *The psychology of affiliation.* Stanford, Calif.: Stanford University Press, 1959.

Schur, E. *The awareness trap: Self-absorption instead of social change.* New York: Quadrangle–The New York Times Book Co., 1976.

Silberman, C. E. *Crisis in the classroom.* New York: Random House, 1970.

Simon, N., & Leder, D. *Why am I different?* Chicago: Albert Whitman, 1976.

Snyder, C. R. *Comparisons.* Millbrae, Calif.: Celestial Arts, 1974.

Snyder, C. R., Shenkel, R. J., & Lowery, C. R. Acceptance of personality interpretations: The "Barnum effect" and beyond. *Journal of Consulting and Clinical Psychology*, 1977, *45*, 104–114.

Storms, M. D., & McCaul, K. D. Attribution processes and emotional exacerbation of dysfunctional behavior. In J. H. Harvey, M. J. Ickes, & R. F. Kidd (Eds.), *New directions in attribution research.* Hillsdale, N.J.: Lawrence Erlbaum Associates, 1976, pp.143–164.

Stouffer, S. A. *Communism, conformity, and civil liberties.* Garden City, N.Y.: Doubleday, 1955.

Suran, B. G. *Oddballs: The social maverick and the dynamics of individuality.* Chicago: Nelson-Hall, 1978.

Tennov, D. *Psychotherapy: The hazardous cure.* Garden City, N.Y.: Anchor Press/Doubleday, 1976.

Tyler, L. E. *The psychology of human differences.* New York: Appleton-Century-Crofts, 1965.

Tyler, L. E. *Individuality: Human possibilities and personal choice in the psychological development of men and women.* San Franciso: Jossey-Bass, 1978.

Valins, S., & Nisbett, R. E. Attribution processes in the development and treatment of emotional disorders. In E. E. Jones, D. E. Kanouse, H. H. Kelley, R. E. Nisbett, S. Valins, & B. Weiner (Eds.), *Attribution: Perceiving the causes of behavior.* Morristown, N.J.: General Learning Press, 1971, pp. 137–150.

Watson, J. B., & Rayner, R. Conditioned emotional reactions. *Journal of Experimental Psychology*, 1920, *3*, 1–14.

White, R. W. Motivation reconsidered: The concept of competence. *Psychological Review*, 1959, *66*, 297–333.

White, R. W. Competence and the psychosexual states of development. In M. R. Jones (Ed.), *Nebraska Symposium on Motivation.* Lincoln: University of Nebraska Press, 1960, pp. 97–141.

Williams, R. J. *Biochemical individuality: The basis for the gene to trophic concept.* New York: Wiley, 1956.

Ziller, R. C. Individuation and socialization: A theory of assimilation in large organizations. *Human Relations*, 1964, *17*, 344–360.

Index